TI-Nspire™ For Dummies

Cheat Sheet

W9-AAT-130

BESTSELLING BOOK SERIES

Editing Text

- Cut: [ctrl][X]
- Copy: [ctrl][C]
- Paste: [ctrl][V]
- Undo: [ctrl][Z] (or [ctrl][esc])
- Redo: [ctrl][Y] (or [caps][esc])

Application-Specific Shortcuts

- Insert data collection console: [ctrl][D]
- Hide/Show entry line in Graphs & Geometry; Go to in Lists & Spreadsheets: [ctrl][G]
- Insert a math expression box in Notes: [ctrl][M]
- Add a function table in Graphs & Geometry and Lists & Spreadsheet: [ctrl][T]
- Recalculate in Lists & Spreadsheet: [ctrl][R]

Inserting Characters and Symbols

- Display the Symbol Palette: [ctrl][⊞]
- Not equal to (¹): [ctrl][=]
- Underscore: [ctrl][⎵]
- Greater than or equal to (³): [ctrl][>]
- Less than or equal to (£): [ctrl][<]
- Semi-colon (;): [ctrl][:]
- Display the Math Template: [ctrl][⊞]
- Infinity symbol (¥): [ctrl][i]
- Dollar sign ($): [ctrl]["]
- Degree symbol (°): [ctrl][/]

For Dummies: Bestselling Book Series for Beginners

TI-Nspire™ For Dummies®

Cheat Sheet

Managing Documents

- Access the tools menu: `ctrl` `⌂`
- Access the context menu: `ctrl` `menu`
- Create New Document: `ctrl` `N`
- Insert New Page: `ctrl` `I`
- Select Application: `ctrl` `K`
- Save Current Document: `ctrl` `S`

Navigation

- Move through fields in reverse order: `⇧` `tab`
- Home: `ctrl` `7`
- End: `ctrl` `1`
- Page Up: `ctrl` `9`
- Page Down: `ctrl` `3`
- Up a level in the hierarchy (i.e. from Full Page view to Page Sorter view): `ctrl` ▲
- Down a level in the hierarchy: `ctrl` ▼

Navigating in Documents

- Switch between applications on a split page: `ctrl` `tab`
- Display previous page: `ctrl` ◄
- Display next page: `ctrl` ►
- Display page sorter: `ctrl` ▲

Wizards and Templates

- Add a column to a matrix: `⇧` `@`
- Add a row to a matrix: `↵`
- Definite integral template: `⇧` `∫`
- Derivative template: `⇧` `∫`

Modify the Display

- Increase contrast: `ctrl` `+`
- Decrease contrast: `ctrl` `−`
- Power off: `ctrl` `on`

For Dummies: Bestselling Book Series for Beginners

by Steve Ouellette

WILEY

Wiley Publishing, Inc.

TI-Nspire™ For Dummies®

Published by
Wiley Publishing, Inc.
111 River Street
Hoboken, NJ 07030-5774
www.wiley.com

For general information on our other products and services, please contact our Customer Care Department within the U.S. at 800-762-2974, outside the U.S. at 317-572-3993, or fax 317-572-4002.

For technical support, please visit www.wiley.com/techsupport.

Wiley also publishes its books in a variety of electronic formats. Some content that appears in print may not be available in electronic books.

Library of Congress Control Number: 2008938385

ISBN: 978-0-470-37934-9

Manufactured in the United States of America

10 9 8 7 6 5 4 3 2 1

WILEY

About the Author

Steve Ouellette, or Mr. O, is currently the Math Department Chair at Westwood High School in Westwood, Mass. Steve holds a bachelor's degree in electrical engineering from Worcester Polytechnic Institute and a master's of arts in teaching degree from Boston University. Steve began his teaching career in 1993 after having worked as an electrical engineer at Otis Elevator Company for five years. His engineering expertise helped fuel Steve's passion for incorporating educational technology in his teaching. In addition to this book, Steve has also authored the *CliffsNotes Guide to TI-Navigator* and the *CliffsNotes Guide to TI-Nspire,* and he relishes the irony that he used to avoid writing assignments during his high school and college years. Steve has enjoyed working on a number of other TI-related projects, most notably as a regular activity writer for the *We All Use Math Everyday* program, a Texas Instruments and NCTM joint venture that provides classroom activities that relate mathematics to the TV series *NUMB3RS* . When he's not lobbying for a cameo role on *NUMB3RS*, Steve enjoys spending time with his family, camping, running with his weekend warrior buddies, and watching the local sports teams compete for championships. His passion for baseball is evident in the name chosen for his 90 pound labradoodle, Wally, named after the mascot for the Boston Red Sox.

Dedication

This book is dedicated to my family; my wife Christine and my three boys Noah, Ben, and Danny.

Author's Acknowledgments

I'd like to thank the good people at John Wiley & Sons who have provided so much support throughout the writing process. First and foremost, I thank my developmental editor, Christopher Morris, for all of his support and expertise. I'm absolutely blown away by his knowledge of the *Dummies* way. I also want to thank my acquisition editors, Amy Fandrei and Tiffany Ma, for helping me adhere to a tight schedule and for all their help related to the content and outline of this book. Additionally, I thank Douglas Shaw, Associate Professor of Mathematics at the University of Northern Iowa, for verifying the mathematical and technical accuracy of this book. There are so many other people that come into play after the acknowledgements are written, so for all the support I know I'll be getting, many, many thanks. Although she hasn't worked directly with me on this project, I must thank Zöe Wykes for all her help with the *CliffsNotes* books. There's no doubt that my work with Zöe helped make the transition to *TI-Nspire For Dummies* a smooth one.

I certainly wish to thank my friends at Texas Instruments for their ongoing support. In particular, I thank the past and present "big three" of the Content Team — Maggie Sherrod, Steven Bailey, and Vince O'Connell. Maggie, your support and unique sense of humor are so much appreciated. Steven, while your role has since changed, I thank you for being my first "boss" and for your ongoing support. And Vince, you have continued to lend a hand on so many fronts. Every time I need something, whether it's an updated device, a piece of software, or a set of Learning Objects, you've been there to help out. There are many other folks that I've come in contact with over the years as a result of my affiliation with Texas Instruments. Although I appreciate the professional growth these relationships have offered, it's the personal friendships that I've formed that have made this experience so wonderful.

On the home front, I wish to thank my teaching colleagues and friends for all your interest and support of this endeavor. In addition to my immediate family, I want to personally thank my mom and dad, Vivianne and Henry Ouellette, my brother Paul Ouellette, his wife Kate, and their children, Alyssa and Christopher, for simply lending an ear. This means the world to me.

Publisher's Acknowledgments

We're proud of this book; please send us your comments through our online registration form located at www.dummies.com/register/.

Some of the people who helped bring this book to market include the following:

Acquisitions, Editorial, and Media Development

Sr. Project Editor: Christopher Morris

Acquisitions Editors: Amy Fandrei and Tiffany Ma

Copy Editor: Mary Lagu

Technical Editor: Dr. Douglas Shaw, University of Northern Iowa

Editorial Manager: Kevin Kirschner

Editorial Assistant: Amanda Foxworth

Sr. Editorial Assistant: Cherie Case

Cartoons: Rich Tennant (www.the5thwave.com)

Composition Services

Project Coordinator: Kristie Rees

Layout and Graphics: Reuben W. Davis, Brent Savage, Ron Terry, Christine Williams

Proofreaders: Jessica Kramer, Christine Sabooni

Indexer: Broccoli Information Management

Publishing and Editorial for Technology Dummies

Richard Swadley, Vice President and Executive Group Publisher

Andy Cummings, Vice President and Publisher

Mary Bednarek, Executive Acquisitions Director

Mary C. Corder, Editorial Director

Publishing for Consumer Dummies

Diane Graves Steele, Vice President and Publisher

Composition Services

Gerry Fahey, Vice President of Production Services

Debbie Stailey, Director of Composition Services

Contents at a Glance

Table of Contents

Introduction

Do you know how to use TI-Nspire to do each of the following?

- ✔ Create and edit documents containing multiple pages and problems
- ✔ Evaluate expressions in the Calculator application and work with fractional or decimal results
- ✔ Graph and manipulate a parabola
- ✔ Manipulate a geometric object and analyze its changing attributes on a coordinate plane in real time
- ✔ Generate a sequence in the Lists & Spreadsheet application
- ✔ Enter data in the Lists & Spreadsheet application and construct a Box Plot of the data in the Data & Statistics application
- ✔ Set up a proof in the Notes application
- ✔ Take pictures of your TI-Nspire handheld screen and insert them in a word processor document
- ✔ Link TI-Nspire applications to represent information algebraically, numerically, graphically, and verbally

If not, then this book is for you. As you read through the pages, you will find straightforward and practical information that is sure to take you well beyond the beginning stage.

About This Book

This book will not tell you everything you need to know about TI-Nspire. However, I do cover all the basics and give you the tools to start creating your own TI-Nspire documents. Additionally, you will see enough examples to gain an appreciation for the *potential* that TI-Nspire has to offer. It's my belief that your experience gained from reading this book (and playing along on your TI-Nspire device) will give you the confidence to forge out on your own.

I outline a lot of concrete steps and processes to perform a variety of tasks. I use specific math applications as the backdrop for these tasks for the purpose of demonstrating how TI-Nspire can be used as a wonderful teaching and learning tool. As you read this book, you will begin to appreciate that TI-Nspire is a very robust device — if you can think it, then TI-Nspire can most likely represent it.

TI-Nspire™ Terminology

TI-Nspire™ learning technology comes with its own unique language. The meaning of most TI-Nspire related words found in this book can be initially understood from their context. However, just to avoid any unnecessary confusion, here are three key terms that you should know right from the get-go:

- ✔ **Handheld:** I use this term when referring to the TI-Nspire product that you quite literally hold in your hand. There are two such handheld devices: the blue TI-Nspire handheld and the gray TI-Nspire CAS handheld with the built-in Computer Algebra System.

- ✔ **Tool:** I routinely make reference to *tool* when talking about some of the features contained in the Graphs & Geometry application. When a tool is activated in the Graphs & Geometry application, its associated icon is displayed in the top left corner of the screen. A tool remains active until you press either (esc) or (tab), or when you begin using another tool. The Triangle tool is one such example. As the name implies, this tool allows you to draw a triangle.

- ✔ **Technology:** The word *technology* can mean a lot of things. In this book, I say *TI-Nspire technology* quite often. In this context, *technology* refers to any TI-Nspire related product, whether it be a TI-Nspire handheld or a TI-Nspire software application such as TI-Nspire Computer Link.

Conventions Used in This Book

When I wrote this book, I had to train myself not to refer to the TI-Nspire unit as a *calculator*. This word is quite misleading, and it suggests that TI-Nspire has a limited amount of computing power. Rather, you will find that I refer to this product as a *device* or *handheld*.

As for pressing keys, I always refer to them by an icon represented by the physical key. For example, rather than say "press the ENTER key," I say "press the (enter) key' or, simply, "press (enter)." Sometimes, I refer to a sequence of keys to push in which case I say "press (ctrl)(?) to grab the object."

To access blue secondary functions, you must first press the (ctrl) key. I always tell you the exact keys to press to access such functions. For example, I say "press (ctrl)(√) to access the square root template."

The NavPad is the circular "donut" located at the top of the keypad with the (⊙) key located in the center. You also see small ◂ ▸ ▴ ▾ symbols located on the NavPad. If I want you to move the cursor in a specific direction, say to the left, I tell you to "press the ◂ key repeatedly." If I simply want you to move the cursor to some other location, I say, "Use the NavPad keys to move the cursor to a new location."

Foolish Assumptions

I assume that you are a beginning user who wants to learn the basics to get up and running with TI-Npsire. Why else would you choose to read a *For Dummies* book? Here are some other assumptions that I've made:

✔ You already own a handheld device or are planning on obtaining one soon.

✔ You are either an educator or a student. Being an educator myself, I found it tempting to write this book from a teacher's perspective. Although I do make some occasional references to teachers, you can expect that this book will work equally well for both.

✔ As you see in Part VII, TI-Nspire comes with two different companion software products. I wrote these chapters under the assumption that you have some basic knowledge of how computers work. As you see in other sections of this book, a basic working knowledge of computers also comes in handy when working with your TI-Nspire handheld.

How This Book Is Organized

This book is organized around TI-Nspire's five core applications. Because TI-Nspire applications often work together, it's hard to talk about them in isolation. However, I've done my best to write this book in such a way that you can jump in pretty much anywhere in the text without having read the pages leading up to it. That being said, I recommend you read this book sequentially to get the most out of it.

Part I: Getting to Know Your TI-Nspire Handheld

In this section, I cover all the basics. This is where I introduce you to the philosophy behind TI-Nspire, the initial set-up procedure, the document model, and all the tips and tricks that allow you to create, edit, and navigate documents quickly and efficiently.

If you are the type that likes to jump around from section to section, go right ahead. However, check this part of the book out first. It gives you the underlying structure to everything TI-Nspire.

Part II: The Calculator Application

This part gets into the first of five core TI-Nspire applications. Here, you learn how to access a range of tools and commands that allow you to work with a variety of mathematical expressions and equations. In this part, I also start getting into how the Calculator application can "talk" to other applications. Finally, I introduce you to the Computer Algebra System of the TI-Nspire CAS handheld.

Part III: The Graphs & Geometry Application

The Graphs & Geometry application represents one of TI-Nspire's most powerful applications. Here, you'll find out how to work in an analytical environment, a plane geometry environment, or a combined analytical/plane geometry environment.

If you have some experience working with dynamic geometry software, you'll appreciate the smooth transition to this application. I hope you'll also recognize that advantages that the Graphs & Geometry application has to offer, especially with its capability to communicate with the other four TI-Nspire applications.

Part IV: The Lists & Spreadsheet Application

Your experience with computer-based spreadsheet applications really pays off here. If words such as *fill down*, *cell*, and *formula* sound familiar, then you'll have little trouble learning how to navigate this application. I also get into combining the Lists & Spreadsheet application with Graphs & Geometry or Data & Statistics to perform regressions and investigate scatter plots.

Part V: The Data & Statistics Application

If you are working with the Lists & Spreadsheet application or the Calculator application, this application is perfectly suited for one and two-variable analysis. In this part, you learn how to create and analyze a host of different statistical graphs including dot plots, histograms, box plots, and scatter plots. I also introduce Data Collection, a feature that works in conjunction with the Graphs & Geometry, Lists & Spreadsheet, and Data & Statistics applications.

Part VI: The Notes Application

The Notes application is the glue that holds together TI-Nspire's four other applications. Simply put, this application allows you to complete the document model, eliminating the need to add paper to your activities as well as providing the continuity that makes your documents flow.

Part VII: TI-Nspire Computer Software

In this part, I talk about how the free TI-Nspire Computer Link software makes a connection between your handheld device and your computer, allowing you to transfer files, take pictures of your handheld screen, back up your device, and upgrade the operating system.

The optional TI-Nspire Computer software allows you to create and edit documents that are completely compatible with those that reside on your handheld device. In addition to providing the nuts-and-bolts of how to use this software, I give you several reasons for why you might want to use it in the first place.

Part VIII: The Part of Tens

In Part VIII, I give you a lot of good information — *quick*. Here, I demonstrate ten small, yet powerful activities that give you a sense of the power behind TI-Nspire. I also summarize ten great shortcuts, periodically mentioned throughout the book, that are sure to save lots of time. Finally, I resolve some common mistakes I have personally made in the past with the hope that you might avoid them.

Icons Used in This Book

This book uses four icons that help to emphasize a variety of points.

The text that follows this icon gives suggestions or shortcuts that help enhance your documents. These helpful little nuggets often pertain to the current material or suggest ways to extend or enhance the use of TI-Nspire.

The text that follows this icon tells you something that is truly worth remembering. I often use this icon to repeat something mentioned earlier in the book or to highlight information that will eliminate potential mistakes down the road.

The text associated with this icon is intended to warn you about more catastrophic mistakes, especially those that are difficult to troubleshoot. I'm thinking about that insidious issue that has no associated warning message. There's nothing more frustrating than dealing with an issue for which there appears to be no solution. This icon eliminates some of those issues.

I use this icon sparingly in this book. It gives you additional technical information that is intended only to satisfy your intellectual curiosity.

Where to Go from Here

This book is not the end-all. In fact, I periodically point you in the direction of some additional resources available to you. These resources include those provided with your TI-Nspire device when you purchased it as well as the abundance of resources found on TI's Web site, education.ti.com.

As for reading this book, I mention earlier that you can read it sequentially or jump around as you see fit. If you are trying to locate something specific, refer to the table of contents or look it up in the index at the back of the book.

Part I

Getting to Know Your TI-Nspire Handheld

The 5th Wave   By Rich Tennant

"What exactly are we saying here?"

In this part . . .

This part gives you all the tools necessary to start creating and editing TI-Nspire documents. From installing the batteries, to managing files, to understanding the document structure, this part is sure to get you comfortable with the nuts and bolts behind TI-Nspire. Just for kicks, I even show you how to send and receive files between two linked handheld devices.

Chapter 1

Using TI-Nspire for the First Time

*I*f you are brand new to TI-Nspire, then I encourage you to start with this chapter. In this chapter, you begin to gain an appreciation of how TI-Nspire can help you understand mathematical concepts in a new way. You also find out about the different TI-Nspire products available and some of the first steps to get up and running with TI-Nspire technology.

The Philosophy behind TI-Nspire

The best way to learn about the philosophy behind TI-Nspire is to read this book and start playing with the device. However, let me whet your appetite now with a few thoughts about how TI-Nspire works and some things you can do with TI-Nspire that really showcase its capabilities.

Multiple representations

It has been demonstrated that students learn mathematical concepts more quickly and in greater depth when concepts are presented in multiple ways, that is, algebraic, graphical, geometric, numeric, and verbal. TI-Nspire technology is all about multiple representations. In fact, TI-Nspire can display up to four different representations on a single screen.

Furthermore, these representations are dynamically linked. As you see in the next section, changes to one representation automatically affect the other representations, in real time, right on the screen. This highly interactive approach allows for students to "see" the math, which enhances their ability to make mathematical connections and solve problems.

Figure 1-1 shows a simple example in which three representations of a concept are displayed. In the first screen in Figure 1-1, I give the algebraic representation of a given word description. In the second screen in Figure 1-1, I give the geometric representation and the numeric representation. Notice that the second screen contains two different applications on the same screen. With TI-Nspire, you have the option of displaying up to four different applications on one screen.

Figure 1-1: Multiple representations.

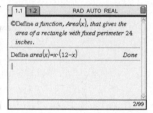 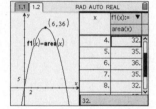

Linking representations

The idea of linking representations is another core feature that separates TI-Nspire from other handheld devices.

Although it's nice to see multiple representations of a mathematical concept, it's really cool to have the option of manipulating one representation and watching the corresponding affect on another representation.

In the first two screens in Figure 1-2, I change the size of a circle and watch the corresponding changes in *radius* and *area* measurements plotted on the coordinate plane in real time. The last screen in Figure 1-2 shows the radius and area data that automatically populates the Lists & Spreadsheet application as the circle is resized. This data represents the coordinates of each point that comprise the scatter plot.

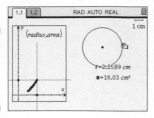 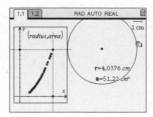

Figure 1-2: Linking representations.

Grab and move

The previous example helps to illustrate the grab-and-move philosophy inherent to TI-Nspire. You can also grab and move certain graphed functions and manipulate the axes themselves.

Imagine graphing $y = x^2$ in the previous example. TI-Nspire gives you the ability to grab the graph itself and change its shape. As you do this, the displayed equation on the screen updates automatically, again, in real time. Match the function to the scatter plot and observe that the equation approximates $y = 3.14x^2$.

The interactive feedback from this simple scenario allows students to explore and identify patterns and to make conjectures based on their observations. What a wonderful and interactive way to demonstrate the formula for the area of a circle!

Save and review work: The document structure

In Chapter 2 you find out how TI-Nspire uses the document structure to engage students in interactive activities. A *document* is a TI-Nspire file that contains problems and pages. With TI-Nspire, you can create, edit, save, and review your documents using many of the same commands and file storage methods found on a computer.

As a student, this provides you with three distinct advantages:

✔ Class assignments and homework documents can be saved on TI-Nspire handhelds and transferred to the teacher's handheld device or computer.

- ✔ Students can pick up where they left off after leaving class.
- ✔ Students can work at home, either on their handhelds or the computers.

As an educator, the document model provides you with these advantages:

- ✔ Teachers can prepare documents in advance and transmit them to students for use individually or in groups.
- ✔ Complicated constructions can be prepared in advance, thereby allowing students to focus on the math.
- ✔ Each student can turn in a unique and complete electronic record of all their mathematical activities. Teachers can use these documents as a form of assessment and provide focused feedback to each student.

The Computer Connection

If you are at all familiar with a PC, then you should find the transition to TI-Nspire quite smooth. For starters, TI-Nspire documents consist of one or more pages, much like a document you might prepare using a word processor. As for working with your documents, you will learn about a variety of shortcuts that are virtually identical to those that you may already be using on your PC. For example, pressing the key sequence (ctrl) + (s) saves your work, (tab) moves you to the next field in a dialog box, (ctrl) + (menu) pulls up the context menu (the equivalent of a right-click on your computer), and so on. As for the right-click reference, get used to me talking about that feature. It's an incredible time-saver that you simply must take advantage of!

The more you remind yourself of this computer connection, the faster you will travel along the learning curve.

TI-Nspire versus TI-Nspire CAS

The TI-Nspire product line includes TI-Nspire and TI-Nspire CAS (both in the handheld version and as a computer application). The blue or blue/yellow (EZ-Spot) TI-Nspire handheld device performs numerical or *floating-point* calculations, much like those performed by the TI-83 and TI-84 product line. The gray TI-Nspire CAS handheld has all the functionality of the TI-Nspire technology with two notable differences:

✔ TI-Nspire CAS technology has a built-in computer algebra system, which allows for symbolic representation of numerical calculations — that is, the solution to $x^2 = 12$ is given as

$$x = -2\sqrt{3}$$

And

$$x = 2\sqrt{3}$$

— and the manipulation of algebraic expressions and processes (that is, you can expand binomials, find derivatives and algebraic expressions, and so on).

✔ TI-Nspire CAS handheld does not include the snap-in TI-84 Plus keypad. (For more on this keypad, see the section "Switching Keypads," later in this chapter.)

Because these devices have so much in common, this book can serve as a valuable resource for either handheld. I've included three chapters (Chapters 8, 12, and 18) that specifically address some of the key features unique to TI-Nspire CAS. Throughout the book, I also occasionally point out some key differences between the two devices.

Installing Batteries and Turning the Unit On

If you are like me, you can't wait to finally open the box and start playing with your TI-Nspire handheld. First, though, you must install the batteries, which are included when you purchase a TI-Nspire handheld device. Here's how to install the batteries on the TI-Nspire handheld:

1. **Remove the sliding cover.**

2. **On the back of the device, slide the tab to the right to release the keypad.**

3. **Slide the keypad down about ¼ inch and lift it out to reveal the battery compartment.**

4. **Insert the batteries, making sure that the + side of each battery faces toward the bottom of the device.**

5. **Place the keypad gently back in place, leaving about a ¼ inch gap at the top.**

6. **Slide the keypad up toward the display screen, applying enough pressure to snap it into place.**

Here's how to replace the batteries on the TI-Nspire CAS handheld:

1. **Remove the battery cover from the back of the handheld.**
2. **Insert the batteries, making sure that the + side of each battery faces toward the top of the device.**
3. **Snap the battery cover back into place.**

To turn on your TI-Nspire device, press the ⓞ key.

Going through the Initial Set-Up of TI-Nspire

After pressing ⓞ for the first time, you see a progress bar indicating that the operating system is loading. Eventually, you are greeted by a screen prompting you to choose a language. This is also your first experience with a dialog box featuring drop-down menus.

To select the language do the following:

1. **Press the center Click key (ⓧ) to reveal the drop-down menu.**
2. **Use the ▲▼ keys on the circular NavPad (more about the NavPad in the next section) to highlight the language.**
3. **Press ⓣ to highlight the OK button (as indicated by a dark box) and press ⓔ.**

If you are happy with the default settings of any dialog box, press ⓔ and the settings take effect and close the dialog box at the same time. There is no need to tab through each field.

Next, you are prompted to select a font size. I happen to like the default medium font. However, if you want to change the font size, feel free to do so by following the same steps used for choosing a language.

Finally, you are greeted by a welcome screen, which describes some of the basic features of your new TI-Nspire device. Feel free to scroll through this document by pressing the ▼ key. You can also press ⓒⓣⓡⓛ③ to page-down through the page. Press ⓔ when you have finished reading to display the TI-Nspire home menu.

Becoming Acquainted with the Keypad

The home menu is where you can create a new document, access existing documents, and add pages to existing documents. It's also where you can adjust your system settings.

Before getting into these nifty features, it's a good idea to acquaint yourself with the TI-Nspire keypad. A basic understanding of the TI-Nspire keypad helps you understand how to start navigating through documents quickly and efficiently.

Using the (esc), (tab), (ctrl), , (⌂), and (menu) keys

Figure 1-3 shows the TI-Nspire keypad. Notice the keys that I describe in this section are located near the top of the keypad. These keys perform a variety of functions that you will find are quite similar to their computer counterparts. Here's a brief description of what each of these keys can do.

- ✔ (esc) **Escape:** This key removes menus or dialog boxes from the screen. For example, imagine that you have just activated the Perpendicular tool in a Graphs & Geometry page. To remove this tool and activate the Pointer tool, just press the (esc) key.

- ✔ (tab) **Tab:** This key allows you to move to the next entry field in a dialog box. It also allows you to move around in certain applications. For example, pressing the (tab) key in the Graphs & Geometry application moves you from the entry line to the work area. In the Lists & Spreadsheet application, the (tab) key moves you from one cell to the adjacent cell.

Figure 1-3:
The
TI-Nspire
keypad.

Try pressing and holding ⇧ (shift key) followed by the ⇥ key. This key sequence moves you backwards through a dialog box, just as it does on a computer.

✔ ⌃ **Control:** This key provides access to the secondary function or character located on a given key. For example, ⌃ ⌂ turns off your TI-Nspire handheld.

✔ ⓧ **Click key:** Pressing this key selects objects on the screen, much like the click button on your computer mouse. Press ⌃ then ⓧ to grab objects. Alternatively, you can press and hold the ⓧ key momentarily to grab an object.

✔ ⌂ **Home:** This key displays the home screen.

✔ (menu) **Menu:** This key displays the menu associated with the current application (called the *application menu*). If you are on a Graphs & Geometry page, you see one menu. If you are on a Lists & Spreadsheet page, you see another completely different menu.

Try pressing and holding ⌃ followed by the (menu) key. This key sequence acts just like a right-click on a computer mouse — it provides you with access to the *context menu*, a list of the specific options available based on the current cursor location or active object. This is the second time I've mentioned this feature and certainly not the last!

✔ (clear) **Clear:** This key works just like the backspace key on your computer. It deletes a single character of text or an entire selected object. Press ⌃ (clear) to erase the entire contents of a field.

The NavPad

The circular wheel on the TI-Nspire keypad is called the NavPad (refer to Figure 1-3). If you look closely, you see the ▲ ▶ ▼ ◀ symbols clockwise from the top of the NavPad. Simply put, pressing these keys allows you to move the cursor or pointer in any direction. It has the same effect as moving a mouse around on a mouse pad.

Accessing menus and submenus

As I've already mentioned, the (menu) key gives you access to the menu options available in the current application. Pressing it once shows the top-level menu options. Some of these menu options have an arrow to their right, indicating that submenu options are available. To access a submenu, press ▼ to scroll down to the desired top-level menu option, then press ▶ to reveal the submenu. You may even find a third level of menu options as shown in Figure 1-4.

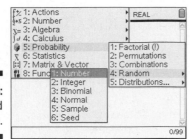

Figure 1-4:
Menus and
submenus.

To move back out of a series of submenus, just press (esc). You need to press (esc) three times to completely remove the layers of menus shown in Figure 1-4.

Configuring the System Settings

Okay, now that you know a bit about the TI-Nspire keypad, it's time to configure the system settings. To access the system settings, press (⌂)⇨System Info⇨System Settings. The first screen in Figure 1-5 shows the first five systems settings fields, with the last field (Exponential Format) expanded by pressing the (⌄) key. The second screen in Figure 1-5 shows the remaining five system settings fields.

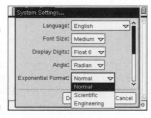

Figure 1-5:
System
Settings
options.

Press (enter) at any time to select the current configuration and close the system settings dialog box.

Your system settings are applied to all documents. For example, if you set Angle to Degrees, then all angle operations in all documents are based on degrees.

Selecting Default restores the original TI-Nspire factory settings.

Changing Your Document Settings

Press ⓐ⇨System Info⇨Document Settings to make changes to the settings for the current document. Changes made to your document settings override your system settings.

With the exception of Language and Font, document settings are the same as system settings.

You have the option to apply the document settings to the system by highlighting Apply to System and pressing ⓧ or ⓔ.

Switching Keypads

The blue TI-Nspire handheld comes with two keypads: the TI-Nspire keypad and a TI-84 Plus Silver Edition keypad When the TI-Nspire keypad is installed, you are using TI-Nspire. When the TI-84 Plus Silver Edition keypad is installed, your handheld device works exactly like any TI-84 Plus Silver Edition device. This means that you actually have two handheld devices!

To change the current keypad, follow these steps:

1. **Remove the sliding cover.**
2. **On the back of the device, slide the tab to the right to release the keypad.**
3. **Slide the keypad down about ¼ inch and lift it out to reveal the battery compartment.**
4. **Place the new keypad gently in place, leaving about a ¼ inch gap at the top.**
5. **Slide the keypad up toward the display screen, applying enough pressure to snap it into place.**

Each time you change keypads and turn the unit on, you must wait for the new operating system to load (as indicated by a progress bar).

I work only with the TI-Nspire keypad in this book. If you are interested in learning more about the TI-84, see the book *TI-84 Plus Graphing Calculator For Dummies* by C. C. Edwards (Wiley).

Chapter 2

Understanding the Document Structure

*I*n Chapter 1, I give you a brief overview of the document structure. In this chapter, I give you the information you need to better understand the file management system inherent in TI-Nspire. I then show you how you can open an existing document, and I give you the tools to move around an open document quickly and efficiently.

Managing Files and Folders

Computers allow you to save files to folders. TI-Nspire does, too. You have complete control over how to name these files, and you have several other options available that allow you to organize your files and folders. These options exist in the My Documents view of TI-Nspire.

The My Documents view

My Documents offers you a way to view all the folders and files on your TI-Nspire handheld. To access the My Documents view, press ⌂⇨My Documents.

The first screen in Figure 2-1 shows that I have five different folders in My Documents. To view the contents of any folder, use the NavPad keys to highlight the folder and press the ⓧ key to expand the folder. Repeat this process if you want to collapse a folder.

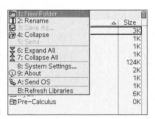

Figure 2-1:
The My
Documents
view.

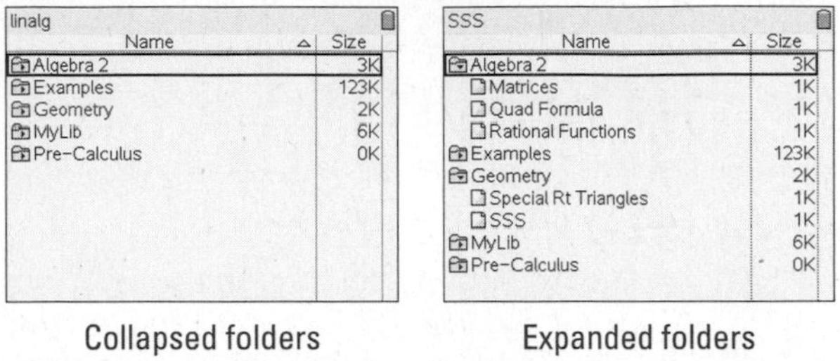

Collapsed folders   Expanded folders

The My Documents application menu

The My Document application menu differs slightly depending on whether you have a folder or file highlighted. To access the My Documents application menu, press the (menu) key. Figure 2-2 shows the menu options available for a highlighted folder (first screen) and a highlighted file (second screen).

Figure 2-2:
The My
Documents
application
menu.

Notice that the My Documents application menu contains an alternate way to expand or collapse folders. Two other related options, Expand All and Collapse All, are available in the My Documents application menu.

Using folders to organize files

The My Documents application menu can be used to help you organize your folders and files. Referring back to Figure 2-1, notice that I have named three folders by subject, Algebra 2, Geometry, and Pre-Calculus. To add another folder, say, Statistics, press ⓐ⇨My Documents⇨New Folder. A new folder, temporarily named Folder1, appears. Using the green alpha keys, type the name of your new folder and press ⏎.

TI-Nspire can hold lots of files so it's a good idea to spend a little bit of time thinking about how you want to use folders to organize your documents.

Renaming files and folders

Perhaps you made a mistake naming a file or folder. Simply highlight the file or folder and press (menu)⇨Rename. A secondary box appears around the highlighted file or folder with the existing name highlighted in gray. Start typing the new name and press (enter) when complete.

File and folder names can be 34 and 36 characters long, respectively. Additionally, you can use almost any character, including spaces, as part of a file or folder name.

Other My Documents application menu items

You may have noticed a few other options located in the My Documents application menu. Two of these options, Save As and Send, are only available if you have a file highlighted rather than a folder. I describe how to use the Send option to send a file to another handheld in Chapter 4. I also talk about how to use Send OS in Chapter 4.

You also have the option to Save As and Open a highlighted file. Selecting the Save As option automatically opens a dialog box that allows you to type a new file name within the same folder. Or, you can select a different folder and then type a new file name. This feature saves a copy and preserves the original file. See Figure 2-3.

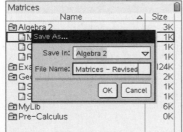

Figure 2-3: Using the Save As command.

The Page Tools menu,

The Page Tools menu, accessed by pressing (ctrl)(⌂) and denoted by the ⚲ symbol, is the one menu that is available no matter where you are in TI-Nspire. Furthermore, the Page Tools menu options never change. For example, you can access the Page Tools menu from a Graphs & Geometry page or from within the My Documents view and you see the same menu choices. Keep in mind, though, that certain menu items may not be available for use, as indicated by the light-gray (and barely legible) font.

The first screen in Figure 2-4 shows the top-level Page Tools options. The second and third screens show the secondary Page Tools options for File and Edit, respectively.

Notice that the Edit menu offers several editing options similar to those found on a computer. Additionally, several of these options can be accessed using keyboard shortcuts, the same ones that are used on a PC computer.

For example, you can Cut the file named Matrices by highlighting the file and pressing (ctrl)(🏠)➪Edit➪Cut. Alternatively, to use the keyboard shortcut, highlight the file and press (ctrl)(x). Here is a complete list of the Page Tools menu options that have corresponding keyboard shortcuts.

> ✔ (ctrl)(🏠)➪File➪New Document (Shortcut: (ctrl)(N))

> ✔ (ctrl)(🏠)➪File➪Save (Shortcut: (ctrl)(S))

> ✔ (ctrl)(🏠)➪Edit➪Undo (Shortcut: (ctrl)(Z) or (ctrl)(esc))

> ✔ (ctrl)(🏠)➪Edit➪Cut (Shortcut: (ctrl)(x))

> ✔ (ctrl)(🏠)➪Edit➪Copy (Shortcut: (ctrl)(C))

> ✔ (ctrl)(🏠)➪Edit➪Paste (Shortcut: (ctrl)(V))

The right-click menu

Let me officially introduce the *right-click option*. When you perform a right-click on a computer, what you are really doing is pulling up a contextual menu or shortcut menu that gives a list of available options depending on the application that is running, the objects that are currently selected, or the cursor location.

To access the contextual menu, press (ctrl)(menu).

Within the My Documents view, the contextual menu includes a collection of options that reside in both the My Documents application menu and the Page Tools application menu. See Figure 2-5.

Figure 2-5:
The contex-
tual menu
associated
with the My
Documents
view.

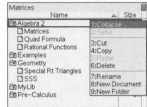 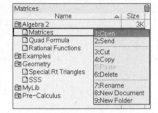

Right-click on a folder   Right-click on a file

One main advantage to using the contextual menu is that you can avoid digging through menus and submenus to find a specific feature or function.

Documents, Problems, and Pages

Now that you've had an opportunity to learn about the file management system of TI-Nspire, it's time to start looking at the files themselves.

Opening, closing, and saving files

To open a file, you must be in the My Documents view. Simply highlight a specific file and press ⏎ or ⊙. You can also highlight a file and press (menu)⇨Open (or (ctrl)(menu)⇨Open). The first page of the file is displayed and you are no longer in the My Documents view. To go back to the My Documents view, press (ⓗ)⇨My Documents.

In the My Documents view, open files are designated by an asterisk symbol (*) to the left of the file name.

There is no menu option to close a file in TI-Nspire. However, you cannot have two files open simultaneously. Therefore, one way to close a file is to open another file. If you made any changes to an open file, you are prompted to save the current open file before the new file opens. Press ⏎ to save the current open file, (tab)⏎ if you don't want to save the current open file but still want to open the new file, or (tab)(tab)⏎ to cancel the operation altogether.

As for saving files, here's how it works. A new document is not saved — it resides in TI-Nspire's local memory, just like a new (but unsaved document) on a computer. To save a new, unnamed document, follow these steps:

1. **Press (ctrl)(⌂)⇨File⇨Save to open the Save As dialog box.**

2. **By default, the cursor is located in the File Name field. Type the file name.**

3. **If you want to specify a different folder location, press (ctrl)(tab) to move up to the Save In field. Press ⓧ to reveal and select an available folder or type a folder name if you want to create a new folder.**

4. **At any time, press (enter) to put your choices into effect and close the dialog box. Alternatively, press (tab) until the OK or Cancel buttons are highlighted and press (enter).**

To save a previously saved document with the current name, press (ctrl)(s) (or (ctrl)(⌂)⇨File⇨Save).

To save an open file under a different name (thus preserving the original file), press (ctrl)(⌂)⇨File⇨Save As.

Any time you create a new document or open an existing document, you are prompted to save the current open document (assuming you have made even the slightest change to the current open document). If you choose to save the file, all changes will be saved and the original configuration will no longer exist. If you choose not to save the file, it will revert back to its configuration when you last opened it — all new work will not be saved.

Understanding how documents are structured

Every time you use TI-Nspire you are either working on an existing document or working with a new document. Again, I remind you that this experience is very similar to your experience working on a computer, especially when using a word processor. However, there are significant differences, too, and I discuss those differences in this section.

The five core applications

TI-Nspire has five applications from which to choose. Here's a list of the applications and a brief description of what each does.

- **Calculator application:** In this application, you perform calculations. You also enter and view expressions, equations, and formulas, all of which are displayed in a format similar to what you see in a textbook. A variety of built-in templates are also available that give you the power to describe just about any mathematical concept symbolically.

- **Graphs & Geometry application:** In this application, you graph equations, expressions, and a variety of functions. Variables and sliders allow you to investigate the effect of certain parameters dynamically. Graphs & Geometry is also where you can explore synthetic geometry concepts, that is, geometry not associated with the coordinate plane. Finally, Graphs & Geometry allows you to integrate coordinate geometry and synthetic geometry. Watch as connections between these two areas are made dynamically, in real time.

- **Lists & Spreadsheet application:** In this application, you investigate numeric data, some of which is captured for the Graphs & Geometry application and some of which resides entirely within the Lists & Spreadsheet application. Like a computer spreadsheet program, this application allows you to label columns, insert formulas into cells, and perform a wide range of statistical analyses.

- **Data & Statistics application:** Used in conjunction with Lists & Spreadsheet, this application allows you to visualize one-variable and two-variable data sets. Data & Statistics allows you to create a variety of statistical graphs including scatter plots, histograms, box-and-whisker plots, dot plots, regression equations, and normal distributions. With this application, you can manipulate a data set (either numerically or graphically) and watch the corresponding change in the other representation. A variety of inferential and descriptive statistical calculations can be performed and linked to a graphical representation.

- **Notes application:** The Notes application enables you to put math into writing. Three templates make the Notes application a robust and integral part of any TI-Nspire document. With the Notes application, you can pose and answer questions, review or write geometric proofs, and provide directions for an activity. The Notes application also allows you to integrate text and virtually any mathematical symbol, expression, or equation.

Dividing documents up into problems and pages

Every TI-Nspire document contains at least one problem. Each problem contains at least one page. Figure 2-6 shows the first three pages of a document titled *01GettingStarted*. Each page has a tab associated with it, and a white tab indicates that the page is active. Inactive pages are designated by a gray tab. A small ▸ symbol located to the right of the last tab indicates that there are additional pages that comprise the entire document.

As for the numbering system itself, the first number indicates the problem number and the second number indicates the page number.

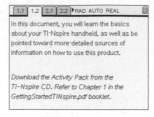

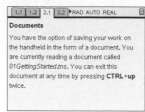

Figure 2-6:
Documents,
problems,
and pages.

Problem 1, page 1   Problem 1, page 2   Problem 2, page 1

Press (ctrl) ▶ to move to the next page in a document. To move to a previous page, press (ctrl) ◀. (Refer to Figure 2-6.)

Understanding how variables interact

The five core TI-Nspire applications do not reside in isolation. In fact, most documents consist of a variety of applications, all working in conjunction with one another. This means that variables defined in one page are available for use in another page, assuming the pages are part of the same problem.

Figure 2-7 helps illustrate this point. In the first screen of Figure 2-7, I have graphed the function $f1(x) = x^2$ in problem 1, page 1. In the second screen in Figure 2-7, I have typed $f1(12)$ and pressed (enter). The result, 144, is displayed because the function $f1(x)$ is the same function defined in problem 1, page 1.

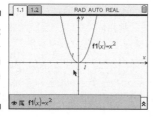

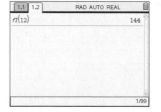

Figure 2-7:
Shared vari-
ables within
the same
problem.

Perhaps I want to use $f1(x)$ again but do not want to change its original defini-tion. To accomplish this, I insert a new problem. In the third screen in Figure 2-7, I have defined $f1(x) = x^3$. Because this page is part of problem 2, you can be assured that $f1(x)$ is still equal to x^2 in problem 1. I can use the same variables for different purposes, assuming they are contained in different problems.

Choose Your Level

TI-Nspire offers three different ways to view your documents:

✔ Full Page view

✔ Page Sorter view

✔ My Documents view

Each view has certain advantages and, when used in combination, these views can allow you to complete a variety of tasks quickly and efficiently.

Full Page view

In the previous section, I talk about how documents are comprised of problems and pages. The Full Page view allows you to see one complete page at a time. The screens shown in Figure 2-7 are all examples of pages shown in the Full Page view.

Moving around within a single page

Use the NavPad keys to move around within a single page. Here are four other tricks that can be used to move easily around a page.

✔ **Press (ctrl) + (1), the equivalent to the End key on a computer.**

This is a very handy key sequence that works in all applications. In the Notes application, you automatically move to the very end of the page.

✔ **Press (ctrl) + (7), the equivalent to the Home key on a computer.**

Pressing this key sequence automatically moves you to the top of a page.

✔ **Press (ctrl) + (3), the equivalent to the Page Down key on a computer.**

Consider you are reading text in the Notes application. A vertical scroll bar located to the right of the page indicates that the contents of a page do not fit in the viewable area. Page down allows you to see blocks of viewable text.

✔ **Press (ctrl) + (9), the equivalent to the Page Up key on a computer.**

Pressing these keys works just like Page Down with the exception that it moves you up through a page.

Dealing with more than one application on a page

With TI-Nspire, you can view up to four applications on a single page. Figure 2-8 shows one such case. In the first screen in Figure 2-8, notice the dark box located around the Lists & Spreadsheet application found in the bottom left corner of the screen, indicating that this application is currently active.

To move to other applications on the same page, press (ctrl)(tab). The second screen in Figure 2-8 shows the result of this action: The top-left application is now active. In general, (ctrl)(tab) always moves you to the next application in a clockwise direction. Just keep pressing (ctrl)(tab) until you reach the desired application.

Figure 2-8:
Moving from application to application within the same page.

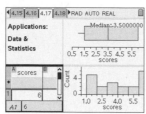

Page Sorter view

The Page Sorter view gives you a bird's-eye view of an open document. To enter the Page Sorter view, press (ctrl) ▲ from within the Full Page view. Figure 2-9 shows the Page Sorter view of the *01GettingStarted* file. Using the NavPad keys, you can highlight any problem or page. If you highlight a problem number, you can press ⓔ to expand/collapse the pages within the problem.

Moving around from page to page and from problem to problem

Move to any page and press (enter) to bring the page in Full Page view. In the second screen in Figure 2-9, I have highlighted problem 2, page 3. The third screen in Figure 2-9 shows this page in Full Page view after pressing (enter).

Figure 2-9:
The Page Sorter view.

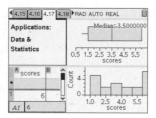

Changing the problem or page order

The Page Sorter view offers a convenient way to change the order of problems and pages within a document. To accomplish this, highlight a page and press (ctrl)(?) to grab the page. Use the NavPad keys to move the page and press (enter) to drop it in place. See Figure 2-10.

Figure 2-10:
Using the
Page Sorter
view to
change
page order.

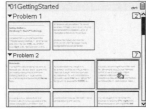

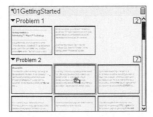

Grab problem 2, page 3   Move to problem 2, page 2

The My Documents view revisited

Toward the beginning of this chapter I talk about how you can access the My Documents view by pressing (on)⇨My Documents. Well, it turns out that you can access the My Documents view a second way.

If you are in Full Page view, press (ctrl) ▲ to move to the Page Sorter view. Press (ctrl) ▲ again to access the My Documents view. If you are already in the Page Sorter view, just press (ctrl) ▲ once to access the My Documents view. You will see that the current open file name is highlighted. Press (enter) to jump back to Full Page view. If you choose to open a different file from within the My Document view, you will be prompted to save the current file (assuming you have made changes to the file).

Chapter 3

Creating and Editing Documents

· ·

In This Chapter

▶ Creating documents consisting of pages and problems

▶ Working with the Page Layout menu to configure screens with two or more applications

▶ Using Cut, Copy, and Paste within the three TI-Nspire views

· ·

*I*n this chapter, I give you the tools you need to create and edit documents. You find out how to insert pages and problems, customize the page layout with as many as four applications, and take advantage of TI-Nspire's convenient editing features to ensure that your documents look and act their best.

Creating a New Document

So you've been reading this book and you are finally getting up the nerve to create a new document. After turning on your TI-Nspire, you are likely to find that you are already in an open document. Here are three ways to open a new document:

✔ Press (ctrl)(⌂)⇨File–>New Document. If you currently have a document open, you may be prompted to save the current file. Press (enter) to save the document, (tab)(enter) to open the new file without saving the current document, or (tab)(tab)(enter) to cancel the transaction. See the first screen in Figure 3-1.

✔ Press (⌂) and select New Document from the options given. Again, you may be prompted to save the current document (if one is open).

✔ Press (ctrl)(N) (shortcut for New Document).

After dealing with the prompt to save the current open document, you see the second screen shown in Figure 3-1. Use the cursor keys to select an application and press (enter). A new page based on the application you choose opens. Because this is the first page of the document, it is denoted problem 1, page 1.

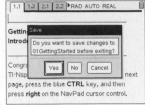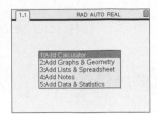

Figure 3-1:
Opening a
new file.

Adding pages to your documents

The first page I add is a Notes page. The first screen in Figure 3-2 shows that I have typed some instructions that refer to the next page. To insert a Graphs & Geometry page (I have chosen this application because I want to graph a function) do one of the following.

✔ Press (ctrl)(⌂)⇨Insert⇨Page and select Graphs and Geometry from the available options. (See the second screen in Figure 3-2.)

✔ Press (⌂)⇨Graphs & Geometry.

✔ Press (ctrl)(I) (shortcut for Insert Page). At the prompt, highlight the Graphs & Geometry application and press (enter).

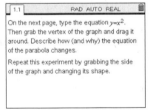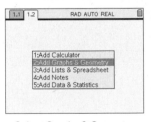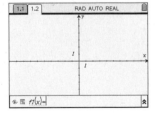

Figure 3-2:
Adding a
page.

A single notes page　　　Select Graphs & Geometry　　　Blank Graphs & Geometry page

The tabs at the top of each page indicate the problem number and the page number. The third screen in Figure 3-2 shows problem 1, page 2.

Adding problems to your document

Recall that a new problem allows you to use the same variables as another problem without creating conflicts. A new problem can be added only by using the Page Tools (🔧) menu. You do this by pressing (ctrl)(⌂)⇨Insert⇨ Problem.

After adding a new problem, you are greeted by a screen prompting you to pick an application, just as when you add a new page.

Saving your work

Very soon after you create a new problem, it's a good idea to save the file. The quickest and easiest way to save your new file is to press (ctrl)(S) (shortcut for (ctrl)(f)⇨File–>Save). Because this file was not previously saved, a dialog box opens, giving you complete control over the file name and the folder in which to save.

Here are the steps to follow to change the folder location or to create a completely new folder:

1. **Press (ctrl)(f)⇨File–>Save or the shortcut key sequence (ctrl)(S).**

2. **The cursor is initially located in the File Name field. Type the name of the file.**

3. **Press (⇧)(tab) to move from the File Name field to the Save In field.**

   You are automatically put in overtype mode.

4. **To create a new folder, just start typing the folder name. Or, if you want to select an existing folder do the following:**

   a. **Press (?) to expand the Save In field to see a list of available folders.**

   b. **Use the NavPad keys to select a folder and press (enter).**

5. **Press (enter) to accept file saving information and close the dialog box. Alternatively, press (tab) until the OK button is highlighted and press (enter) or (?).**

If you don't want to change the folder location, complete Steps 1 and 4. As you continue to work on your document, you can periodically save your work by pressing (ctrl)(S).

Configuring a Page Layout

TI-Nspire allows you to display up to four applications on one screen. Of course, you need to balance your desire to display several different representations of a problem with a need to keep the screen as uncluttered as possible.

Configuring pages with up to four applications

Consider that you want to solve the equation $x^2 - x - 1 = 0$ using the zero feature in Graphs & Geometry and confirm your answer using the Numerical Solve command in the Calculator application.

In the first screen in Figure 3-3, I have found the positive solution to this equation by plotting a point and dragging it through the x-axis (more about how to do this in Chapter 9). To add a Calculator page to the same screen, press (ctrl)(⌂)⇨Page Layout–>Select Layout. In the second screen in Figure 3-3, notice the several layout options available. I chose Layout 2, which brings up the third screen in Figure 3-3.

Figure 3-3:
Changing
the page
layout.

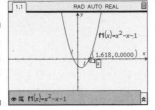 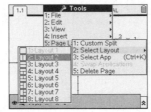 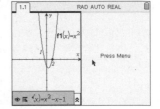

Notice the dark box surrounding the Graphs & Geometry application in the third screen in Figure 3-3. This means that this is the current active application. To activate the new application on the right side of the screen, press (ctrl)(tab). Then press (menu) and select Add Calculator.

The Switch Applications tool, designated by the ⊞ icon above the (tab) key, is accessed by pressing (ctrl)(tab). This tool is available only when two or more applications are displayed on a single page. Each time you access this tool, the next application located in a clockwise direction becomes active.

The first screen in Figure 3-4 shows the result (a dark box on the right side of the screen) of using the Switch Applications tool. The second and third screens in Figure 3-4 show that I have pressed (menu) and selected a Calculator page. I also invoked the Numerical Solve command to verify the graphical solution to $x^2 - x - 1 = 0$. To access the Numerical Solve command from the Calculator application, press (menu)⇨Calculations⇨Numerical Solve. The complete expression that I used in the last screen in Figure 3-4 is nSolve($f1(x)=0,x,1,3$). This expression indicates that I wish to look for the solution to $x^2 - x - 1 = 0$ on the interval from $x = 1$ to $x = 3$.

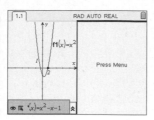 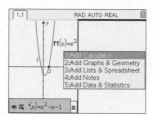 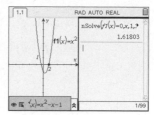

Figure 3-4:
Using the
Switch
Application
tool.

Creating a custom split

In the first screen in Figure 3-5, I've decided to add a third application, Lists & Spreadsheet, to the current screen. I added this third application by pressing (ctrl)(⌂)⇨Page Layout⇨Select Layout⇨Layout 7. My goal is to generate a rather famous sequence to see how it might relate to the solution to the equation $x^2 - x - 1 = 0$. As you can see, it's hard to see the values in the spreadsheet because there's so little room. I will use the Custom Split tool to see if I can improve upon the space utilization. Here's how:

1. **Press (ctrl)(⌂)⇨Page Layout⇨Custom Split to activate the Custom Split tool.**

   The second screen in Figure 3-5 shows the image of the NavPad located at the intersection of the three applications.

2. **Press the keys on the NavPad to adjust the vertical split down the middle of the page and the horizontal split between the two right-hand applications.**

3. **Press (enter) when you are happy with the split and to exit the Custom Split tool. See the third screen in Figure 3-5.**

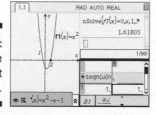 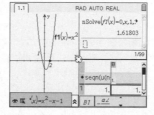 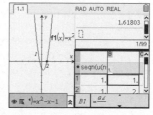

Figure 3-5:
Using the
Custom Split
tool.

You must press Enter after configuring the custom split. If you press (esc) after configuring the split, your changes do not take effect and the custom split tool closes.

Using the swap applications tool

Although the Custom Split tool helped a bit, what I'd really like to do is swap the position of the Graphs & Geometry application (located on the left side of the screen) with the Lists & Spreadsheet application (located on the bottom-right corner of the screen). Fortunately, the Swap Applications tool located in the Page Layout menu accomplishes this task. Follow these steps:

1. **Press (ctrl)(tab) until one of the applications you want to swap is activated (as indicated by the dark box surrounding the application).**

2. **Press (ctrl)(⌂)⇨Page Layout⇨Swap Applications to activate the Swap Application tool.**

   Notice that the Graphs & Geometry application is pulsing and the ⟨⟩ icon is located in the Calculator application (as shown in Figure 3-6). Pressing (enter) swaps these two applications. Keep in mind, though, that I want to swap the Graphs & Geometry and Lists & Spreadsheet applications.

3. **Use the NavPad to move the ⟨⟩ icon to the Lists & Spreadsheet application and press (enter) to make the swap with the Graphs & Geometry application.**

   The third screen in Figure 3-6 shows the result of this change (after a bit of additional clean up). Much better!

Figure 3-6:
Using the
Swap
Applications
tool.

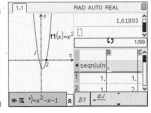 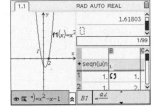 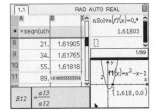

Notice in the third screen in Figure 3-6, the ratio of consecutive terms of the famous Fibonacci sequence has a value (the Golden Ratio), which is approximately equal to the solution to $x^2 - x - 1 = 0$!

Changing a page layout

Being the indecisive person that I am, I have decided that I really don't want the Calculator page cluttering my screen. Therefore, I'd like to go back to a layout that includes only two applications, the Graphs & Geometry application and the Lists & Spreadsheet application. If you access the Select Layout tool, you see that the layouts with only two applications on a page are not available (because I currently have three applications on the page). My only options at this point are to select a different three-application layout or choose the layout with four applications on one screen.

However, all is not lost. I first need to delete the Calculator application. Then I can select a layout with two applications. Here are the steps to accomplish this task:

1. **Press <kbd>ctrl</kbd><kbd>tab</kbd> until the Calculator application is active.**

2. **Press <kbd>ctrl</kbd><kbd>⌂</kbd>⇨Page Layout⇨Select App to select the Calculator application. Alternatively, use the shortcut key sequence, <kbd>ctrl</kbd><kbd>K</kbd>.**

   You know the application is selected because the dark box surrounding the application is flashing.

3. **Press <kbd>clear</kbd> to delete the application.**

   Notice that the Calculator application is removed and replaced by a blank screen with the words "Press Menu" located in the middle. At this point, you have the option to put another application in its place. However, my goal is to eliminate the application completely and configure the screen for two applications. See the first screen in Figure 3-7.

4. **Press <kbd>ctrl</kbd><kbd>⌂</kbd>⇨Page Layout⇨Select Layout.**

You will notice that the layouts with two applications are now available to be selected. Highlight your choice and press <kbd>enter</kbd>. See the second and third screens in Figure 3-7.

Figure 3-7:
Changing
the page
layout.

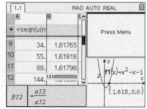 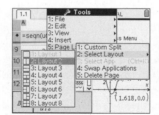 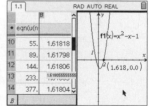

Managing Documents: Cut, Copy, and Paste

A number of options are available to quickly edit or manipulate existing documents. Some of these options I mention in Chapter 2. In this section, I talk briefly about how Cut, Copy, and Paste can be used in each of the three document views.

In the My Documents view

Recall that you can access the My Documents view two different ways — by pressing (⌂)⇨My Documents or by pressing (ctrl) ▲ twice from the Full Page view (or once from the Page Sorter view).

Perhaps you have a file that's already been created. You want to keep that file as is but also want to copy it and edit it for a slightly different purpose. From within the My Documents view, just highlight the file and press (ctrl)(C) (shortcut for copy) and (ctrl)(V) (shortcut for paste). You see a second file appear underneath the original file with the same name preceded by the words *Copy of.* You can then highlight the file name and press (ctrl) (menu)⇨Rename to change the name to whatever suits you.

If you copy a file to a different folder, the original file name is used without the words *Copy of.*

You can cut ((ctrl)(X)), copy ((ctrl)(C)), or paste ((ctrl)(V)) any file or folder from within the My Documents view.

In the Page Sorter view

Recall that the Page Sorter view is accessed by pressing (ctrl) ▲ once from the Full Page view. Alternatively, you can press (ctrl)(⌂)⇨View⇨Page Sorter from the Full Page view. However, I think this second option is more time consuming and not worth the effort.

From within the Page Sorter view, you can also use Cut, Copy, and Paste to perform a variety of edits. For example, you can cut (or copy) any page by highlighting the page and pressing (ctrl)(X) (or (ctrl)(C) for Copy). When a page has been cut (or copied) it can be pasted back into the same problem or to another problem. You can even paste a cut (or copied) page into another document assuming it's the last thing you cut (or copied).

If you copy a page into another problem that uses the same variables, you are greeted by the message "Cannot add to a problem because one or more variables of the same name already exist and cannot be overwritten."

You cannot highlight a problem number in the Page Sorter view and use the Cut, Copy, and Paste commands. However, to delete an entire problem from within the Page Sorter view, just highlight the problem number with the NavPad keys and press (⌫). After you delete a problem, all subsequent problems are renumbered.

Copying an entire page from within the Full Page view

Pressing (ctrl)(K) from within the Full Page view, followed by (ctrl)(C) and (ctrl)(V)(,) splits the page vertically and inserts a copy of the entire page side-by-side with the original page.

Perhaps you want to copy an entire page and paste the copy to a new page, all from within the Full Page view. To accomplish this, follow these steps:

1. Press (ctrl)(K) from within the Full Page view to select the entire page.

2. Press (ctrl)(I) to insert a new page.

3. Press (esc) to remove the prompt for choosing an application, revealing the words Press Menu in the center of the screen.

4. Press (ctrl)(V) to paste the copied page.

From within a page

Cut, Copy, and Paste work the same way from within the Full Page view. To cut or copy text, a mathematical expression, and so on, hold down the shift key ((shift)) and press the NavPad keys until you have selected what you are interested in. Press (ctrl)(X) to cut the selected region (or (ctrl)(C) for Copy) and save it to the clipboard. Then use Paste either in the same page or a different page.

Figure 3-8 shows the result of copying and pasting text within the same page.

Figure 3-8: Using Copy and Paste within the Full Page view.

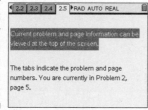

Highlight text

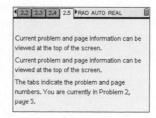

Paste text

The Undo and Redo Commands

We all make mistakes once in a while. Sometimes these mistakes seem catastrophic, especially if you just cut or deleted a large quantity of text, entire pages, or a complete document. Not to worry! To undo a series of changes, use the Undo command, denoted by ↺, by pressing (ctrl)(esc) repeatedly until you have restored your work. You can also access the Undo command by pressing (ctrl)(menu)⇨File⇨Undo or the shortcut key sequence (ctrl)(Z), the same key sequence that is used on a computer.

The Redo command enables you to move forward through a series of commands that were just undone. Press (ctrl)(menu)⇨File⇨Redo, or use the shortcut keys (ctrl)(Y) to access the Redo command.

Keep these two options in mind at all times. They work everywhere and allow you to eliminate mistakes in a flash. Wouldn't it be nice if life had an Undo command!

Chapter 4

Linking Handhelds

● ●

In This Chapter

▶ Sending files from one handheld to another

▶ Transferring the operating system from one handheld to another

● ●

*I*n Chapter 24, I tell you how to communicate between your TI-Nspire handheld and your computer. In this chapter, I tell you how to communicate between two TI-Nspire handhelds.

In Chapter 24, I talk about how you can check for updates and install them on your TI-Nspire handheld via Computer Link software. In this chapter, I also tell you how to transfer the TI-Nspire operating system from one handheld to another.

Sending and Receiving Files

Your TI-Nspire handheld comes with two different USB cables. One cable has a standard USB connector on one end and a small Mini-A USB connector on the other end. This cable is used to communicate between the TI-Nspire handheld and the computer.

The other cable has the small Mini-A USB connector on both ends. I call this the *unit-to-unit cable,* and I use it to transfer files between two TI-Nspire handhelds. To connect two handhelds follow these steps:

1. **Insert one end of the unit-to-unit cable into either handheld and press firmly to establish the connection.**

2. **Insert the other end of the same cable into the second handheld. Press firmly.**

To send a document, follow these steps:

1. **Press ⌂⇨My Documents to enter the My Documents view.**

2. **Highlight the document you want to send and press (menu)⇨Send.**

The file transfer automatically begins. When the process is complete, you see screens similar to those shown in the first two screens in Figure 4-1.

The third screen in Figure 4-1 shows what happens if the receiving calculator already contains a file with the same name — TI-Nspire appends a number after the file name and does not overwrite the original file.

Figure 4-1:
Transferring documents between two hand-helds.

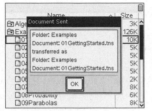 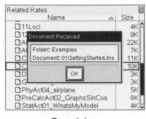 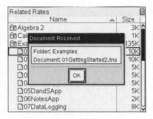

Sending   Receiving   Dealing with
handheld message   handheld message   a duplicate file name

 I always put the sending handheld on the left and the receiving handheld on the right. That way, I never forget which calculator is doing the sending.

No action is required on the part of the receiving handheld. In fact, it does not even need to be powered on. This happens automatically when the unit-to-unit cable is attached.

 The sending handheld always attempts to put a sent document in a folder on the receiving handheld that has the same name as the sender's folder. If no such folder exists on the receiving handheld, the sender creates a folder with this name and places the received document in this folder.

Here are some other rules that are followed when sending documents from one handheld to another:

✔ There is a 255-character maximum length for a document name. If the document already exists with the same name on the receiving handheld, the file name is truncated to allow for renaming the file as described earlier in this section.

✔ All variables associated with a sent file are included in the transferred file.

✔ If a problem arises (usually because the cables are not pressed in fully), transmission will time out after 30 seconds.

Sending OS

It's always a good idea to periodically check whether you have the latest operating system. If you do, you can take advantage of any new features that TI has come up with for your TI-Nspire handheld.

In this section, I tell you how to transfer the TI-Nspire operating system from one handheld to another. For starters, connect the two handheld devices with the unit-to-unit cable as described in the previous section. Then follow these steps on the sending handheld:

1. **Press** ⓐ⇨**My Documents to enter the My Documents view.**

2. **Press** (menu)⇨**Send OS.**

The file transfer automatically begins, as indicated by the message "Sending OS *<version number>*. Do not unplug cable." on the sending handheld. Additionally, you see a progress bar on the sending handheld. Keep in mind, the transfer may take several minutes to complete. You do not see a progress bar (or any action for that matter) on the receiving handheld.

After the transfer is complete, you see messages on both handhelds. The sending handheld displays the message shown in Figure 4-2. The receiving handheld shows a progress bar indicating that the new operating system is being installed.

Figure 4-2: Transferring OS between two handhelds.

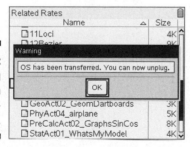

After the updated operating system is installed on the handheld, you are taken through the same initial setup screens (that is, Choose Language and Font Size), as described in Chapter 1.

The automatic power-down feature of TI-Nspire is disabled during transfers. Therefore, it's a good idea to check your batteries before starting an operating system transfer by pressing ⓐ⇨Handheld Status. If the battery status is low, install a new set of batteries.

Part II
The Calculator Application

The 5th Wave — By Rich Tennant

"It says here if I subscribe to this magazine, they'll send me a free desktop calculator. Desktop calculator?!!! WHOOAA — Where have I been?!!"

In this part . . .

This part takes a look at the first of five core TI-Nspire applications. As the name implies, I show you how to enter and evaluate numerical expressions. I also show you how to access functions and commands in the Calculator application menu as well as the Catalog. Additionally, I cover how variables are defined and used in the Calculator application and how this concept helps the Calculator application "talk" to other TI-Nspire applications.

I also dedicate a chapter to TI-Nspire CAS, the gray hand-held device with the built-in computer algebra system. Specifically, I talk about how CAS functionality looks and acts in the Calculator application.

Chapter 5

Entering and Evaluating Expressions

In This Chapter

▶ Working with primary and secondary keys

▶ Dealing with results in different forms

▶ Using the Calculator history and Last Answer to work efficiently in the Calculator application

▶ Understanding the Calculator Application menu

▶ Accessing commands, symbols, and templates from the Catalog

▶ Evaluating expressions in multiple ways

*1*n this chapter, I show you how to use the Calculator application to do what its name implies — perform a wide variety of calculations. However, the name *Calculator application* is somewhat of a misnomer. As you will see in subsequent chapters in this part of the book, the Calculator application can communicate with all other applications and perform a variety of tasks that go well beyond the basics.

Evaluating Expressions Using Primary and Secondary Keys

In this section, I show you how to evaluate mathematical expressions directly from the primary keys (as defined by the functions or characters located directly on the keys themselves) and the secondary keys (as defined by the blue functions or characters located toward the top of some keys). For example, ⬡ is the primary key for the sine function and the secondary key for the inverse sine function. To access a secondary key, press ⬡ followed by the primary key.

To add a Calculator page, press (ctrl)(1)⊏>Add Calculator.

Let's start with a very simple expression, entered and evaluated by pressing primary keys only. In the first screen in Figure 5-1, I typed ③③③④⑤ to find the value of 3 + 3 ÷ 5. The result of this calculation, found by pressing (enter), is shown in the second screen in Figure 5-1. Notice that two things happen after you press (enter). The original typed expression is shown with a stacked fraction, and the result is also expressed as a stacked fraction. When possible, TI-Nspire displays expressions and results in *pretty print* — that is, in the format that you typically see in a math textbook or other print source.

As for the fractional result, TI-Nspire attempts to display all rational values as fractions. Later on in this chapter, I show you how to force a rational result to be displayed in decimal form.

In the last screen in Figure 5-1, I typed ③(ctrl)④①② to find the value of 3 times the square root of 12. Notice that the result is expressed as a decimal. This happens any time a result is an irrational number (that is, when the decimal portion does not terminate or repeat and cannot be written in fractional form). Again, I also want to point out that the typed expression looks just as you would expect to see it in a textbook.

When using TI-Nspire CAS, the expression

$$3\sqrt{12}$$

returns the exact value

$$6\sqrt{3}$$

Refer to Chapter 8 for more information about the symbolic representation of results associated with TI-Nspire CAS.

Figure 5-1:
Evaluating expressions with primary and secondary keys.

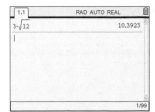

The square root symbol is a blue secondary key, located on the key. To access such keys, you must press (ctrl) first.

This result is shown to four decimal places. To change the number of displayed digits, press ⌂⇨System Info⇨Document Settings (or System Settings). A dialog box opens and the first field, Display Digits, allows for changing the number of displayed digits.

Changes made to the Document Settings affect only the settings within the current document. Changes made to the System Settings affect all documents.

Consider that you want to evaluate $\log_5 25$. The logarithm function is a secondary key located on the ㏒key. The first screen in Figure 5-2 shows that a logarithm template appears after pressing ctrl㏒. Notice the two small dashed rectangles (or fields) with the cursor located in the leftmost field. This first field defines the base of the logarithm and the second field gives the value for which I want to evaluate this logarithm. Type ⑤ to specify the base. To move to the next box, press tab. Type ②⑤ and press enter to complete the calculation, as shown in the second screen in Figure 5-2.

Figure 5-2: Working with fields in a mathematical expression.

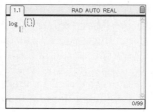 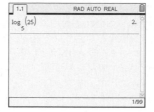

Always use the tab key to move from field to field in a mathematical expression.

If you leave the first field in the logarithm template blank, TI-Nspire uses a default base of 10.

Dealing with Very Large and Very Small Results

If you are familiar with the TI-84 graphing calculator, very large and very small results are often automatically put into scientific notation. This is not necessarily true of TI-Nspire. Take, for example, the calculation ⑤÷②㏒⑦④ (five-halves raised to the 74th power). The first screen in Figure 5-3 shows the exact result as a stacked fraction in excruciating detail! This result is roughly equivalent to 2.8×10^{29}.

Now try evaluating two-fifths raised to the 74th power (press ⌘②⌘⑤⌃ ⌃⑦④). This extremely small result, approximately equal to 3.57×10^{-30}, is also displayed as a stacked fraction in all its glory. See the second screen in Figure 5-3.

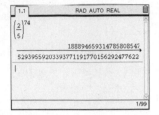

Figure 5-3:
Very large
and very
small
results.

Very large or very small results often do not fit on a single screen. To view an entire result, press ▲ once to highlight the answer. Then use the ◀▶ keys to scroll through and view the entire answer.

So just how large an exponent can you raise five-halves to? Try raising this number to the 1419th power. TI-Nspire displays the answer as a stacked fraction. Now try an exponent of 1420. This time, the result is displayed in scientific notation. Now try raising five-halves to the 2513th power. TI-Nspire cannot handle this calculation and displays an Error Overflow message. TI-Nspire CAS deals with overflow issues by displaying the result as ±μ and displaying the message Overflow replaced by μ or -μ at the bottom of the page.

Controlling the Form of a Result

Clearly you are sometimes better off seeing an answer expressed as a decimal or in scientific notation. Here are three ways to force an approximate result, ranked in order from easiest to hardest:

- ✔ **Press ⌃⌨ to evaluate an expression.** This action invokes the Approximately Equal To feature, a secondary function represented by the symbol ≈.

- ✔ **Include a decimal point somewhere in your calculation.** For example, type ③⌃③⌃⑤⌃ to evaluate my first example in decimal form.

- ✔ **Use the Approx command to force a result in decimal form or scientific notation.** This command can be typed using the green alpha keys. It can also be found in the catalog menu, which I talk about later in this chapter.

The last two methods described here are shown in Figure 5-4.

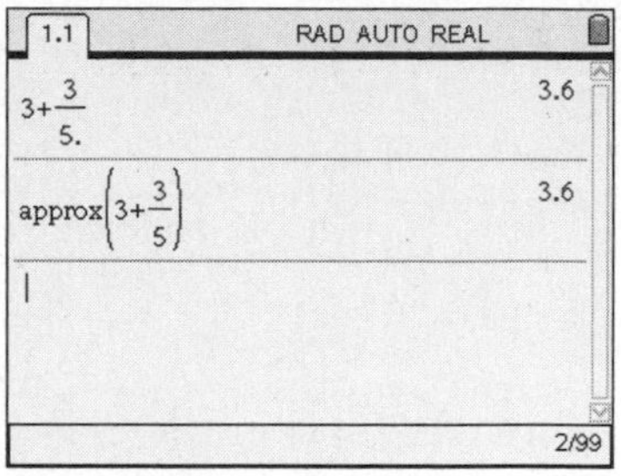

Figure 5-4:
Forcing a
result in
decimal
form or
scientific
notation.

1.1	RAD AUTO REAL	
$3 + \dfrac{3}{5.}$		3.6
$\text{approx}\left(3 + \dfrac{3}{5}\right)$		3.6
		2/99

Using History

TI-Nspire offers a convenient way to access previously used commands. This allows for a quick way to perform similar calculations without the need to re-type a long expression.

Accessing previously used commands

Consider that you want to use the quadratic formula to solve the equation $x^2 + 3x - 9 = 0$. For starters, I accessed the fraction template, a secondary function located on the ⊕ key. This pastes the fraction template to the entry line with a blank numerator field and a blank denominator field. Type the numerator first. Next, press ⓣ to move to the denominator, type ②, and press ⊜ to evaluate the expression. See the first screen in Figure 5-5.

The second solution to this equation can be evaluated by making a slight edit to the expression just entered. Here are the steps to follow:

1. **Press ▲ twice to highlight the previous expression (see the second screen in Figure 5-5).**

2. **Press ⊜ to paste this expression to the entry line.**

3. **Use the keys on the NavPad to move the cursor to the right of the + sign in the numerator of the expression.**

4. **Press ⓒ to clear the + sign and press ⊝ to insert a subtraction sign.**

5. **Press ⊜ to evaluate this revised expression. See the third screen in Figure 5-5.**

Figure 5-5:
Accessing
and
evaluating
previously
used
expressions.

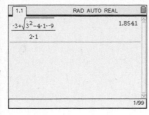 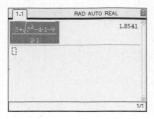 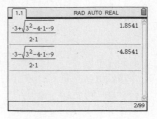

You can fill a total of 99 lines on a single Calculator page. If you do not clear your history (see the next section for how to do this), then any of up to 98 previous entries can be pasted to the entry line.

Clearing the calculator history

If your history contains many entries, you may notice a slowdown in the processing speed of your TI-Nspire handheld. To clear this history, simply press (menu)⇨Actions⇨Clear History.

If you choose to clear the history, all previously defined variables and functions retain their current values. Use the Undo feature ((ctrl)(esc)) to restore the history if you mistakenly delete it.

Using the Last Answer

Each time you perform a calculation, the result is stored to TI-Nspire's local memory as the variable **Ans**. As a result, you can quickly access this stored variable and use it in subsequent calculations.

Consider, for example, that you want to teach students how to evaluate an algebraic expression, such as $2x^2 + 1$ for $x = -8$. This problem can be easily evaluated by entering the entire expression once on the entry line. However, perhaps you want to take students through the process, step-by-step, to place additional emphasis on the order of operations. Here's how the Last Answer feature can accomplish this task. Also refer to Figure 5-6.

1. **Type –8 on the entry line and press (enter).**

   This stores the number –8 to the last answer variable Ans.

2. **Press the (x²) key.**

   This action automatically pastes the variable Ans to the entry line and raises it to the second power. (See the first screen in Figure 5-6.)

3. **Press ⊜ to square the last answer.**

   This stores the number 64 to the variable Ans. (See the second screen in Figure 5-6.)

4. **Press ⊛⊙ to multiply the last answer by 2.**

   The entry line reads Ans•2.

5. **Press ⊜ to evaluate this expression.**

   This stores the number 128 to the variable Ans.

6. **Press ⊙⊙ to paste the expression Ans−1 to the entry line. Press ⊜ to find that the value of $2x^2 + 1$ for $x = -8$ is equal to 127. (See the last screen in Figure 5-6.)**

Figure 5-6:
Using the
Last Answer
variable,
Ans.

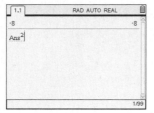

The last answer variable, Ans, is automatically pasted to the entry line if, after evaluating an expression, you press ⊕, ⊙, ⊛, ⊙, or ⊙.

Notice occurrences to the variable Ans in the entry line are replaced with their numerical values after you press ⊜.

Using the last answer variable in an expression

In the last section, I show you how the last answer variable can be automatically pasted to the entry line by pressing ⊕, ⊙, ⊛, ⊙, or ⊙.

You can also access the last answer variable by pressing ⊙⊙. This is very helpful if you want to take your last answer from a calculation and use it one or more times in a subsequent calculation. For example, consider that I have a cylinder of known volume and height (for example volume = 50 and height = 10), and I'm interested in finding the volume of a sphere with the same radius. Using the formula for volume, I can solve for the radius as shown in the first screen in Figure 5-7. The last answer from this calculation, accessed by pressing ⊙⊙, is used as the radius to find the volume of the sphere (see first and second screen in Figure 5-7).

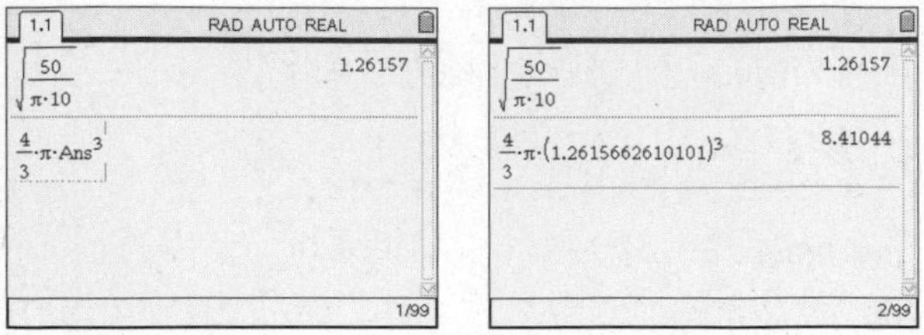

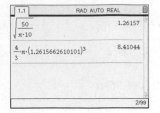

Figure 5-7:
Using
⟨ctrl⟩⟨(-)⟩ to
access the
last answer
variable.

Using the last answer variable to generate a sequence

You can also use the last answer variable to generate a sequence such as 2, 5, 14, 41, . . . Each term of this sequence is found by multiplying the previous value by 3 and subtracting 1. Follow these steps to generate successive terms of this sequence.

1. **Press** ⟨2⟩⟨enter⟩.

   This action stores the first value of the sequence, 2, to the last answer variable.

2. **Press** ⟨×⟩⟨3⟩⟨-⟩⟨1⟩ **to paste the expression Ans•3–1 to the entry line.**

3. **Press** ⟨enter⟩ **to evaluate this expression.**

   Notice that the expression Ans•3–1 is replaced by 2•3–1, indicating that the value of Ans in the preceding step is equal to 2.

4. **Continue to press** ⟨enter⟩ **to generate additional terms of this sequence.**

See the first screen in Figure 5-8.

The second and third screens in Figure 5-8 show how to generate a more complicated sequence of numbers. Perhaps you recognize the numerators and denominators of each fractional answer as terms from the Fibonacci sequence.

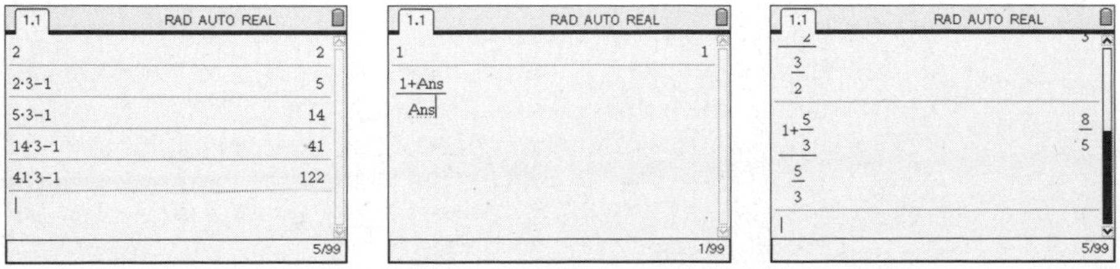

Figure 5-8:
Using the
last answer
variable to
generate a
sequence.

Copying, Pasting, and Editing Expressions and Answers

Earlier in this chapter, I tell you how to use the NavPad to highlight an expression in the Calculator history and press ⏎ to paste the entire expression to the entry line. You may have noticed that pressing the ▲ key alternatively highlights previous answers and expressions from the Calculator application history. When a previous answer or expression is highlighted, you have the option of pressing ⓒⓣ c to copy the answer or expression to local memory. You can then use ⓒⓣ v to paste this copied item as often as you want in future calculations.

For example, perhaps you are using the distance formula to find the distance between two points. After entering and evaluating the expression for the first time, press ▲ twice to highlight the original expression, press ⓒⓣ c, press ▼ twice to move back down to the entry line, and press ⓒⓣ v to paste the expression to the entry line. You can then use the NavPad keys and the ⌫ key to edit the expression. See Figure 5-9.

Figure 5-9:
Copying and pasting expressions.

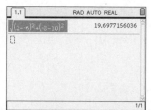 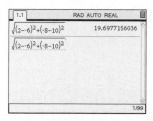 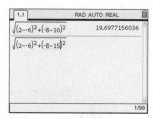

Highlight an expression   Paste the expression   Edit the pasted expression

You can also highlight an expression and simply press ⏎ to paste it to the entry line. However, the method described in this section allows you to press ⓒⓣ v to paste the expression as often as desired for subsequent calculations.

Keep in mind, too, that you can also copy an answer and use it in future calculations.

You can also copy just a part of an expression from the Calculator history. To do this, follow these steps:

1. **Use the ▲ key to highlight a previous expression.**

2. **Press ◄ or ► to move the cursor to the left or right of the part of the expression you want to highlight.**

3. **Press and hold the ⟨⟩ and use the ‹ or › keys to drag the highlighting to the left or right.**

4. **Press ⟨ctrl⟩⟨C⟩ to copy the highlighted item.**

Exploring the Calculator Application Menu

Each application in TI-Nspire has its own unique application menu, accessed by pressing the ⟨menu⟩ key. Some top-level applications (the first menu choices you see after pressing ⟨menu⟩) have submenus as indicated by the small ▯ located to the right of the menu choice. To view a submenu, highlight the menu choice using the NavPad and press ⟨enter⟩ or ⟨▸⟩. If you happen to be working with the Functions & Programs menu, you can get as far as a fourth menu level.

Press the ⟨esc⟩ or ‹ to back out of a submenu.

The Calculator application menu has so many different tools that I simply cannot provide a sufficient description of each tool. Rather, I give you a sampling of some of my favorite tools from each top-level menu choice. My hope is that this brief tour makes you want to explore these menus in more detail.

Working with Number tools

Notice that the top-level menu choices are grouped by topic. For example, press ⟨menu⟩⇨Number to access a variety of choices for working with numbers, including fractions, decimals, prime factorization, greatest common divisor, and so on. Figure 5-10 provides a brief sampling of some of the tools found in the Number menu.

Figure 5-10:
The Number
submenu.

Convert to Decimal,
Factor,
Least Common Multiple

Remainder, Proper Fraction,
Get Numerator,
Round

Mod, Ceiling, Complex
Conjugate, Magnitude,
Convert to Polar

If you do not know the syntax of a function or command, you can look it up in the reference material provided with your TI-Nspire device. Alternatively, you can access the command from the Catalog (see the next section of this chapter), which also provides help with the proper syntax.

Numerical calculations

Press (menu)⇨Calculations to access the numerical calculations submenu. The names of the commands are fairly self-explanatory. Keep in mind that you can use these calculations with previously defined functions such as those that might be graphed in the Graphs & Geometry application. See Figure 5-11 for a sampling of these tools.

Figure 5-11:
The
Calculations
submenu.

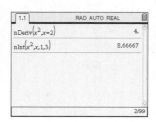 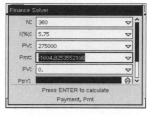

Numerical Solve,
Numerical Function Minimum,
Numerical Funtion
Maximize

Numerical Derivative,
Numerical Integral

Using the Finance Solver
to find the payment on a loan

Notice the syntax for the Numerical Solve, Numerical Function Minimum, and Numerical Function Maximum. The last two numbers indicate the interval in which to look for the solution, minimum, and maximum values, respectively. If you don't specify this interval, TI-Nspire returns the value that is closest to the origin.

Probability and statistics

Press (menu)⇨Probability to access the probability menu.

If you refer to the first screen in Figure 5-12, notice I have used the Factorial, Permutations, and Combinations commands in the first three lines. These three functions are invoked by first pressing (menu)⇨Probability. The last three lines in this screen are part of the Random submenu (press (menu)⇨Probability⇨Random). The last line in this screen uses the Random Normal command to give two random numbers from a normal distribution with mean 60 and standard deviation 5.

Press (menu)⇨Statistics to access the statistics menu. The second screen in Figure 5-12 shows the Statistics submenu. Notice that all but the Stat Results choice have a third-level submenu.

Many of the items in this menu are used in conjunction with other applications, mainly the Lists & Spreadsheet application. Data is usually located in the Lists & Spreadsheet application . Additionally, some commands can be nested within other commands. The third screen in Figure 5-12 shows two such examples. The first line in this screen shows how to find the mean of 50 random integers from 1 to 6. The second line in this screen shows how to find the sum $1^2 + 2^2 + 3^2 + \ldots + 10^2$.

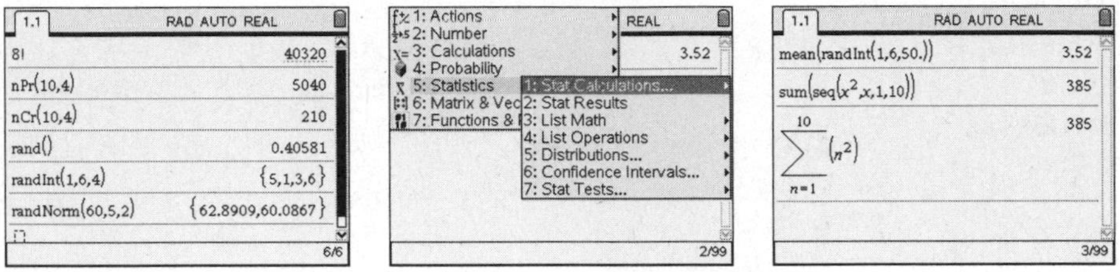

Figure 5-12: The Probability submenu and the Statistics submenu.

1.1	RAD AUTO REAL
8!	40320
nPr(10,4)	5040
nCr(10,4)	210
rand()	0.40581
randInt(1,6,4)	{5,1,3,6}
randNorm(60,5,2)	{62.8909,60.0867}
	6/6

	REAL
1: Actions	
2: Number	
3: Calculations	3.52
4: Probability	
5: Statistics	1: Stat Calculations...
6: Matrix & Vec	2: Stat Results
7: Functions &	3: List Math
	4: List Operations
	5: Distributions...
	6: Confidence Intervals...
	7: Stat Tests...
	2/99

1.1	RAD AUTO REAL
mean(randInt(1,6,50.))	3.52
sum(seq(x^2,x,1,10))	385
$\displaystyle\sum_{n=1}^{10}(n^2)$	385
	3/99

The last line in the third screen of Figure 5-12 shows that there is a much easier way to find the sum $1^2 + 2^2 + 3^2 + \ldots + 10^2$. Press (ctrl)(x²) to access the math template, highlight the summation template, and fill in the fields as I did. I talk more about the math template later in this chapter.

Exploring matrices

Press (menu)⇨Matrix & Vector to access the matrix menu.

Many of the items contained in the matrix menu work with a matrix that you must first define. For example, check out the first screen in Figure 5-13. I pressed (menu)⇨Matrix & Vector⇨Reduced Row-Echelon Form to paste the Rref command to the entry line. The easiest way to define a matrix as the argument for the Rref command is via the math template. Follow these steps to accomplish this task:

1. **Press (ctrl)(x²) to open the math template.**

2. **Highlight the variable size matrix template. See the first screen in Figure 5-13.**

3. Press (enter) open the Create a Matrix dialog box shown in the second screen in Figure 5-13. Use the ▲▼ keys to set the number of rows and columns.

4. Press (enter) to paste a blank matrix with the specified dimensions to the argument of the Rref command.

5. Enter each element of the matrix, pressing (tab) each time to move to the next field.

6. Press (enter) to execute the command. See the last screen in Figure 5-13. I also used the last answer feature with the Transpose command to transpose the rows and columns of my answer.

Figure 5-13: Creating a matrix and using the Matrix & Vector submenu.

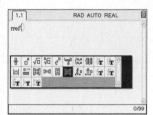 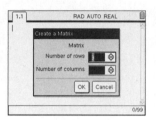 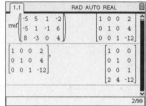

You can accomplish so much using the Matrix & Vector submenu that I encourage you to refer to your user's guide for additional information.

Using the Catalog (📖) Menu

The catalog, accessed by pressing the 📖 key, contains a list of all system functions, commands, symbols, and expression templates. These items can be pasted to the entry line of the Calculator application.

Moving from category to category

Press the 📖 key to open the Catalog. Within the Catalog, five categories are indicated by the numbered tabs located at the top of the screen. I show the first three categories of the Catalog in Figure 5-14. Here's a brief description of what each category represents:

✓ **Category 1:** Contains a list of all commands, functions, and symbols, in alphabetical order.

✓ **Category 2:** Contains a list of all math functions, sorted by topic area.

▶ **Category 3 (the Symbol Palette): Contains a list of all mathematical symbols.**

▶ **Category 4 (the Math Template): Contains a list of mathematical templates including square root, piecewise functions, and matrices.**

▶ **Category 5: Shows a list of all Public Library objects.**

To move from one category to the next, just type the number associated with each category. For example, press ④ to access the math template.

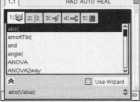

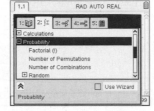

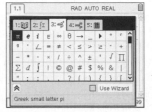

Figure 5-14:
The Catalog.

Alphabetical list of commands   List of math functions   The symbol palette

Accessing functions and commands

When you are in a desired category, use the NavPad keys to highlight your choice and press ⓔ to paste it to the entry line. Keep in mind that the items contained in the second tab are grouped by topic. To expand a topic, such as Probability, highlight the topic name and press the ⑦. See the second screen in Figure 5-14.

The alphabetical list contained in the first category of the Catalog is quite extensive. Fortunately, a few tricks allow you to access specific commands quickly. If you know the name of a command, press the letter corresponding to the first letter of the command. For example, to access the Rand command, press ⓡ to jump to those commands beginning with R. Then use the NavPad to scroll down to the Rand command. When your command has been highlighted, press ⓔ to paste it to the entry line.

No matter what tab is active in the Catalog, press ⓒⓣⓡ⑦ to page-down through the entire list. You can also press ⓒⓣⓡ① to page-up through the list.

To jump to the last item in the Catalog, press ⓒⓣⓡ⑨ (the equivalent to the End key on your computer). To jump to the first item in the Catalog, press ⓒⓣⓡ③ (the equivalent to the Home key on your computer).

Determining syntax

Notice on the first screen in Figure 5-15 that the bottom of the screen shows the syntax associated with the rounding command, Round. To see an expanded view of this syntax (or any command or symbol in the Catalog), press ⓣab to highlight the bottom portion of the screen and then press ⓧ to expand this area (see the second screen in Figure 5-15). Depending on the command that you have highlighted, you may see several rows of syntax.

Any part of the syntax that is contained in brackets is optional. For example, the Round command will, by default, round up to the number of Display Digits specified in the Document Settings. The optional second number in the argument determines the number of decimal places to include in the result. The third screen in Figure 5-15 shows the result of Round(12.365) and Round(12.365,2).

Figure 5-15:
Using syntax help to execute a command.

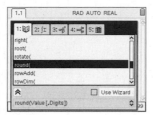 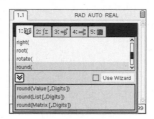 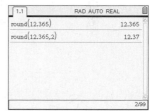

 You may have noticed the wizard box in Figure 5-15. To check this box, press ⓣab until the word *Wizard* becomes highlighted and press ⓧ. When this box is checked, certain functions (such as the LinRegMx command) open with labeled boxes to help you enter arguments in an expression.

 When you first open the Catalog, the most recently used category and command (or symbol, template, and so on) is highlighted. Pressing ⓣab once moves you to the syntax box located at the bottom of the screen. Pressing ⓣab again moves you to the wizard check box. Pressing ⓣab a third time highlights the numbered tabs, allowing you to move through each tab by pressing the ◀▶ keys on the NavPad. Finally, pressing ⓣab a fourth time brings you back to your command (or symbol, template, and so on) once again. Think of this as a counterclockwise rotation through the different fields of the Catalog. To move in a clockwise direction, press ⓒaps ⓣab.

 To paste an item to the entry line, you must continue to press ⓣab until the item you want to use is highlighted.

Alternative ways to access the symbol palette and the math template

The third and fourth categories can also be directly accessed via secondary keys. To access the symbol palette, press (ctrl)(⌨). To access the math template, press (ctrl)(π|²ₓ).

Evaluating expressions in multiple ways

TI-Nspire's primary and secondary keys, application menu, and catalog provide for a lot of power when it comes to working in the Calculator application. It also means you often have many ways to complete a task.

Earlier in this section, I evaluated the expression $\log_5 25$. It turns out that you can use several different ways to evaluate this expression. Here's a list of these methods, in no particular order:

✔ Press (ctrl)(log10ˣ) to access the logarithm template from a secondary key.

✔ Press (ctrl)(π|²ₓ) to access the math template. Highlight the logarithm template and press (enter) to paste it to the entry line.

✔ Press (⌨)(4) to access the math template through the catalog.

✔ Press (⌨)(1) to access the alphabetical list of functions and commands and then follow these steps:

   a. Press (L) to jump down to those functions and commands that begin with L.

   b. Use the NavPad keys to highlight Log (and press Enter to paste the command to the entry line).

   c. Complete the expression by typing **log(25,5)** and press (enter).

✔ Type (L)(O)(G) using the alpha keys to invoke the same command that is found in the Catalog menu. Then follow step *c* from the preceding list to complete the expression and find its value.

Clearly, some of these options are more efficient than others. However, those of you who like choices should be quite happy. The many options also demonstrate the versatility of TI-Nspire.

Chapter 6

Working with Variables

*T*his chapter is all about variables — how to create variables, name variables, and use variables to enhance your experience working with TI-Nspire. Keep in mind that variables are shared among applications within the same problem. And it is because of this sharing that TI-Nspire can dynamically represent math concepts in multiple ways.

The Rules for Naming Variables

TI-Nspire offers a great deal of flexibility when it comes to naming variables. However, a few variable names are off-limits. Here's the official list of do's and don'ts when it comes to naming variables:

✔ Variables can be 1 to 16 characters long and may consist of letters, digits, and the underscore character.

✔ TI-Nspire does not distinguish between uppercase and lowercase letters.

✔ The first character cannot be a digit.

✔ Spaces are not allowed.

✔ If an underscore is used as the first character, the variable is considered a type of unit. Units do not allow subsequent underscores in the name.

✔ System variables, functions, and command names cannot be used as variables. Examples include Ans, fMax, and Mean.

Storing Variables

There are a variety of reasons why you might want to store a variable. Here's a list of some of those reasons.

- **Store a number.** You may want to store a number to a variable if you expect that you will need to use the number again in subsequent calculations. This is especially helpful if the number is irrational (or quite long) and you want to store the entire result for future use.

- **Define a function.** The ability to define a function with a meaningful name is a powerful option. In fact, TI-Nspire has dispelled the myth that functions must have names like $f(x)$ or $g(x)$. Now you can create functions whose names actually tell you what the function does. My two examples from this chapter, $area(s)$ and $surface\_area(r, h)$, illustrate this point.

- **Store a list.** Lists can be quite long and cumbersome. By storing a list as a variable, you have the ability to recall the list using a single variable name, rather than by retyping all the elements contained in the list.

- **Store a matrix.** Matrices can also be long and cumbersome, particularly if the matrix contains several rows and columns. Storing a matrix can save you a lot of time and effort.

In general, storing variables can be a great time saver. It also ensures that subsequent actions that utilize stored variables are precise and accurate. Finally, there are many, many situations in which a stored variable can facilitate and enrich a mathematical exploration. You will certainly see many of these types of applications as you read other chapters in this book.

Some variables are stored automatically depending on the functions you access while using TI-Nspire. For example, each time you perform a calculation, the last answer is stored to the variable Ans. If you perform a regression on a data set, several variables are created such as Stat1.r (correlation coefficient), stat.resid (list of residuals), and stat1.regeqn (regression equation). These examples also serve to remind you of the types of variables that TI-Nspire can store. The variable Stat1.r is a *number*. The other two variables, stat.resid and stat1.regeqn, are a *list* and a *function*, respectively.

Variables can only be shared among pages that are part of the same problem. If you define a variable in Problem 1, then this variable can only be accessed from within Problem 1. Furthermore, I can define a variable with the same name in a second problem, knowing that these two variables will not conflict with one another. They can take on completely separate values or meanings. Chapter 7 discusses the use of variables in applications outside the Calculator application. You cannot create a global variable across all problems in the TI-Nspire.

You also have the option of deciding what variables you want to store. The next two sections explain how to do this.

Using the store variable (⟨ctrl⟩ ⟨sto▸ var⟩) key

The Store Variable operator is a secondary key, accessed by pressing ⟨ctrl⟩⟨sto▸ var⟩. When using this method to store a variable, follow these three steps:

1. **Type the item you want to store on the entry line. This might be a value, list, matrix, or expression.**

2. **Press ⟨ctrl⟩⟨sto▸ var⟩ to invoke the Store command (as indicated by a small right arrow).**

3. **Type the variable name and press ⟨enter⟩ to store the variable.**

An alternate method for storing a variable

A colon followed by an equal sign (press ⟨∶⟩⟨=⟩) also tells TI-Nspire to store a variable. This method works just the opposite of the ⟨ctrl⟩⟨sto▸ var⟩ method. That is, you must first type the variable name, press ⟨∶⟩⟨=⟩, and type the value, list, matrix, or expression to be stored.

The first screen in Figure 6-1 shows several examples of how variables can be stored using the first method. The second screen in Figure 6-1 shows how these same variables can be stored using the second method.

Figure 6-1: Storing variables using two different methods.

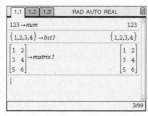
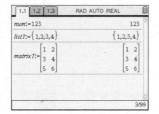

Using the Define command

The Define command offers yet another way to store a variable. Here's an example of how you can create your own function in the Calculator application using the Define command.

1. **Press (menu)⇨Actions⇨Define to paste the Define command to the entry line.**

2. **Type the name of your function using function notation. You must include the independent variable within parentheses.**

3. **Press ⊜ and type the function rule in terms of the independent variable that you have selected.**

4. **Press (enter).**

The first screen in Figure 6-2 shows an example of a user-defined function that gives the area of an equilateral triangle, *area*(*s*), with side length *s*. The second screen in Figure 6-2 shows an example of a user-defined function that gives the surface area of a cylinder, *surface_area*(*r, h*), in terms of the input variables *r* and *h*.

Keep in mind that these functions can also be defined using the methods described in the previous two sections. For example, I can define the function *surface_area*(*r, h*) by typing `surface_area(r,h):=2·ω·r²+2· ω·r·h`.

The third screen in Figure 6-2 shows how to evaluate these functions for specific values of the independent variables. I have accessed these user-defined functions by pressing the (sto→var) key and selecting the defined function from the list. You can also type the function using the keypad. I talk more about recalling a stored variable in the next section.

Figure 6-2:
Using the
Define
command
to store a
function.

Stored functions can be graphed in the Graphs & Geometry application. However, you must specify *x* as the independent variable for this to work. For example, to graph *A*(*s*), type *A*(*x*) next to the first available function in the Graphs & Geometry application.

You can also use the Define command to store a variable as a number, list, or matrix. Just invoke the Define command, type the variable name, press ⊜, and type the number, list, or matrix.

Multiple variables can be stored simultaneously by separating each store command with a colon (press $\odot$). For example, num1:=10:num2:=20 stores 10 to the variable num1 and 20 to the variable num2.

Recalling a Variable

After a variable has been stored, you will inevitably want to recall the variable for use in a command, expression, or other application. In this section, I give you two ways to recall a stored variable.

Typing a variable name

If you know the name of the variable you want to use, feel free to type the variable name using the keypad. This method generally works fine if the variable name is relatively short and does not contain fancy symbols that are hard to find.

As shown in the first two screens in Figure 6-3, I have used this method to recall the variable num. As you type, the letters appear in italics. When the variable name is complete, the entire variable name turns nonitalicized and bold (see first screen in Figure 6-3). Press 🔘 to see the value of the variable as shown in the second screen in Figure 6-3.

Using the 🔘 key

The 🔘 key provides a quick way to access variable names. Press 🔘, scroll through the variable list using the NavPad keys to highlight your choice, and press 🔘 to paste it to your current location. The third screen in Figure 6-3 shows an example of the list that appears after you press the 🔘 key.

Figure 6-3:
Recalling a
variable.

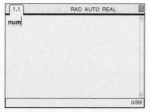

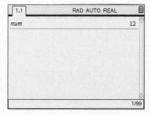

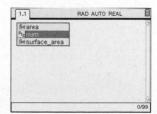

Complete variable
turns bold, non-italic

The value of the variable

Access the variable
from a list

When pressing the ⌨ key, small icons located to the left of each variable name indicate the variable type. The table below gives the meaning of each icon.

Table 6-1	Stored Variable Icons
Icon	*Description*
ƒ⋅⊢	Function
⊢⋅⊣	List
⊞⊞	Matrix
0_{1_2}	Number

The two methods described in this section for recalling variables work in any TI-Nspire application.

Updating a variable

Consider that you just stored a variable with a certain value (or function, matrix, or list). If you store the variable again with a new value (or function, matrix, or list), the variable takes on this new value.

You can also use the variable itself to define the same variable with a new value.

The first screen in Figure 6-4 shows some examples in which variables are stored to new values. In the first line, I have stored 10 to the variable num. On the second line, I've stored 16 to the same variable. On the third line I've recalled num to show that it has taken on this new value. On the fourth line, I've performed a more complicated expression containing num and stored the result, 248, back to num. On the last line I've recalled num to show that it has taken on this new value.

The second screen in Figure 6-4 shows some examples of how a stored matrix can be updated using the alternative method of storing variables.

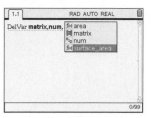

Figure 6-4:
Updating
variables.

Deleting Variables

Variables can be deleted from within the Calculator application via the DelVar command (press (menu)⇨Actions⇨Delete Variable). Keep in mind that you can only delete a variable that is contained within the current problem. The DelVar command can be used to delete several variables at a time by separating each variable to be deleted with a comma.

Figure 6-5 shows that I have deleted three variables using the DelVar command.

Figure 6-5:
Deleting
variables.

After you invoke the DelVar command, press (stovar) to bring up a list of stored variables and select the variable to be deleted from this list. If you call up a function, it also brings up a set of parentheses, which must be deleted by pressing (clear) once.

If you mistakenly delete a variable, press (tab)(esc) to undo the deletion.

Chapter 7

Using the Calculator Application with Other Applications

*T*here is so much that you can do by working strictly within the Calculator application. However, this application does not work in isolation. In this chapter, I show you some examples that illustrate how the Calculator application can work in conjunction with other applications. This capability really extends the power of the Calculator application.

Defining Variables To Be Used Elsewhere

This is a fundamental idea that applies to any TI-Nspire application. If you define a variable, it is available for use in any page in TI-Nspire, assuming that you work on pages within the same problem. To recall the variable, you have two options:

  ✔ Press ⬡ and select the desired variable from the list.

  ✔ Type the variable name using the keypad. If you choose this option, the variable name displays as nonitalicized and bold after the last character is typed. This indicates that you are working with a stored variable.

Variables can only be shared among pages that are part of the same problem. If you define a variable in Problem 1, this variable can only be accessed from within Problem 1. Furthermore, I can define a variable with the same name in a second problem, knowing that these two variables will not conflict with one another. They can take on completely separate values or meanings.

Using the Calculator Application with the Graphs & Geometry Application

The Calculator application and the Graphs & Geometry application are a perfect fit. In this section, I show you several examples of how you can establish the lines of communication between these two powerful applications.

Defining a function and graphing it in Graphs & Geometry

In Chapter 6, I define a function, *area(s)*, that gives the area of an equilateral triangle with side of length *s*. Using the 🔲 key, I can call up this function from within the Graphs & Geometry application for the purpose of analyzing this function graphically. In the following list, I show you once again how to define this function in the Calculator application and then how to graph it in the Graphs & Geometry application.

1. **Use the Define command to define *A(s)*.**

   Refer to Figure 6-2 for how to do this.

2. **Open a new Graphs & Geometry page.**

   By default, you are in graphing mode with the cursor located on the entry line next to the first available function.

3. **Press 🔲 to view a list of variables and select** area **from the list.**

   See the first screen in Figure 7-1. You also have the option of typing the variable name using the green alpha keys.

4. **You must type parentheses and include the variable *x* as the independent variable (even though you used *s* when defining the function).**

   See the second screen in Figure 7-1.

5. **Press 🔲 to graph the function and adjust the window settings accordingly.**

   I added some lines and included a moveable point, with coordinates, on the graph. See the third screen in Figure 7-1.

Because I graphed the function *area(s)* in the Graphs & Geometry application as *f1(x)*, I can now access this function in two ways, *area* and *f1*. For example, from within a calculator page I can type area(4) to find the area of an equilateral triangle with side length 4. Alternatively, I can evaluate f1(4) and obtain the same result.

Figure 7-1:
Graphing
a function
defined
in the
Calculator
application.

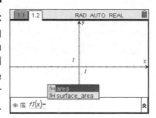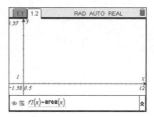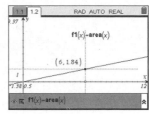

Graphing a function with two input variables

In Chapter 6, I define a function, *surface_area(r,h)*, that gives the surface area of a cylinder as a function of the radius, *r*, and height, *h*. This is a trickier function to graph because there are two input variables. To get around this issue, I created a slider in the Graphs & Geometry application to give the height, *h*, a fixed value, but with the option of changing this height by dragging the slider. In effect, I'm defining *h* as a constant but still giving myself the option of varying it. See Chapter 9 to learn how to use a slider.

The first screen in Figure 7-2 shows the graph of this scenario with *h* set to 3.5. The second screen in Figure 7-2 shows this same scenario with *h* changed to 7.5. Notice that the point on the graph corresponding to *x* = 8 has corresponding *y*-values of 578.05 and 779.11 for *h* = 3.5 and *h* = 7.5, respectively.

Figure 7-2:
Graphing
a function
with two
independent
variables.

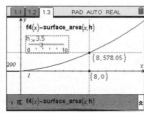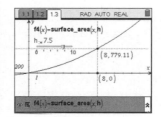

Using nfMax and nfMin to find max and min in the Calculator application

In Figure 7-3 I show you a classic optimization problem in which squares of side length *x* are cut from the corners of a standard 8.5 in. by 11 in. piece of paper. The resulting flaps are folded up to create an open-topped box. The challenge is to determine the cut length, *x*, that will produce a maximum value.

The first screen in Figure 7-3 shows the captured data obtained by dragging the indicated point located on the left side of the screen. The second screen shows that I have graphed a function that represents the volume of the open-topped box for a cut length of x.

In the third screen in Figure 7-3, I have called up this function, $f1(x)$, and used it within the nfMax command to find the value of x, 1.58542, that produces the maximum volume (see the first line of the Calculator page). In the second line, I've embedded the nfMax command within the function $f1(x)$. The result is that TI-Nspire first calculates the value of x that produces the maximum volume and then uses this value to find the corresponding maximum volume, 66.1482, given by the function $f1(x)$.

Figure 7-3:
Using nfMax
to analyze
a function
defined in
the Graphs
& Geometry
application.

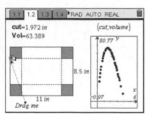
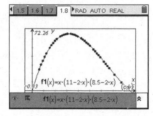
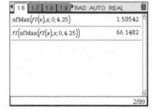

The $(x, f1(x))$ pair that give the maximum value of this function can also be found directly in the Graphs & Geometry application. See Part III to learn how to do this.

In Figure 7-4, I show another classic optimization problem. This time, I am trying to find the radius of a standard soda can with fixed volume 355 ml that produces the least surface area. Notice in the third screen in Figure 7-4 I have used the nfMin command on the first line to find the value of x that gives the least amount of surface area. On the second line, I've embedded this function within $f5(x)$ to calculate the corresponding minimum surface area.

Figure 7-4:
Using nfMin
to analyze
a function
defined in
the Graphs
& Geometry
application.

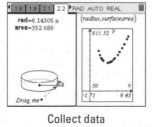
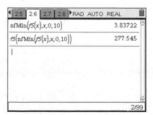

Collect data   Graph $f5(x)$ to match   Use nfMin to analyze
                       the data   a function

You learn more about how these constructions are made in Part III of this book. I describe how to produce the scatter plots shown in Figures 7-3 and 7-4, which utilize the Data Capture feature, in Chapter 16.

Evaluating a function in the Graphs & Geometry application

In Figure 7-3, I reference the function $f1(x)$ defined in the Graphs & Geometry application and use it with the nfMax command to find the value of x that produces a maximum value. The idea of referencing a function defined in the Graphs & Geometry application is an important feature and one that bears repeating here.

To evaluate a function defined in the Graphs & Geometry application at a specific value for the input variable, follow these steps.

1. **Type the name of the function using the keypad or press ⬡ to call up a list of functions.**

2. **After you type the function name, press ⬡ to open a set of parentheses. If you access a function using the ⬡ key, a set of parentheses is automatically included.**

3. **Type any numerical value within the parentheses and press ⬡ to evaluate the function for this value. If you mistakenly attempt to evaluate a function for a value for which it's not defined, an error message appears.**

Using NDeriv and NInt to graph in G & G

You also have the option of calling up functions or commands typically used in the Calculator application from within the Graphs & Geometry application. First, I show you how to graph the derivative of $y = x^3$ using the nDeriv (numerical derivative) command.

1. **Position the cursor next to the first available function line in the Graphs & Geometry application.**

2. **Press ⬡ to open the Catalog. If necessary, press ⬡ to activate the first category containing the alphabetical listing of all commands, functions, and symbols.**

3. **Press ⓝ to jump to those items beginning with N. Scroll down and highlight nDeriv and press ⬡ to paste this command to the Graphs & Geometry entry line.**

   See the first screen in Figure 7-5.

4. **Type the argument that is shown in the second screen in Figure 7-5 and press ⊕ to graph the derivative of** $y = x^3$ **as shown in the third screen in Figure 7-5.**

Figure 7-5:
Using
nDeriv from
the Catalog
to graph a
derivative.

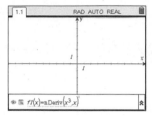

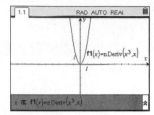

The syntax that I used for the nDeriv command is nDeriv(*expression, variable*). For the *variable* part of the argument, I typed x to obtain a graph for all x, not just a single value. Had I typed $x = 2$ for *variable*, I would have graphed the horizontal line $y = 12$ (because the derivative of $y = x^3$ at $x = 2$ is 12).

I can use the nInt (numerical integral) command to go in the opposite direction, that is, to graph the anti-derivative of a function. The syntax for this command is nInt(*expression, variable, lower bound, upper bound*). By typing nInt($3x^2$, x, 0, x), I can produce the graph $y = x^3$, which is the definite integral of $3x^2$ with lower bound 0 and upper bound x.

Graphing a step function in G&G

Many other functions can be graphed by accessing commands commonly used in the Calculator application. The *greatest integer function*, $y = int(x)$, is one such graph which can be created by following these steps:

1. **Position the cursor next to the first available function line.**

2. **Press ⊕ to open the catalog. If necessary, press ① to activate the first category containing the alphabetical listing of all commands, functions, and symbols.**

3. **Press ① to jump to those items beginning with I. Scroll down and highlight** Int **and press ⊕ to paste this command to the Graphs & Geometry entry line.**

4. **Type** x **for the argument and press ⊕ to complete the graph.**

The first screen in Figure 7-6 shows the graph of the greatest integer function. I've also included the graph of the anti-derivative from the previous section as well as the graph of the absolute value function (which uses the Abs command from the catalog).

Figure 7-6:
Using other
functions
from the
Calculator
application
for
graphing.

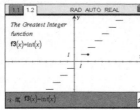 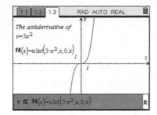 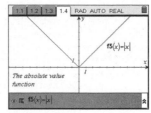

Rather than use the Catalog, I can type a function directly using the alpha keys. That's how I graphed the absolute value function in Figure 7-6. I simply typed Ⓐ Ⓑ Ⓢ and the command was recognized as indicated by the non-italicized font. After pressing ⏎, the Abs command is replaced by the vertical bars that are used to denote absolute value, just as you see in a textbook.

Using the Calculator Application with the Lists & Spreadsheet Application

In the previous section, I tell you how the Calculator application and the Graphs & Geometry application talk to one another. It turns out that the Calculator application talks to any application, including the Lists & Spreadsheet application.

Performing regressions

In Chapter 15, I discuss how to perform a regression from within the Lists & Spreadsheet application. You can also perform a regression on data contained in the Lists & Spreadsheet application from within the Calculator application.

Chapter 15, Table 15-1 contains United States Immigrant Population (in millions) for years after 1900. The first screen in Figure 7-7 shows how the *year* versus *Immigrant Population* data looks in the Lists & Spreadsheet application. To learn more about how to configure the Lists & Spreadsheet application for this data, see Chapter 15. You may also want to take a look at Figure 15-7. This figure shows a scatter plot of the data which suggests that a cubic model is a good choice.

To perform a cubic regression on this data in the Calculator application, press (menu)⇨Statistics⇨Stat Calculations…⇨Cubic Regression.

A dialog box opens as shown in the second screen in Figure 7-7. As with any dialog box, you can press ⓣ to move from one field to the next or ⓢⓣ to move backwards through a field.

The names used for X List (*year*) and Y List (*impop*) are the same names found at the top of each column containing the data in the Lists & Spreadsheet application. You can type these names using the green alpha keys or press ⓥ and select *year* to specify the location of the X List and *impop* for the Y List.

Press ⓔ after configuring the dialog box to perform the regression. All the results of the regression are pasted to the Calculator page as shown in the third screen of Figure 7-7.

Figure 7-7:
Performing a cubic regression from within the Calculator application.

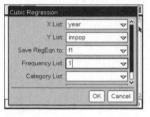 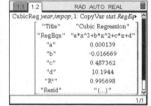

The cubic regression results yield the equation $f1(x) = 0.000139x^3 - 0.0167x^2 + 0.487x + 10.194$. Notice the *Coefficient of Determination*, R^2, is very close to 1. This suggests that the regression equation is a good fit for the data.

A variety of variables are stored by TI-Nspire after a regression. To view this list, press the ⓥ key. Using the ▲▼ keys, you can scroll through this list and paste a variable to the entry line in the Calculator page.

For example, try selecting the variable Stat.Resid and pressing ⓔ to paste it to the entry line. Press ⓔ again to produce a list of *residuals*. This list represents the difference between the *y*-value of each data point and the corresponding *y*-value associated with the regression equation.

I stored the regression equation to $f1(x)$. As with any stored function, I can evaluate this function for specific values of *x* or use it within a command (such as nfMax).

Storing lists from the Calculator application to L&S

The Calculator contains a variety of commands that are useful in generating lists of data. One such example is the Sequence command, accessed by pressing ⓜ⇨Statistics⇨List Operations⇨Sequence. The syntax for this command is seq(*Expression*, *Variable*, *Low*, *High*[, *Step*]. For example, the command seq(2*x* + 1,*x*,0,50,5) generates the list {1, 11, 21, 31, …,101}. The Random submenu (press ⓜ⇨Probability⇨Random) offers another place where lists of data can be produced.

If you are interested in investigating the outcomes of rolling two dice 50 times, here's how to accomplish this task:

1. **Insert a Lists & Spreadsheet page and name the first column** *red_die* **and the second column** *blue_die*.

2. **Insert a Calculator page and press** ⓜ⇨**Probability⇨Random⇨ Integer. This pastes the command randInt to the entry line. Configure this command to read** `randInt(1,6,50)`.

3. **Press** ⓒⓣⓡⓛ ⓢⓣⓞ `var` **to invoke the Store command.**

4. **Press** `var`, **highlight** *red_die* **from the list, and press** ⓔⓝⓣⓔⓡ.

5. **Press** ⓔⓝⓣⓔⓡ **again to execute the command.**

   You see the list of numbers displayed on the Calculator page. This data is also stored to the Lists & Spreadsheet page under the column titled *red_die*. (See Figure 7-8.)

   Repeat Steps 2 through 5, this time storing 50 random integers from 1 to 6 to the list named *blue_die*.

Figure 7-8:
Storing two-dice data to the Lists & Spreadsheet application.

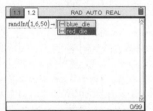

| Storing random integers to *red_die* | Results displayed on the Calculator page | Results stored to the Lists & Spreadsheets application |

Performing statistical analyses on data

Data contained within the Lists & Spreadsheet application can be analyzed from within the Calculator application. For example, it might be interesting to view the one-variable statistical results of the *Total* list from the two-dice sum experiment. Follow these steps.

1. **Press (menu)⇨Statistics⇨Stat Calculations…⇨One-Variable Statistics.**

2. **Press (enter) to indicate that you want to analyze one list.**

   If you have additional lists, change Num of Lists to match the number of lists you are interested in analyzing.

3. **Configure the dialog box as shown in the first screen in Figure 7-9.**

4. **Press (enter) to close the dialog box and perform the statistical analysis.**

   See the second screen in Figure 7-9.

Figure 7-9:
Performing
one-variable
statistical
analysis
from within
the
Calculator
application.

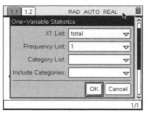 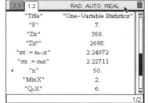

 A variety of statistical results are generated by the One-Variable Statistics command. Refer to Chapter 15 for a description of what each result means.

 Many of the statistical results generated by the One-Variable Statistics command can be invoked individually from within the List Math submenu (press (menu)⇨Statistics⇨List Math). For example, the command Sum of Elements (denoted Sum) yields the sum of all the elements of a specified list. In general, all the commands found within the List Math submenu must contain either a list or a list name as their arguments.

 You can sort lists or perform a variety of other manipulations of lists from within the Calculator application. Many of the commands that allow you to perform such manipulations are found in the Lists Operations submenu (press (menu)⇨Statistics⇨List Operations). For example, the command Sort Ascending (denoted SortA) sorts a specified list from lowest value to highest value.

Other variations on the two-dice example

In the previous section, I show you how to execute two separate commands to store 50 random integers from 1 to 6 to two separate lists. You can execute both of these commands on a single entry line by separating them with a colon. The exact syntax for this command is `randInt(1,6,50)→red_die:randInt(1,6,50)→blue_die`. Press ⏎ to populate both lists in the Lists & Spreadsheet page with 50 random integers from 1 to 6 simultaneously.

To find the sum of these dice, name the third column in the spreadsheet *Total*. Then go back to the Calculator page and type the command `red_die + blue_die→total` and press ⏎. Take a look at the Lists & Spreadsheets page. The third column contains 50 numbers, with each value equal to the sum of the two numbers found in the first and second columns.

If you want to generate an entirely new set of two-dice data, use the Calculator history to re-execute the `randInt(1,6,50)→red_die:randInt(1,6,50)→blue_die` and `red_die + blue_die→total` commands. See Chapter 5 for more information on how to use the Calculator history.

Chapter 8

Using the Calculator Application with TI-Nspire CAS

*T*he acronym *CAS* stands for *Computer Algebra System*. A computer algebra system facilitates the symbolic manipulation of mathematical expressions and equations. For example, consider the solution to the equation $x^2 = 12$. A computer algebra system, such as the one built into the gray TI-Nspire CAS handheld, returns the answers

$$x = -2\sqrt{3}$$

and

$$x = 2\sqrt{3}$$

The blue TI-Nspire unit performs numerical or *floating-point* calculations. Hence, the solutions to the equation $x^2 = 12$ are given as –3.464 and 3.464.

Throughout this book, I refer to the blue numeric TI-Nspire handheld as simply TI-Nspire. I refer to the gray CAS unit as TI-Nspire CAS.

The TI-Nspire CAS device does not come with a removable keypad. Therefore, you cannot operate this unit as a TI-84 Plus Silver Edition graphing calculator.

In this chapter, I demonstrate the symbolic manipulation capabilities of TI-Nspire CAS as they apply to the Calculator application. In Chapter 12, I discuss how TI-Nspire CAS can be used with the Graphs & Geometry application. In Chapter 18, I show you how TI-Nspire CAS can be used with the Lists & Spreadsheets application.

A brief history of computer algebra systems

Computer algebra systems were first invented in the early 1970s. Examples of computer-based CAS systems include Maple, Mathematica, Derive, and MathCAD. Derive requires relatively little memory and processing power. As a result, it can be used on older machines with limited capabilities. Furthermore, Derive helped make possible the introduction of the TI-92 in 1995, one of the first devices that offered computer algebra capabilities in handheld form.

Texas Instruments introduced the successor to the TI-92, the TI-89 series, in 1998. The TI-89 is similar to the TI-92 except that it is smaller and does not have a QWERTY keyboard. As a result, the TI-89 is allowed on most standardized tests. Texas Instruments introduced its latest CAS device, TI-Nspire CAS, in 2007. TI-Nspire and TI-Nspire CAS are also allowed on most standardized exams.

The remaining chapters do not pertain exclusively to the TI-Nspire CAS handheld. TI-Nspire and TI-Nspire CAS have a significant amount in common, and just about everything you read in this book most certainly applies to both.

Evaluating Expressions

In this section, I show you how the results of simple calculations are given, by default, symbolically. I then show you how to force approximate results.

Finding symbolic representations of numerical calculations

Check out the first screen in Figure 8-1. I've entered some expressions by using a combination of primary and secondary keys. As you can see in the first two lines of these screens, TI-Nspire CAS returns results in symbolic form. That is, results are given as exact values — the way you typically see them in textbooks or other printed materials. You can see on the third line of this same screen that TI-Nspire CAS attempts to display algebraic expressions in simplified form. In the case of the product of two rational expressions, common factors are divided out, and the result is displayed as a single, simplified rational expression. TI-Nspire CAS can even handle complicated expressions such as the one shown in the last line of the first screen in Figure 8-1. Notice that warning message located at the bottom of first screen in Figure 8-1. The complete message reads "Domain of the result might be larger than the domain of the input." This message occurs because the domain of the input is the set of all real numbers greater than zero, whereas the domain of the output is the set of all real numbers greater than or equal to zero.

As a comparison, I've typed the first three expressions on the TI-Nspire handheld as shown in the second screen in Figure 8-1. The first two results are given as decimal approximations. The rational expression on the third line returns an error message because the variables x and y are not defined and, therefore, do not have a numerical value. Had I stored numerical values to x and y, TI-Nspire would return the numerical result of this expression evaluated at these stored values.

Figure 8-1:
Comparing
evaluated
expressions
on TI-Nspire
CAS and
TI-Nspire.

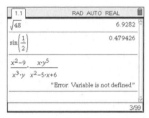

TI-Nspire CAS   TI-Nspire

TI-Nspire and TI-Nspire CAS do not always display results as decimals. Answers that are rational numbers are almost always given in fractional form. However, the examples shown in the second screen in Figure 8-1 have irrational answers and, therefore, must be given as decimal approximations.

Finding approximate results

At times, it is advantageous to view the decimal approximation of an answer. As you do with TI-Nspire, press (ctrl)(enter) to evaluate an expression and force a result as a decimal. This action invokes the *Approximately Equal to* feature, a secondary function represented by the symbol . Here are two additional ways to obtain an approximate result:

- **Include a decimal point somewhere in your calculation.** For example type (3)(÷)(3)(÷)(5)(.) to evaluate the first example in decimal form.
- **Use the Approx command to force a result in decimal form or scientific notation.** This command can be typed using the green alpha keys. It can also be found in the catalog menu.

The TI-Nspire CAS Application Menu

Take a look at the screens in Figure 8-2. These screens represent the top-level Calculator application menus for both TI-Nspire devices. Both devices have submenus titled Actions, Number, Probability, Statistics, Matrix & Vector, and

Functions & Programs. Within these submenus are a variety of functions, commands, and additional submenus that are virtually identical in both devices.

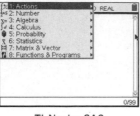

Figure 8-2:
The
TI-Nspire
CAS and
TI-Nspire
Calculator
application
menus.

TI-Nspire CAS   TI-Nspire

However, note two differences. On the TI-Nspire CAS unit, the Calculations menu that resides on TI-Nspire is replaced by the Algebra menu. Figure 8-3 shows the contents of these two menus.

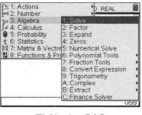

Figure 8-3:
The
TI-Nspire
CAS
Algebra
menu and
TI-Nspire
Calculations
menu.

TI-Nspire CAS   TI-Nspire

All the functions in the TI-Nspire Calculations menu are located elsewhere on the TI-Nspire CAS device. In fact, you can find the last five commands in the Calculations submenu on TI-Nspire CAS by choosing (menu)⇨Calculus⇨ Numerical Calculations. You reach the Numerical Solve command on TI-Nspire CAS by choosing (menu)⇨Algebra⇨Numerical Solve.

Of course, all menu items are in the Catalog.

The Calculus menu on TI-Nspire CAS does not have a counterpart on TI-Nspire. It contains a variety of powerful functions described in detail later in this chapter.

Doing algebra

Early in this chapter, I demonstrate how TI-Nspire CAS can perform symbolic manipulation of numerical and algebraic expressions. As impressive as that is, the CAS capabilities found in the Algebra submenu are nothing short of powerful. In this section, I highlight some of the functions and commands in the Algebra submenu. Keep in mind that the name associated with each function reveals much about what it can accomplish.

To find the syntax associated with a command, look it up in the alphabetical listing of commands and functions found in the Catalog. To see an expanded view of this syntax (or any command or symbol in the Catalog), press (tab) to highlight the bottom portion of the screen and then press ⊚ to expand this area. Depending on the command that you have highlighted, you may see several rows of syntax.

The Solve command

Choose (menu)⇨Algebra⇨Solve to invoke the Solve command. As the name implies, this command returns the solution(s) to an equation, inequality, or system of equations.

Figure 8-4 shows some examples of what this command can do.

Figure 8-4: Using the Solve command.

The first screen in Figure 8-4 shows how the Solve command can solve a single equation, an inequality, and a system of equations, with solutions displayed in symbolic form. As for systems, you can include as many equations, separated by the word *and*, as you want. Just make sure that you also specify the variables for which you want to solve.

The first line in the second screen in Figure 8-4 shows how the solution to a *dependent* system is displayed. The infinite number of solutions is indicated by an expression in terms of the constant *c2*. This constant can equal any real number and gives the set of ordered pairs that lie on the line $2x - y = -3$.

The last two lines in the second screen show how TI-Nspire reacts to equations with no real number solutions.

Try solving the equation $a \cdot x^2 + b \cdot x + c = 0$ for the variable x by typing **solve(a·x2+b·x+c=0,x)**. TI-Nspire CAS returns the quadratic formula! Make sure that you press ⊛ between variables. Otherwise, TI-Nspire CAS may mistakenly think that ax and bx are single variables.

The equation $x^2 - 4x + 8 = 0$ has no real number solutions. However, it does have two *complex* solutions. To find complex solutions, choose (menu)⇨Algebra⇨Complex⇨Solve. This command, denoted cSolve, returns the complex solutions $x = 2 + 2i$ and $x = 2 - 2i$ for this equation.

The Factor command

Choose (menu)⇨Algebra⇨Factor to invoke the Factor command. This command factors numerical and algebraic expressions. Take a look at the first two lines of the first screen in Figure 8-5. TI-Npsirc CAS attempts to factor any expression as much as possible with linear, rational, and real factors. The expression shown in the second line is not factorable based on these conditions.

Notice in the third and fourth lines, I've included a comma followed by a variable. By specifying a variable, TI-Nspire CAS produces linear factors (that is, factors in which the degree of the specified variable is 1) as long as these factors contain only real numbers.

The fifth and sixth lines are intended to illustrate that TI-Nspire CAS provides some sorting when it does its factoring. For example, notice that the fifth line is sorted with respect to the variable x (by *sorted*, I mean that x shows up first in the factors). In the sixth line, I've specified that I want to factor with respect to the variable b. As a result, the factors in the result lead with this variable.

Now, I turn my attention to the second screen in Figure 8-5. The first line returns the original expression because the polynomial $x^4 - 3x^3 + 3x - 12$ is *prime*, meaning it cannot be factored into linear, rational factors. However, by specifying that I want to factor in terms of the variable x (as shown the second line), I make TI-Nspire produce linear factors with decimal approximations of irrational numbers. This provides for a nice way to find the zeroes of a polynomial.

Finally, take a look at the third line of this screen, which illustrates that the Factor command factors numbers, too. The fourth line gives an example of what you get when you try to factor a prime number.

The computing time required to factor large composite numbers can be quite long. If you are interested only in determining whether a number is prime or composite, try using the isPrime command. This command returns the word *true* if the number is prime and *false* if the number is composite. See the fifth line of the second screen in Figure 8-5.

Figure 8-5:
Using the
Factor com-
mand.

1.1	RAD AUTO REAL
factor(x^2-y^2)	$(x+y)\cdot(x-y)$
factor(x^2-y)	x^2-y
factor(x^2-y,x)	$(x+\sqrt{y})\cdot(x-\sqrt{y})$
factor(x^2-3,x)	$(x+\sqrt{3})\cdot(x-\sqrt{3})$
factor(x^3-b^3)	$(x-b)\cdot(x^2+b\cdot x+b^2)$
factor(x^3-b^3,b)	$-(b-x)\cdot(b^2+b\cdot x+x^2)$

6/6

1.1	RAD AUTO REAL
factor$(x^4-3\cdot x^3+3\cdot x-12)$	$x^4-3\cdot x^3+3\cdot x-12$
factor$(x^4-3\cdot x^3+3\cdot x-12,x)$	
$(x-3.09212)\cdot(x+1.54117)\cdot(x^2-1.44905\cdot x+2.9$	
factor(360)	$2^3\cdot3^2\cdot5$
factor(12841)	12841
isPrime(104729)	true

5/5

The Expand command

Choose (menu)⇨Algebra⇨Expand to invoke the Expand command. This command works just the opposite of the Factor command. It multiplies out expressions in factored form, including those containing exponents.

As you can see in the first screen in Figure 8-6, other similarities exist between the Expand and Factor commands. If you specify a variable to expand with respect to, TI-Nspire adjusts the order by which the variables are presented.

The second screen in Figure 8-6 illustrates that the Expand command also gives the partial fraction expansion for rational expressions. In the third screen, I've used the Expand command again with the same rational expression. However, I've also specified the variable x. Because I did so, TI-Nspire CAS provides a more complete partial fraction expansion.

Figure 8-6:
Using the
Expand
command.

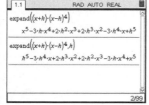 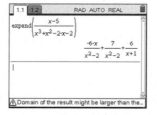 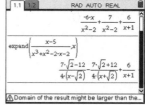

Other commands found in the Algebra submenu

The Solve, Factor, and Expand commands form the cornerstone of the Algebra submenu. However, several other items are contained in the Algebra submenu worth mentioning. The following is a list of some of these functions and a brief description of what they do:

- **Zeros:** The syntax for this command is Zeros(*Expression*, *Variable*). This command produces a list of the values of the specified *variable* that make the *expression* equal zero.

  Sometimes the Zero command returns the empty set because the zeros are complex. To find complex zeros, choose (menu)⇨Algebra⇨Complex⇨Zeros.

- **Polynomial Tools:** This submenu contains the following polynomial commands:

  - *Remainder of Polynomial:* The syntax for this command is polyRemainder(*Expression1*, *Expression2*) and returns the remainder when *Expression1* is divided by *Expression2*.

- *Quotient of Polynomial:* The syntax for this command is `polyRemainder(Expression1, Expression2)` and returns the quotient when *Expression1* is divided by *Expression2*, less the remainder.

- *Greatest Common Divisor:* The syntax for this command is `polyGcd(Expression1, Expression2)` and returns the greatest common rational factor of *Expression1* and *Expression2*.

- *Coefficients of Polynomial:* The syntax for this command is `polyCoeffs(Expression)` and returns the numerical coefficients, in list form, of the polynomial *Expression*. Coefficients are given in order from the highest degree term down to the lowest degree term. For example, `polyCoeffs(5x + x³ - 3)` returns the list {1, 0, 5, -3}. Notice that a zero is given for the missing x^2 term.

- *Degree of Polynomial:* The syntax for this command is `polyDegree(Expression)` and returns the degree of the polynomial.

✔ **Trigonometry:** This submenu contains the following trigonometry commands:

- *Expand:* The syntax for this command is `tExpand(Expression)` and returns the expansion of sines and cosines whose angles are integer multiples, sums, and differences. For example, the expression `tExpand(sin(α+θ)` returns the angle-sum identity `cos(α)·sin(θ)+sin(α)·cos(θ)`. This is a great command to use if you forgot the sum, difference, double, and half-angle trigonometric formulas.

- *Collect:* The syntax for this command is `tCollect(Expression)` and returns an expression in which powers and products of sines and cosines are converted to linear combinations of sines and cosines of multiple angles, angle sums, and angle differences. Basically, the tCollect command reverses the results obtained by the tExpand command. For example, the expression `tCollect(2·(cos(θ))²-1` gives `cos(2·θ)` as a result.

The α symbol, as well as other Greek characters, can be found in the Symbol Palette (press ⌃⌨). The θ character has its own button located at the bottom-left corner of the keypad.

Exploring calculus using CAS

Choose menu⇨Calculus to access the Calculus submenu as shown in the first screen in Figure 8-7. Many of these functions can also be accessed via the Math Template as shown in the second screen in Figure 8-7. Starting with the first icon to the right of the shaded icon in the Math Template, you have the Sum template, Product template, First Derivative template, Higher Order Derivative template, Definite Integral template, Indefinite Integral template, and Limit template.

Figure 8-7:
Accessing
Calculus
functions.

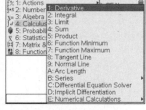

The Calculus submenu

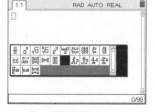

The Math Template

Like the Algebra submenu, the CAS technology allows for symbolic manipulation of algebraic expression as well as numerical calculations. You'll understand what I mean by this as you read this section.

The Derivative, Integral, and Limit commands form the cornerstone of the Calculus submenu, and I provide some detail as to how these functions work in the next three sections. I also provide a brief overview of some of the other items contained within the Calculus submenu.

Taking derivatives

Choose (menu)⇨Calculus⇨Derivative to invoke the Derivative command. A template containing two fields is pasted to the entry line. The current active field (as indicated by the blinking cursor) allows you to type the variable that you are finding the derivative with respect to. Type this variable and then press (tab) to move to the second field enclosed in parentheses. Type the expression that you want to find the derivative of here and press (enter) to find the derivative.

Figure 8-8 provides some examples of how to use the Derivative command. Here are a few comments about the first screen in Figure 8-8:

- **The first line shows a common use of the Derivative command.** Notice that TI-Nspire CAS displays an answer identical to what might appear in a textbook.

- **In the second line, I typed (x)(^) in the first field.** This tells TI-Nspire CAS to give the second derivative. To find higher order derivatives, press (^) followed by the derivative order.

- **The third line gives an alternative method of finding higher order derivatives.** I simply nest a number of derivative commands equal to the derivative order.

Here are some comments about the second screen in Figure 8-8:

✔ **In the first line, I typed** ⊗⊛⊟① **in the first field.** This tricks TI-Nspire CAS into giving the anti-derivative of the expression contained in the second field.

✔ **In the second line, I show you that TI-Nspire CAS can use function notation to provide the symbolic representation of the product rule.**

✔ **In the third line, I show you how to find the derivative of a list of expressions.** Make sure that you separate each expression with a comma and enclose the entire list in curly braces.

Finally, here are some comments about the third screen in Figure 8-8:

✔ **The first line shows TI-Nspire CAS's attempt at finding the symbolic rule for the quotient rule.**

✔ **In the second line, I've nested the derivative command in the Common Denominator command to obtain quotient rule in a form consistent with what's found in many textbooks.** This is another important reminder that you can mix and match commands as needed.

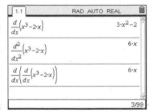
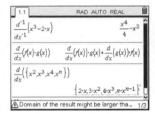
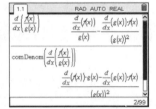

Figure 8-8:
Using the
Derivative
command.

Working with integrals

Choose (menu)⇨Calculus⇨Integral to invoke the Integral command. A template containing four fields is pasted to the entry line. The two leftmost fields are where you specify the lower and upper limits of integration. Leave these fields blank if you want to evaluate an indefinite integral. Type the expression to be integrated in the field contained in the parentheses. The rightmost field is where you type the variable to integrate with respect to.

Figure 8-9 provides some examples of how to use the Integral command. Here are a few comments about the first screen in Figure 8-9:

✔ **In the first line, the lower and upper limits of integration are omitted and the anti-derivative, less the constant of integration, is given.**

✔ **In the second line, I've included an expression for which the indefinite integral cannot be represented analytically.** As a result the coefficient, a, is written before the integral symbol, and the expression containing e is left in integral form.

> ✔ **The third line shows that, although the indefinite integral cannot be found for the same expression containing the number *e*, a corresponding definite integral can be evaluated.**

Here are two comments about the second screen in Figure 8-9:

> ✔ **The first line shows that TI-Nspire provides an exact answer for a definite integral whenever possible.**

> ✔ **The second line shows that I can force a decimal approximation by pressing** (ctrl) (⬧enter).

Figure 8-9:
Using the
Integral
command.

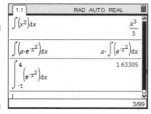 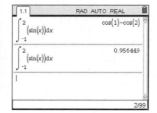

Evaluating limits

Choose (menu)⇨Calculus⇨Limit to invoke the Limit command. A template containing four fields is pasted to the entry line. Type the variable in the leftmost field. Type the approaching value of the variable in the next field. Type ⊕ or ⊖ in the next field if you want to evaluate a one-sided limit. Leave this field blank if you want to evaluate the limit from both sides. Type the expression in the rightmost field.

Figure 8-10 provides some examples of how to use the Limit command. Here are a few comments about the first screen in Figure 8-10:

> ✔ **In the first line, I evaluate the limit of $x2 - 3x + 1$ as *x* approaches 2.**

> ✔ **In the second line, I've used the definition of the derivative to find the derivative of the tangent function.**

> ✔ **In the third line, I've evaluated a limit at infinity.** Notice that TI-Nspire CAS does a great job displaying the exact answer of this result. I accessed the symbol for the infinity character by pressing (ctrl) (📇). You can also access the infinity symbol by pressing (ctrl)(*i*).

Here are two comments about the second screen in Figure 8-10:

> ✔ **The first two lines show how to evaluate a left- and right-sided limit, respectively.**

> ✔ **The last line shows that the general limit of this absolute value expression is not defined.**

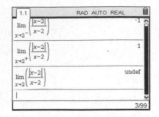

Figure 8-10:
Using the
Limit
command.

Other commands found in the Calculus submenu

Here are some other items contained in the Calculus submenu worth mentioning, including a brief description of what they do:

▱ **Tangent Line (& Normal Line):** The syntax for this command is
`tangentLine(Expression, Variable, point)`. This command
returns the equation of the tangent line to the equation y = *expression* for an *x*-value equal to *point*. The Normal Line command works
exactly the same way, except that it returns the equation of the line
perpendicular to the tangent line at the same *point* on the curve y =
expression.

▱ **Arc Length:** The syntax for this command is `arclen(Expression,`
`Variable, Start, End)`. This command gives the arc length of a
function (given by *Expression*) from x = *Start* to x = *End*. Try evaluating `arclen(f(x), x, a, b)` to obtain the textbook formula for the
arc length along a curve.

▱ **Differential Equation Solver:** The syntax for this command is
`deSolve(1`st` or 2`nd` Degree Differential Equation,`
`Independent Variable, Dependent Variable)`. For example, the
command `deSolve(y'=a·y, x, y)` returns the general solution $y = cke^{a \cdot x}$,
where **k** is an integer suffix from 1 to 255. For example, the first time
you execute this command, TI-Nspire CAS returns the solution $y = c1e^{a \cdot x}$
where **c1** is an arbitrary constant. Subsequent occurrences of this
arbitrary constant are denoted **c2**, **c3**, and so on. To find a particular
solution, include the initial condition(s) with the differential equation.
For example, the command `deSolve(y'=a·y and y(0)=1, x, y)`
returns the solution $y = e^{a \cdot x}$.

Press ⊙ once to denote a first derivative and press ⊙ twice to denote a
second derivative.

For a second order differential equation, you must provide two initial
conditions. Each initial condition must be preceded by the word *and*.

▱ **Implicit Differentiation:** This command gives the implicitly defined
derivative of an equation in which one variable is implicitly defined
in terms of another variable. The syntax for this command is
`impDif(Equation, Independent Variable, Dependent`
`Variable)`. For example, the command `impDif(x`2`+y`2`=r`2`, x, y)`
returns the result $-x/y$.

Part III
The Graphs & Geometry Application

In this part . . .

This part gets into one of TI-Nspire's most powerful applications. You learn how the analytical side of this application is used to graph functions, inequalities, scatter plots, polar equations, and parametric equations. On the plane geometry side, I show you how this application can be used to dynamically represent just about any geometric drawing or construction, all without a ruler or compass. I then show you examples of how to work in both environments simultaneously.

As with Part II, I dedicate the last chapter in this part to highlight some of the ways the computer algebra system functionality of TI-Nspire CAS can be used with the Graphs & Geometry application.

Chapter 9

Working in the Analytic View

*I*n this chapter, I talk about the analytic side of the Graphs & Geometry application. By this, I mean the functionality built into TI-Nspire that enables you to graph and analyze functions, inequalities, parametric equations, and polar equations. A number of tools are available to customize your graphs and to make the subsequent analysis quick and painless.

Graphing Functions

Press ⓒtrⓛⓘ⇨Add Graphs & Geometry to insert a new Graphs & Geometry page into a current document. Or, open a new document and press ⓜenⓤ⇨Add Graphs & Geometry.

By default, your new Graphs & Geometry page opens in an analytic window that you can recognize by the coordinate graph displayed on the screen. Also, notice the blinking cursor located on the *Entry Line*, the narrow space located at the bottom of the screen. The Entry Line is used to type functions, inequalities, configure scatter plots, and so on.

In Chapter 15, I use data on U.S. Immigrant population and U.S. Total Population for the years since 1900 to construct a scatter plot and perform a regression. The equation that models U.S. Immigrant population (in millions) for years since 1900 is given by $y = 0.000139x^3 - 0.0167x^2 + 0.487x + 10.194$. The cursor is automatically located next to the first available function on the Entry Line, which means you are ready to type the equation. Here are the steps to follow to type the equation and view its graph:

1. **Start typing the equation, making sure that you press ⓧ for the independent variable. Here's how to include exponents:**

   - **Press ⌃ to move into exponent mode.**

   - **Type the exponent.**

   - **Press ▸ to move out of exponent mode.**

   The first screen in Figure 9-1 shows the complete equation on the Entry Line.

To apply an exponent of 2, you press ⓧ. After you press this key, the exponent of 2 appears, and then you are automatically moved out of exponent mode.

2. **After typing the equation, press ⏎ to activate the graph.**

   The second screen in Figure 9-1 shows the result after this second step. Notice that your equation appears in the *Work Area*, the space above the Entry Line. The graph itself is somewhat hard to see. I tell you how to adjust the window settings later in this chapter.

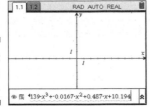

Figure 9-1: Graphing a function.

Moving from the Entry Line to the Work Area

After you graph an equation, the cursor remains on the Entry Line and is positioned to the right of the next available function (in this case that's $f2(x)$). To move to the Work Area, press ⓔˢᶜ. Alternatively, press ⓣᵃᵇ twice to move to the Work Area.

You know you are in the Work Area because a moveable cursor appears in this area and the Entry Line turns dark gray.

To move back to the Entry Line, press ⓣᵃᵇ once.

Hiding the Entry Line

Sometimes it's desirable to hide the Entry Line. This is particularly helpful if you are done graphing equations and want the Work Area to be slightly larger.

To hide the Entry Line, press (menu)⇨View⇨Hide Entry Line. To bring the Entry Line back into view, press (menu)⇨View⇨Show Entry Line.

There's also a much easier way to toggle between **Hide Entry Line** and **Show Entry Line**. Simply press the shortcut key sequence (ctrl)(G).

Adjusting the window settings

Referring to Figure 9-1, clearly the window settings do not effectively reveal the graph. Recall that the *x*-values of this function represent years since 1900, starting with $x = 0$. The *y*-values are positive. Therefore, it makes sense to focus on the first quadrant only.

To grab the entire graph, move the cursor to some open space and press (ctrl)(✱). You see the crunched up paper symbol with a hand, ✌, indicating that the entire coordinate plane can be translated in any direction. Use the NavPad keys to move the graph so that the origin is located at the bottom-left corner of the screen. Press (esc) to release the coordinate plane. See the first screen in Figure 9-2.

The graph is now completely out of view because the maximum *x*- and *y*-values are too small. Press (menu)⇨View⇨Show Axes End Values to see the maximum (and minimum) end values. The maximum *x*-value should be near 100 because this value corresponds to the year 2000. TI-Nspire allows you to grab the tick marks on the axes themselves to change these end values. Here's how:

1. **Move the cursor over the *x*-axis, preferably near the far right side of the *x*-axis. Both axes start to pulse and the word *axes* appears on the screen.**

2. **Press (ctrl)(✱) to grab both axes.**

3. **Press the NavPad keys to drag the tick marks. Moving to the left increases the scale. Moving to the right decreases the scale.**

4. **Press (esc) when the maximum *x*-value reaches just over 100 to release the axes.**

Perhaps you want to increase the scale on the *y*-axis only to completely fill the space in the Work Area with your graph. Follow these steps:

1. **Move the cursor over the *y*-axis. Again, both axes start to pulse and the word *axes* appears on the screen.**

2. **Press ⌢⊙ to grab just the *y*-axis.**

3. **Press the NavPad keys to drag the tick marks, moving up to decrease the scale and moving down to increase the scale.**

4. **Press (esc) to release the axis.**

The last two screens in Figure 9-3 show how to drag both axes and a single axis, respectively.

Figure 9-2:
Adjusting
the window
settings.

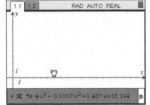

Translating the entire
coordinate plane

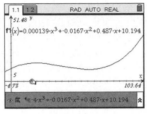

Adjusting
both axes

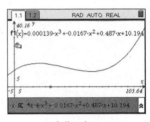

Adjusting
one axis

Here are two more options that can be used to adjust the window settings:

✔ **Move the cursor to an axis end value (assuming it's in view) and press ⊙ twice to highlight the current end value.** Type a new end value and press ⌢ to put the change into effect.

✔ **Press (menu)⇨Window⇨Window Settings.** This action opens a dialog box and enables you to type your minimum and maximum end values as well as the scale. Press ⌢ to put the changes into effect.

Changing your graph's attributes

TI-Nspire gives you the option of changing your graph's weight (thin, medium, thick), style (continuous, dotted, dashed), label style, and whether it is continuous or discrete. Press (menu)⇨Actions⇨Attributes to invoke the Attributes command. Alternatively, move your cursor to the graph and press (ctrl)(menu)⇨Attributes.

After opening the attributes menu, press the ▲▼ keys to move through the different options (weight, style, and so on). Use the ◄► keys to view the different options within each attribute. The corresponding attribute changes on the graph as well.

To put an attribute into effect, you must use the NavPad keys to select it and then press ⊙. To exit the attribute menu without making a change, press ⊙.

Figure 9-3 shows some examples of different attributes you can assign to a graph.

Figure 9-3: Changing your graph's attributes.

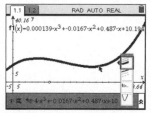 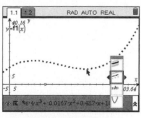 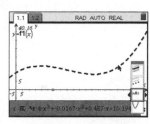

Thick and continuous

Medium, dotted and $y=f1(x)$ label

Medium, dashed and $y=f1(x)$ label

Analyzing your graph

Some of the more common analyses that are performed on a graphed function include evaluation, finding local maximum and minimum values, and locating zeros. The Point On tool offers a convenient way to accomplish each of these tasks. Here are the steps:

1. **Press** ⓘ**⇨Points & Lines⇨Point On to invoke the Point On tool.**

2. **Use the NavPad to move the cursor to your graph. A ghosted image of the coordinates at this location appears along with the words** *point on.*

3. **Press** ⊙ **to create the point.**

4. **Press** ⊙ **to exit the Point On tool.**

Now move over the point until the ☜ symbol appears and press ⊙⊙ to grab the point. Using the NavPad, move your point along the graph. Notice when you approach a local maximum value, an uppercase *M* appears accompanied by the coordinates of this local extreme value. As you pass through a local minimum, you see a lowercase *m*. As you pass through a zero (*x*-intercept) a lowercase *z* appears.

Figure 9-4 shows the Point On tool in action as well as the location of the maximum and minimum values on this graph.

Figure 9-4: Using the Point On tool to analyze a graph.

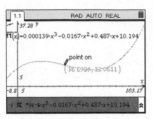
Using the Point On tool

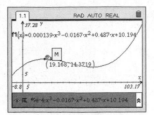
A local maximum

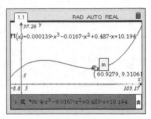
A local minimum

Notice that the coordinates of my point are given to the nearest ten-thousandth. To change this level of precision, hover your cursor over the *x*-coordinate so that the ꔷ symbol appears and the coordinate blinks. Press the ꔷ repeatedly to increase the number of displayed digits and press the ꔷ key to decrease the number of displayed digits. Repeat this process for the *y*-coordinate as well as for any other measurements located on your Graphs & Geometry page.

You cannot change the number of displayed digits on a label such as **f1**(*x*).

As you hover the cursor over the *x*-coordinate, try clicking ꔷ twice to allow for editing of the *x*-coordinate. Type a new *x*-coordinate value and press ꔷ. Watch the point jump to its new location. You can also perform a similar task by editing the *y*-coordinate. For functions that are not one-to-one (meaning in some instances the *y*-values are not unique), TI-Nspire jumps to a point with the specified *y*-value closest to the current location.

You also have the option of using the Trace tool to perform a similar analysis. Press ꔷ⇨Trace⇨Graph Trace to invoke this tool. A moveable point and its coordinates are automatically placed on the graph. Use the ◀▶ keys to move this point along the graph. You can periodically drop points on your graph by pressing ꔷ. Keep in mind that this action does not take you out of trace mode.

While in trace mode, try pressing ▲ or ▼ once. This action reveals a dashed vertical line which provides an alternate visual reference. That is, you can see how the current trace location relates to the *x*-axis. You can still press the ◀▶ keys to move along the curve, however, the Drop Point feature is disabled. Press ▲ or ▼ once more to revert to the default trace mode.

Press ꔷ to exit Graph Trace. Remember, any points that you dropped along the way remain on your graph.

Hiding or deleting a graph

You can hide a graph without actually deleting it. To accomplish this task quickly, move your cursor to the graph and press (ctrl)(menu)⇨Hide/Show. Keep in mind that your graph still exists — it's just hidden from view.

To reveal a hidden graph, you must press (menu)⇨Actions⇨Hide/Show to invoke the Hide/Show tool. The Hide/Show icon (an eye) is displayed in the top-left corner of the screen, indicating that this tool is currently active. Additionally, a ghosted image of all hidden objects appears, including your hidden graph. Move your cursor to the graph until the ∅ icon appears and press ⑨ once. Press (esc) to exit the Hide/Show tool.

When the Hide/Show tool is active, the symbol ✎ is used to indicate that an object is currently in view and can be hidden by pressing ⑨.

To delete a graph, move your cursor to the graph and press (ctrl)(menu)⇨Delete.

If you mistakenly delete a graph, press (ctrl)(esc) to invoke the Undo feature.

An alternate method of graphing a function

Referring back to our U.S. Immigrant population example, it may be interesting to graph the total U.S. population on the same screen. In this section, I show you an alternative method of graphing a function. Before doing so, change your y-axis end value to 320 using one of the methods described earlier in this chapter. I also recommend pressing (ctrl)(G) to hide the Entry Line.

An equation that models the total U.S. population (in millions for years after 1900) is given by $y = 80.563 \cdot 1.013x$. Here's the alternative method I use to graph this function:

1. **Press (menu)⇨Actions⇨Text to invoke the Text tool.**

2. **Move your cursor to some open space and press (enter) or ⑨ to open a text box.**

3. **Type 80.563·1.013x and press (enter) to close the text box.**

4. **Press (esc) to close the Text tool.**

5. **Drag this text expression (press (ctrl)(⑨)) to the x-axis and notice that a ghosted image of this graph appears. Press (enter) to graph this function.**

You should approach the *x*-axis very slowly for this graphing method to work.

The sequence of screens in Figure 9-5 shows how this method works.

Figure 9-5:
Using an
alternative
method to
graph a
function.

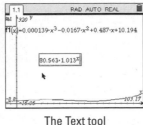

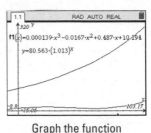

| The Text tool | Drag to the *x*-axis | Graph the function |

TIP

Move back to the expression $y = 80.563 \cdot 1.013x$ that is automatically placed on the screen. Press ⓧ twice to allow editing of this equation, and press ⏎ to put your changes into effect. Any changes that you make are automatically reflected in the graph. You can also use this method to edit labels resulting from functions graphed via the Entry Line.

TIP

In general, you can use the Text tool for a variety of reasons, even if it's just to annotate your graphs by providing additional information. Later, you see how the Text tool can be used to perform numerical calculations. Keep in mind, too, you can mix text with mathematical symbols or expressions using the primary and secondary keys as well as the symbol palette and math template.

Analyzing two functions simultaneously

The Trace tool enables you to analyze two functions simultaneously. Press (menu)⇨Trace⇨Graph to start tracing along **f1**(*x*). Press ▲ to move the second graph and allow for tracing along $y = 80.563 \cdot 1.013x$. Press ▲ again to simultaneously trace both graphs. Continue to press ▲ to cycle through these three options. See Figure 9-6.

Figure 9-6:
Tracing
graphs
individually
and simulta-
neously.

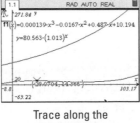

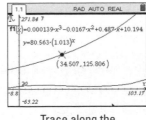

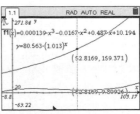

| Trace along the lower graph | Trace along the upper graph | Trace two graphs simultaneously |

You can only drop points while using the Trace tool if you are tracing along a single graph.

Drawing and constructing geometric objects in the analytic window

TI-Nspire gives you the option of adding geometric objects (points, perpendicular lines, circles, polygons, and so on) to your analytic window. These objects can add some type of functionality to your graph or serve as a way of enhancing the overall look in the analytic window. For example, earlier in this chapter (in the section, "Analyzing your graph"), I show you how to use the Point On tool to trace along a graph.

Continuing with the U.S. Immigrant and U.S. Population example, I now show you how the perpendicular line tool can enhance this investigation.

1. **Press (menu)⇨Construction⇨Perpendicular to open the Perpendicular tool (notice the Perpendicular icon in the top-left corner of the screen).**

2. **Move the cursor (denoted by the ⌀ symbol) to the x-axis until the ⌗ symbol appears.**

   Make sure that you are not pointing to a tick mark. If you are, your perpendicular line is restricted to the tick marks when dragged along the x-axis. Sometimes this is preferable; however, for the purpose of this example, I am interested in continuous movement.

3. **Press (⌖) or (enter) twice to construct the perpendicular line.**

4. **Press (esc) to exit the Perpendicular tool.**

The first screen in Figure 9-7 shows the result of adding this perpendicular line. I also changed the line attribute from continuous to dotted. Notice that I also changed the point attribute on the x-axis from solid to hollow. I do this for all points that will eventually be dragged.

I'm now interested in using the Intersection Point(s) tool to construct the intersection of my perpendicular line with each function. Here's how:

1. **Press (menu)⇨Points & Lines⇨Intersection Point(s) to open the Intersection Point(s) tool (notice the icon for this tool in the top-left corner of the screen).**

2. **Move the cursor to the perpendicular line and press (⌖).**

3. **Move the cursor to the bottom graph and press (⌖). Notice the intersection point is constructed.**

4. **While the Intersection Point(s) tool is still active, repeat Steps 2 and 3 to construct the intersection of the perpendicular line and the top graph.**

5. **Press (esc) to exit the Intersection Point(s) tool.**

The second screen in Figure 9-7 shows the result of adding these points of intersection.

Now it's time to add the coordinates of each of these points, including the point on the *x*-axis. Follow these steps:

1. **Press (menu)⇨Actions⇨Coordinates & Equations to open the Coordinates & Equations tool (notice the icon for this tool in the top-left corner of the screen).**

2. **Move the cursor to one of the three points (make sure you see a ghosted images of its coordinates) and press (?) or (enter) twice.**

3. **While the Coordinates & Equations tool is still active, repeat Step 2 to display the coordinates of the other two points.**

4. **Press (esc) to exit the Coordinates & Equations tool.**

The third screen in Figure 9-7 shows the result of adding the coordinates to each point. I've also changed the displayed precision of each coordinate (hover over the coordinate and press (⊤) repeatedly) to the nearest hundredth.

Figure 9-7: Construc-ting a perpen-dicular line and points of intersection.

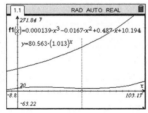 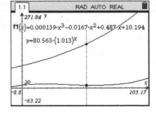 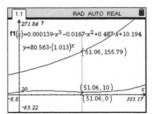

Try changing the value of the *x*-coordinate of the hollow point on the *x*-axis. Watch the perpendicular line jump to its new location. What a great way to evaluate both functions simultaneously!

You cannot change the coordinates of the points of intersections with the graphed functions. These points are constrained by the perpendicular line, which is dependent on the hollow point constructed on the *x*-axis. If you try to make a change, you are greeted by the message "Cannot accept change: Invalid input."

Performing calculations

Virtually any number that appears on your Graphs & Geometry screen is eligible to be part of a calculation, including the coordinates of graphed points. In this section, I show you how to find the quotient of the *y*-coordinate of the bottom graph and the *y*-coordinate of the upper graph. This quotient represents the percent of the total U.S. population that is immigrant for the year given by the corresponding *x*-value.

To perform a calculation, you must use the Text tool to type an expression to be evaluated. Use *dummy variables* (no pun intended) to serve as placeholders for the numerical values that become part of the calculation. Before attempting this calculation, hide the labels that give the equations of each graph (the right-click method is the fastest way to accomplish this task). Next, follow these steps:

1. **Press ⒨⇨Actions⇨Text to open the Text tool. Type your expression and press ⒠ to close the text box and ⒠ to exit the Text tool.**

   In my example, I typed ①⓪⓪⊗Ⓐ÷Ⓑ because I want to express my quotient as a percent. The variables *a* and *b* serve as dummy variables, or placeholders, for the *y*-coordinates that will become part of the calculation.

2. **Press ⒨⇨Actions⇨Calculate to invoke the Calculate tool.**

3. **Move the cursor over the text from Step 1 (notice the word *expression* appears), and press ⓧ once to accept this expression.**

4. **As you move away from the expression, notice the words "Select a? (or press VAR)." Move to the *y*-coordinate of the ordered pair located at the intersection of the perpendicular line and the bottom function [in this case, it is (51.06, 10)] and press ⓧ once. This action selects this coordinate as the value of *a* in the calculation.**

5. **Start moving the cursor again, and notice the words *Select b* (or press VAR). Move to the *y*-coordinate of the ordered pair located at the intersection of the perpendicular line and the top function (in this case, it is (51.06, 155.79)) and press ⓧ once.**

6. **Move the cursor to the right of the expression and press ⓧ to drop it in place.**

7. **Press ⒠ to exit the Calculate tool.**

The sequence of screens in Figure 9-8 shows the results of this calculation.

Figure 9-8:
Using the
Calculate
tool.

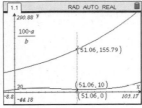
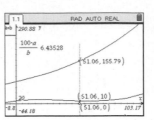
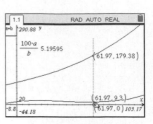

Type an expression   Complete the calculation   Dynamically update
the calculation

Notice in the last screen, I have dragged the point on the *x*-axis and the calculation automatically updates. For example, the percentage of the total U.S. population that was immigrant in 1962 (61.97 is close enough) was approximately 5.2%.

You can also edit the *x*-coordinate of the hollow point on the *x*-axis to jump to any *x*-value. The calculation updates accordingly.

Using Measurement Transfer

The Measurement Transfer tools allow you to transfer the result of a calculation, a numeric text value, or a measurement to a circle, ray, or vector. You can also use this tool to transfer a measurement to an axis, which is what I do in this section. Specifically, I'm interested in transferring my percent measurement to the *y*-axis. Here are the steps:

1. **Press ⓜ⋯⋯⟩Construction⟩Measurement Transfer to invoke the Measurement Transfer tool.**

2. **Move the cursor to the result of the calculation (or numeric text value or measurement) and press ⓧ.**

3. **Move the cursor to the *y*-axis and press ⓧ.**

4. **Press ⓔⓢⓒ to exit the Measurement Transfer tool.**

Notice a point appears on the *y*-axis with a *y*-coordinate equal to the current value of the calculation. Try dragging the hollow point on the *x*-axis and watch as the point on the *y*-axis moves up and down.

Figure 9-9 shows the results of using the Measurement Transfer tool. I've adjusted the *y*-axis to provide a better window for seeing this result. The first two screens show the movement of the transferred measurement as the *x*-axis point is dragged. In the third screen, I've added a perpendicular line through the transferred measurement and constructed the intersection point, denoted (*x*, *y*), with the other perpendicular line.

Figure 9-9:
The
Measure-
ment
Transfer
tool.

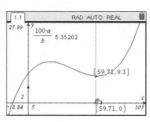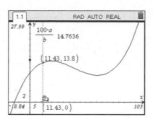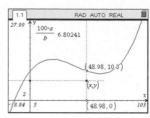

Using the Locus tool and Geometry Trace

The point (x, y) on my graph is now part of a new function, which gives the percent of the total U.S. population that is immigrant for years since 1900. The Locus tool and Geometry Trace provide two options for "seeing" the entire function given by the path of this point as the point on the *x*-axis is dragged.

Here's how to use the Locus tool to investigate this new function:

1. **Press (menu)⇨Construction⇨Locus to invoke the Locus tool.**

2. **Move the cursor to point (x, y), the point whose path I'm interested in viewing) and press (⬚).**

3. **Move the cursor to the point on the *x*-axis, the driver point, and press (⬚).**

4. **Press (esc) to exit the Locus tool.**

The first screen in Figure 9-10 shows the result of using the Locus tool. I've changed its attributes to dashed to provide some contrast from the other graphed function.

Geometry Trace offers another way to see this relationship. Press (ctrl) (menu)⇨Delete to delete the locus and follow these steps:

1. **Press (menu)⇨Trace⇨Geometry Trace to invoke the Geometry Trace tool.**

2. **Move the cursor to point (x, y), the point whose path I'm interested in viewing, and press (⬚).**

3. **Move the cursor to the point on the *x*-axis, the driver point, and press (ctrl) (⬚) to grab the point.**

4. **Use the NavPad keys to move the grabbed point along the *x*-axis and watch the trace appear on the screen.**

5. **Press (esc) to exit the Geometry Trace tool.**

Figure 9-10: Using the Locus tool and the Geometry Trace tool.

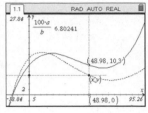

Constructing a locus

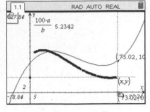

Using Geometry Trace

The locus I created in this section is tied to the analytical window. That is, if I adjust the window settings, the locus adjusts accordingly. On the other hand, the Geometry Trace is not tied into the analytical window. Rather, think of it as a geometric object overlaid on top of the analytic window. If you move or adjust the coordinate plane, the Geometry Trace does not move with it.

Press (menu)⇨Trace⇨Erase Geometry Trace to erase the Geometry Trace.

Adding a tangent line to a graph

In this section, I start with a fresh Graphs & Geometry page (I think I've pretty much exhausted the U.S. population problem) and graphed the equation $f(x) = x^3 - 3x^2 - 2x + 6$.

The Tangent Line tool is a great option for exploring the instantaneous rate of change of a nonlinear function. Here's how it works:

1. **Graph your function using the first available function on the Entry Line.**

2. **Adjust the window to reveal all local maximum and minimum values as well as the zeros.**

3. **Press (menu)⇨Points & Lines⇨Tangent to open the Tangent Line tool.**

4. **Move your cursor onto the function graph and press ⊙ to construct the tangent line.**

5. **Press (esc) to exit the Tangent Line tool.**

The first screen in Figure 9-11 shows the result of these steps. You can drag the point of tangency to move the tangent line along the graph.

The second screen shows an alternative approach to this problem. Here, I've constructed a line perpendicular to the x-axis. I then constructed the point of intersection of this perpendicular line with the function. Finally, I constructed the tangent to this point of intersection. Under this scenario, I can move the tangent line by dragging the point of intersection between the *x*-axis and the perpendicular line. I like this option a bit more because the tangent line moves along the curve more smoothly.

Using the Measurement tool

The Measurement tool can be used to enhance the tangent line problem from the previous section. Here's how you can find the slope of the tangent line:

1. **Press (menu)⇨Measurement⇨Slope to access the Measurement (Slope) tool.**

2. **Position the cursor on the tangent line and press ⓧ.**

3. **Move the measurement to some open area, and press (enter) to drop it in place.**

4. **Press (esc) to exit the Measurement (Slope) tool.**

The third screen in Figure 9-11 shows the slope calculation with text added for effect.

Figure 9-3:
Using the
Tangent
line and the
Measure-
ment tool.

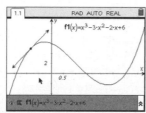 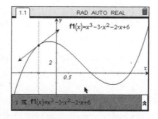 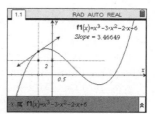

For a nice effect, try using Measurement Transfer to transfer the slope measurement on the *y*-axis. Then construct a perpendicular to the *y*-axis through this point and construct the point of intersection with the two perpendicular lines. Using the Locus tool or Geometry Trace, investigate the path of this intersection point as the vertical line is dragged. What a nice way to explore the derivative of this function.

Adding a function table

To add a function table to a graph, press (menu)⇨View⇨Add Function Table. This action automatically splits the screen and adds a Lists & Spreadsheet application with, by default, *x*-values incrementing by 1 and their corresponding *y*-values. Use the ▲▼ keys to scroll through the Function Table.

You have the option to change the Function Table settings. Press (menu)⇨Function Table⇨Edit Function Table Settings to open a dialog box and customize Table Start, Table Step, and the settings for the Independent and Dependent variables.

Adding a Function Table changes the page layout from one application to two applications. Use the Undo feature repeatedly to restore the page with a single Graphs & Geometry application. Alternatively, try the following.

1. **With the Lists & Spreadsheet application active, press (ctrl)(K) to select the entire application.**

2. **Press (clear) to delete the application (as noted by the words "Click here to add an application" located in the vacated space).**

3. **Press (ctrl)(⌂)⇨Page Layout⇨Select Layout⇨Layout 1.**

Other investigations

So far, I've showcased many of the tools used within the analytic view of the Graphs & Geometry application. The following sections introduce a few other noteworthy tools and features.

Manipulating a graph

Several types of functions have graphs that can be directly manipulated on the screen. To accomplish this task, simply press (ctrl)(⌖) to grab the graph and then use the NavPad keys to perform a transformation. As an example, consider the graph of $y = x^2$. Two different options are possible:

- ✔ **Perform a translation. Position the cursor on the vertex of the graph until the ÷ symbol appears, and press (ctrl)(⌖) to grab the graph. Use the NavPad keys to translate the graph and press (esc) when complete.**

  Notice the equation of the graph is updated automatically, in real time, as you move the graph as shown in the first screen in Figure 9-12.

- ✔ **Perform a stretch. Position the cursor on a side of the parabola until the ⤢ symbol appears and press (ctrl)(⌖) to grab the graph. Use the NavPad keys to stretch the graph and press (esc) when complete.**

  Notice the equation of the graph, specifically the value a in front of the parentheses, is automatically updated as shown in the second screen in Figure 9-12.

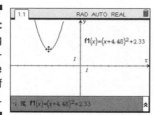 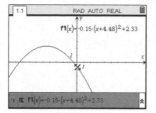

Figure 9-12: Performing transformations on the graph of $y = x^2$.

Performing a translation   Performing a stretch

You can only perform a transformation on quadratic functions that are written in vertex form, $y = a(x + h)^2 + k$. Had I typed $x^2 + 0x + 0$ rather than x^2, I would not be able to perform a transformation.

Here is a complete list of the different functions that can be transformed using the same procedures just described:

- ✔ Linear function of the form $y = b$, where b is a constant.

- ✔ Linear function of the form $y = ax + b$, where a and b are constants.

- ✔ Quadratic function of the form $y = ax^2 + bx + c$, where a, b, and c are constants.

- ✔ Exponential function of the form $y = eax + b + c$, where a, b, and c are constants.

- ✔ Exponential function of the form $y = beax + c$, where a, b, and c are constants.

- ✔ Exponential function of the form $y = deax + b + c$, where a, b, c, and d are constants.

- ✔ Logarithmic function of the form $y = a\ln(cx + b) + d$, where a, b, c, and d are constants.

- ✔ Sinusoidal function of the form $y = a\sin(cx + b) + d$, where a, b, c, and d are constants.

- ✔ Cosinusoidal function of the form $y = a\cos(cx + b) + d$, where a, b, c, and d are constants.

All of the previously mentioned functions can be translated and stretched. However, in the case of the first two linear functions, the stretch looks more like a rotation about the y-intercept as indicated by the ◌ symbol.

With a bit of practice, you will quickly learn where to find the positions on the graph where the ÷ (translation) and ✗ (stretch) symbols appear. For example, translate the graph of $a\sin(cx + b) + d$ by positioning the cursor at a point halfway between the maximum and minimum values. Any other point on the graph allows you to stretch the graph.

Using a slider

In the previous section, I mention that $y = e^{ax + b} + c$ is one type of function that can be transformed. What if I want to transform an exponential function with a base other than e? Better yet, what if I want to explore the graph of $y = ab^x$ where a and b can take on any range of values? To perform this investigation, use the Slider feature and follow these steps:

1. **Press (menu)⇨Actions⇨Insert Slider.**

   This action inserts a slider box on the screen. By default, the slider values range from 0 to 10 with an initial value of 5 and step size of 1. Notice that a grayed out $v1$ is displayed in the upper-left corner of the slider box. This is where you name your slider variable in the next step.

2. **Type a variable name (using standard variable-naming conventions) and press (enter).**

   This step inserts the variable name of your choice in the top-left corner of the slider box. I typed a for my variable name, as shown in the first screen in Figure 9-13.

   After this step, you can move the slider box anywhere on the screen by moving the cursor over the box and pressing (ctrl)(click).

3. **Add additional sliders as needed.**

   I have added a second slider for the constant b in the function $y = abx$.

4. **Type your function on the entry line using the variables defined in your sliders.**

   You can also access these variables by pressing the (var) key. After pressing (enter), the function is graphed with the initial values of 5 for each slider value.

5. **Position the cursor on the slider bar (indicated by the symbol) and press (ctrl)(click) to drag the slider and change the value.**

   Watch your graph update automatically as demonstrated in the second screen in Figure 9-13.

 Try moving your cursor to the slider box and pressing (ctrl)(menu) to access the context menu. This gives you the option of change the slider settings as shown in the third screen in Figure 9-13. You also have the option of animating the slider. This action moves the slider back and forth between the minimum and maximum slider values. Access the slider context menu a second time to stop the animation.

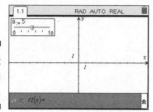
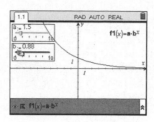
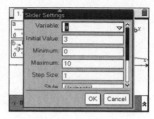

Figure 9-13:
Working
with sliders.

Finding the area under a curve

Consider I want to find the area under the curve $y = x^3 - 3x^2 - 2x + 6$. This is the equivalent of finding the value of a definite integral. Here are the steps to follow:

1. **Graph your equation.**

2. **Press (menu)⇨Measurement⇨Integral to invoke the Integral tool.**

3. **Move the cursor to the graph and press ⓧ to select the graph for which you want to evaluate your integral.**

4. **Press the ◂▸ keys to move to left endpoint of the region for which you want to find the area and press ⓧ.**

   As you move the cursor, notice the dotted line indicating the current left endpoint location. See the first screen in Figure 9-14.

5. **Press the ◂▸ keys to move to right endpoint and press ⓧ.**

   Notice the shaded region and its corresponding area are displayed on the screen. You can move the area measurement anywhere on the screen. See the second screen in Figure 9-14.

6. **Press (esc) to exit the Integral tool.**

7. **Drag either endpoint to adjust the region for which you are finding the area.**

   As shown in the third screen in Figure 9-14, I've used the Text tool to label my endpoints a and b as well as the area measurement. I've also use the Coordinates & Equations tool to display the coordinates of points a and b and then added text next to each coordinate for further clarification.

Figure 9-14:
Finding the
area under
a curve.

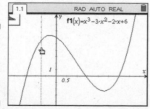
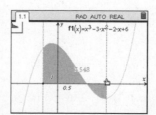
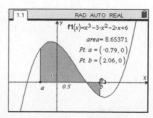

Graphing Inequalities

With TI-Nspire, you can graph a single inequality or multiple inequalities. To graph an inequality follow these steps:

1. **Move to the Entry Line with the cursor positioned to the right of the first available function.**

2. **Press the ⌨ repeatedly until the function name is deleted.**

3. **Type your inequality and press ⌨ to view its graph.**

   Press ⊘ for less than, ⊙ for greater than, ⊘⊜ for less than or equal to, and ⊙⊜ for greater than or equal to. You can also use the symbol palette (press ⌨⌨) to access these symbols.

4. **Repeat Steps 1 through 3 to graph additional inequalities.**

Figure 9-15:
Graphing
inequalities.

Type the inequality
on the Entry Line

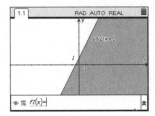

Graph the
inequality

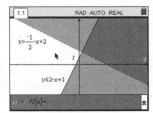

Graph additional
inequalities

Here are few additional things I'd like to point out about inequality graphing:

✔ **You have the option of using the Text tool to type your inequality.** Drag the text expression to the *x*-axis to graph the inequality.

✔ **Less than (<) and greater than (>) inequalities have dashed boundary lines.**

✔ **Less than or equal to (≤) and greater than or equal to (≥) inequalities have solid boundary lines.**

✔ **Use the Intersection Point(s) tool (press ⌨⇨Points & Lines⇨Intersection Points) to find the intersection point of your inequalities.**

Graphing Parametric Equations

Press (menu)⇨Graph Type⇨Parametric to switch to parametric graphing mode. Alternatively, move to the Entry Line and press (ctrl)(menu)⇨Parametric. Next, follow these steps:

1. **Type the *x*-component equation, using *t* as the independent variable.**

   TI-Nspire uses the notation $x1(t)$ for the first *x*-component, $x2(t)$ for the second *x*-component, and so on. You can graph up to 99 parametric curves.

2. **Type the *y*-component equation, using *t* as the independent variable.**

   TI-Nspire uses the notation $y1(t)$ for the first *y*-component, $y2(t)$ for the second *y*-component, and so on.

3. **Edit the interval for the variable *t* and the *tstep* increment.**

   By default, parametric graphing is configured in radians with $0 \le t \le 2\pi$ and *tstep* = $\pi/24$.

4. **Press (enter) to graph the parametric curve.**

Figure 9-16 shows an example of a parametric graph.

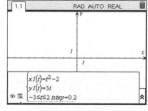
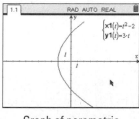
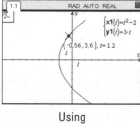

Figure 9-16: Graphing parametric equations.

| The Parametric Entry Line | Graph of parametric equation | Using Graph Trace |

In the second screen in Figure 9-16, I pressed (ctrl)(G) to hide the Entry Line.

In the third screen in Figure 9-16, I use Graph Trace (press (menu)⇨Graph⇨ Graph Trace) to trace along the graph. Each time I press ◂ or ▸ the trace moves by a value of *t* equal to *t*-step.

Many of the features of function graphing (for example, changing attributes, adding a Function Table, adding geometric objects to a parametric graph) are available in parametric graphing mode.

Graphing Polar Equations

Press (menu)⇨Graph Type⇨Polar to switch to polar graphing mode. Alternatively, move to the Entry Line and press (ctrl)(menu)⇨Polar. Next, follow these steps:

1. **Type the equation, using θ as the independent variable.**

   Press the gray ⊚ key to access the θ symbol.

2. **Type the interval for the variable θ and the θ *step* increment.**

   By default, polar graphing is configured in radians with $0 \le \theta \le 2\pi$ and θ *step* = π/24.

3. **Press ⊚ to graph the polar curve.**

Figure 9-17 shows an example of a polar graph.

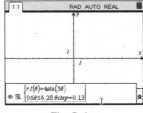
The Polar
Entry Line

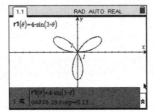
Graph of polar
equation

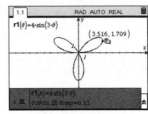
Using the
Point On tool

Figure 9-17:
Graphing
polar
equations.

In the third screen in Figure 9-17, I use the Point On tool (press (menu)⇨Points & Lines⇨Point On) to trace along the graph.

As with parametric graphing, many of the features of function graphing are available in polar graphing mode.

Chapter 10

Working in the Plane Geometry View

The Plane Geometry view enables you to perform a variety of *synthetic geometry* investigations (that is, geometric explorations that do not use a coordinate plane). This is where you draw or construct triangles, circles, regular polygons, parallel and perpendicular lines, as well as a host of other complex geometric objects. Whatever you can conjure up can be created in electronic form on TI-Nspire.

TI-Nspire also has the tools that allow you to perform just about any analysis on your geometric constructions.

I cannot, of course, take you through every possible investigation the Plane Geometry view has to offer. Rather, it is my hope that you begin to gain an appreciation for what you can accomplish in this view as well as the confidence to continue your own explorations.

Removing the Analytic Window

Recall from Chapter 9 that a new Graphs & Geometry page opens in the default Analytic View. To remove this view, press (menu)⇨View⇨Plane Geometry View. With the exception of the scale shown in the top-right corner, the entire page is blank. Consider this view to be your drawing canvas.

Working with Geometric Objects

In this section, I showcase those tools found in the Points & Lines menu and the Shapes menu. Just for kicks, I have changed my Page Layout to include two Graphs & Geometry pages side by side, both set up for the Plane Geometry view. The Points & Lines menu is on the left, and the Shapes menu on the right. Take a peek at Figure 10-1 to see how this layout looks.

Press (ctrl)(⌂)⇨Page Layout⇨Select Layout⇨Layout 2 to select the layout with two applications, side by side. Press (ctrl)(tab) to activate the second application, and press (menu)⇨Add Graphs & Geometry to select the Graphs & Geometry application. Finally, press (menu)⇨View⇨Plane Geometry View. (Chapter 3 explains how to return your TI-Nspire to a single layout view.)

The Points & Lines menu

Press (menu)⇨Points & Lines to access the Points & Lines menu. In Chapter 9, I talk about how to use the Point On and Intersection Point(s) tools. These tools are also available in the Plane Geometry view.

The Line, Segment, and Ray tools are all drawn using nearly identical methods. Here are the steps for drawing a line:

1. **Press (menu)⇨Points & Lines ⇨Line to access the Line tool.**

   Notice the icon associated with this tool located in the top-left corner of the application.

2. **Move your cursor anywhere on the screen and press ⓧ to mark a point through which the line will pass.**

   As you move the cursor, notice the ⌀ symbol and the prompt "point." You can also use an existing point as the starting point for a line, segment, or ray. As you move closer to an existing point, look for the ⌗ symbol. This is TI-Nspire's way to telling you that you are locked in on that point.

3. **Move the cursor to another area on the screen and perform one of the following tasks:**

   • Press ⓧ to draw the line so that the line contains only the single point constructed during Step 2.

   • Press (tab) followed by ⓧ to draw the line with a second point located at the current cursor location.

   • You can move the cursor to an existing point. Look for the ⌗ symbol indicating that you are locked in on the point and press ⓧ to draw the line.

4. **Press (esc) to exit the Line tool.**

   Follow the steps outlined in the previous list to use the Ray tool. The Segment tool requires two points and, therefore, Step 3 is modified as shown here.

5. **Move the cursor to another area on the screen and press ⊚ to draw the segment.**

You can create a line segment of a specific length by using the Compass tool in the Construction menu. All you have to do is use the Compass tool to create a circle with a specific radius. Then draw a radius (segment) with that length and hide the circle.

After Step 2, try holding down the ⊚ key while you complete your drawing. This allows you to draw precisely horizontal or vertical objects as well as objects with angles to the horizontal in increments of 15 degrees.

Figure 10-1 shows the Line, Segment, and Ray tools in action.

Figure 10-1:
Graphing
lines,
segments,
and rays.

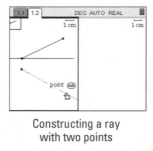
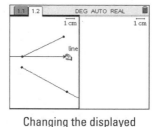

Marking the first point · Constructing a ray with two points · Changing the displayed length of a line

As you know, lines go on forever in both directions, and rays go on forever in one direction. However, TI-Nspire typically displays lines and rays with finite length. As shown in the last screen of Figure 10-1, you move your cursor to the end of a line or ray (in the case of the ray, the end that *should* go on forever). A blinking arrowhead appears. Press (ctrl)⊚ to grab the end of the line (or ray), and use the ◀▶ keys to extend or shorten its displayed length.

Please note that this refers to changing the *appearance* of a line (or ray). These objects still behave as if they go on forever.

The Shapes menu

Within the Shapes menu you find the Circle, Triangle, Rectangle, Polygon, and Regular Polygon tools. The first steps for drawing any of these objects are listed here.

1. Choose (menu)⇨**Shapes and select a tool from the list.**

2. **Move the cursor to an exiting point or any open space on the page and press** (⊚) **to mark the starting point.**

   This starting point is a vertex for the triangle, rectangle, and polygon and the center of the circle and regular polygon.

From here, depending on the tool you have selected, follow these steps:

✔ **Circle tool**

3. **Use the NavPad to adjust the size of the circle and press** (⊚) **to lock it in place.**

   As with the Line and Ray tools, you have the option of pressing (tab) and then (⊚) to draw a second point on the circle.

✔ **Triangle tool**

3. **Use the NavPad to move the cursor to the location of the second vertex of the triangle and press** (⊚) **to lock it in place.**

4. **Use the NavPad to move the cursor to the location of the third vertex of the triangle and press** (⊚) **to lock it in place.**

✔ **Rectangle tool**

3. **Use the NavPad to move the cursor to the location of the second vertex of the rectangle and press** (⊚) **to lock it in place.**

4. **Use the NavPad to move the cursor to the location of the third vertex of the rectangle and press** (⊚) **to lock it in place.**

   If you are drawing a rectangle, there are constraints on the location of this third vertex. It must be located on a line perpendicular to the first side of the rectangle and through the second vertex drawn in Step 3.

✔ **Polygon tool.**

3. **Use the NavPad to move the cursor to the location of the second vertex of the polygon and press** (⊚) **to lock it in place.**

4. **Repeat Step 3 to add additional vertices to your polygon.**

5. **Press** (enter) **to lock in the last vertex.**

✔ **Regular Polygon tool.**

3. **Use the NavPad to move the cursor away from the center of the regular polygon and press** (⊚) **to establish the radius and first vertex of the regular polygon.**

   This step creates a 16-sided regular polygon.

4. **Use the NavPad to move the cursor in a counterclockwise direction. This action increases the number of sides of the regular**

polygon. You can move in the clockwise direction to decrease the number of sides of the regular polygon.

Look for a number enclosed in brackets indicating the current number of sides.

5. Press to complete the drawing.

Press (esc) to exit the current tool.

Figure 10-2 shows the results of using these tools.

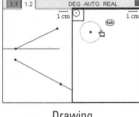 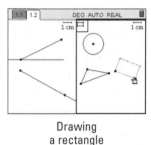 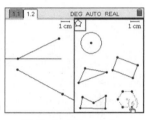

Figure 10-2: Using the Shapes tools.

Drawing a circle   Drawing a rectangle   Changing the number of sides of a regular polygon

Labeling objects and adding text

TI-Nspire allows you to add labels to any object. You can also add text that is not attached to any object in particular. To label an object follow these steps:

1. **Press (menu)⇨Actions⇨text to initiate the text tool.**

2. **Move the cursor to the object (that is, a point, line, rectangle, and so on) until the object starts blinking and its name appears. Press ⓧ to open a text box.**

Sometimes multiple objects are located at the current cursor location (as indicated by the name of the current active object and the image of the (tab) key). Press (tab) to cycle through and activate each available object. Press ⓧ when the desired object's name appears to open the text box for that object.

3. **Type your label and press to close the text box.**

4. **Press (esc) to exit the Text tool.**

When you manipulate a drawing or construction, object labels stay with the object.

An object label can be moved within a small distance of the object it is associated with.

Follow a similar procedure to add free-moving text to a diagram. *Free-moving text* is text that is not associated with a specific object. This type of text is used to annotate your sketches, provide additional information, and so on. You know your text is not associated with an object if the object name does not appear when you first open the text box. Such text can be moved anywhere within an application.

The samples of text shown on the left side of the screen in Figure 10-3 are all examples of object labels. The samples of text shown on the right side of the screen in Figure 10-3 are all examples of free-moving text.

Figure 10-3:
Adding
labels and
text.

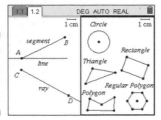

Moving and resizing objects

You can move or resize any object. However, you face some constraints based on the type of drawing you have constructed. For example, consider the rectangle in Figure 10-3. This object can be grabbed and moved or resized. But no matter what you do to change its shape, it always remains a rectangle.

The objects on the left side of the screen in Figure 10-3 can be moved and resized in virtually any direction. Keep in mind that the line and segment on this side of the screen share a common point *A*. If I choose to move the line, the segment invariably moves as well.

To move or resize an object, you must position the cursor on the object (or a part of the object) and press (ctrl)(⬚) to grab the object (as indicated by the ✍ symbol). Then use the NavPad to move the object.

As you move near an object, TI-Nspire displays the word that describes the current object that can be grabbed. If multiple objects are near the cursor, TI-Nspire also displays the (tab) symbol. By pressing the (tab)(›)(›), you can cycle through all the objects near the cursor location until you find the one that you want to grab (or label, hide, change attributes of, and so on).

In Figure 10-4, I show you some examples of how objects can be translated, rotated, and resized. Here's a brief description of how these actions relate to Figure 10-4.

- ✔ **First screen in Figure 10-4.** Here, I've grabbed point *A*. By moving the point, I simultaneously translate the line (meaning it moves without rotation) and rotate and resize the segment. Had I grabbed the segment (but not an endpoint) the segment and line would both translate. Had I grabbed point *B*, I could resize and rotate the segment without affecting the line.

    I can rotate the ray by grabbing either point *C* or point *D*. I can translate the ray by grabbing the ray (but not an endpoint).

- ✔ **Second screen in Figure 10-4.** Here, I grabbed the line (but not an endpoint). The line rotates about point *A*, and the segment is unaffected.

- ✔ **Third screen in Figure 10-4.** Here, I grab the second point that was constructed, which allows for resizing and rotating of the rectangle. Had I grabbed the first point that was constructed, I could accomplish a similar task.

To translate the entire rectangle, grab any side. To resize the rectangle without rotating it, grab either of the last two vertices that were constructed.

Figure 10-4:
Moving and resizing objects.

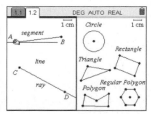 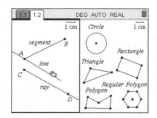 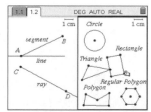

This may seem like a lot of rules and, to be honest, I often forget them myself. My suggestion to you is to experiment grabbing different objects and observing the corresponding effect. If you don't like the effect, press (ctrl)(esc) to undo the transformation.

Suppose you want to change the size of your circle. You may first try grabbing the center point, only to find out that this action translates the circle. Try grabbing the circle itself and notice that this action, in fact, changes the circle's size.

Selecting multiple objects

You may want to select multiple objects for two reasons. First, multiple selected objects can be translated. Second, all selected objects can be deleted by pressing the ⌧ key once.

To move all objects on a screen, move your cursor to open space and press ⌃⟐. You see the crunched up paper symbol (⟑), indicating that all objects on the screen can be translated using the NavPad.

Here are two methods that can be used to select multiple objects:

   ✔ **Method 1**

   1. **Move to an object until it begins to flash and press ⟐.**

   2. **Continue moving to additional objects until they begin to flash, pressing ⟐ each time.**

   ✔ **Method 2**

   1. **Press ⓜⓔⓝⓤ⇨Actions⇨Select to invoke the Select tool.**

   2. **Consider a rectangle surrounding the objects you wish to select. Move to one of the vertices of this rectangle and press ⏎.**

   3. **Move to the opposite corner of this rectangle and press ⏎ again to select the group of objects.**

Keep in mind that any object that is even partially contained within the rectangle is selected.

To deselect individual objects from a group, move the cursor to the desired object and press ⟐. To deselect all objects, press ⓔⓢⓒ.

After objects have been selected, press the ⌧ key to delete them.

To move selected objects, move the cursor to one of the selected objects until the ⊹ symbol appears. Press ⌃⟐ and use the NavPad to move the group.

The first screen in Figure 10-5 is a result of using Method 1. The segment and ray are selected, and I've moved the cursor to the ray. Notice the ⊹ symbol, which indicates that I'm ready to grab and move the selected objects. Although the line has not specifically been selected, it too moves because it's attached to the segment.

The second screen in Figure 10-5 shows the second method in action. The third screen shows that everything has been selected except the text for *Circle*, *Triangle*, and *Polygon,* as well as the circle itself.

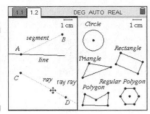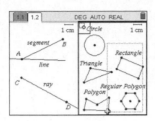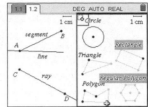

Figure 10-5:
Selecting
multiple
objects.

 If you want to delete all objects in an application, press (menu)⇨Actions⇨Delete all. Press (enter) at the warning prompt to delete the objects, or (esc) if you decide against it.

Changing an Object's Attributes

In Chapter 9, I talk about how to change the attributes of a graph. You can also change the attributes of a geometry object in the Plane Geometry View. Press (menu)⇨Actions⇨Attributes to invoke the Attributes command. Then, move to the object whose attributes you want to change and press (?) or (enter). Alternatively, move your cursor to the object whose attributes you want to change and press (ctrl)(menu)⇨Attributes.

After opening the attributes menu, press the ▲▼ keys to move through the different options (weight, style, and so on). Use the ◆ keys to view the different options within each attribute. You see the corresponding attribute change on the graph as well.

To put an attribute into effect, you must use the NavPad keys to select it and then press (enter). To exit out of the attribute menu without making a change, press (esc).

Many of the attribute options in the Plane Geometry view are the same ones that are available in the Analytic view (see Chapter 9). You may also want to check out the Fill attribute, which is available in either view. This attribute can be used to change the interior shading of any closed figure drawn using the Shapes menu. See Figure 10-6.

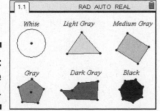

Figure 10-6:
Using the
Fill attribute.

Notice in Figure 10-6, I have removed the scale. To do this, press
(menu)⇨View⇨Hide Scale. To reveal the scale after it's been hidden, press
(menu)⇨View⇨Show Scale.

Using the Lock Feature

The lock feature can be used to lock a numerical value or a point. This feature is found in the Attributes menu, which can be accessed using one of the methods described in the previous section.

The first screen in Figure 10-7 shows how to lock a vertex of a triangle. If you do this, the point cannot be moved unless it is first unlocked.

The second and third screens in Figure 10-7 show a nifty mathematical reason for locking the perimeter of a triangle. By using Geometry Trace ((menu)⇨Trace⇨Geometry Trace), you can trace the path of the vertex of a triangle with fixed perimeter. This tracing results in an ellipse because the sum of the lengths of the two sides of the triangle that meet this vertex must be constant.

Figure 10-7:
Using the
Lock
feature.

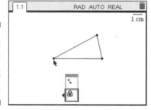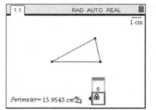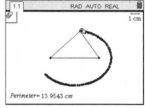

You may also want to try locking the perimeter of a rectangle. This can facilitate finding the maximum area for a fixed perimeter.

Constructing Geometric Objects

The act of creating a geometric construction can provide a rich mathematical experience. Especially when used with the dynamic click-and-drag feature of TI-Nspire. To access the Construction menu, press (menu)⇨Construction.

Perpendicular lines

To construct a perpendicular line, you must already have a segment, line, or ray. Then follow these steps:

1. **Press (menu)⇨Construction⇨Perpendicular to invoke the Perpendicular tool (notice the icon located in the top-left corner of the screen).**

2. **Click the segment, line, or ray through which you want your perpendicular line to pass.**

3. **Move the cursor to an existing point or to any point on the screen through which you want the perpendicular line to pass.**

   As you move the cursor, notice a ghosted image of the perpendicular line is displayed on the screen.

4. **Press ⊚ to set the perpendicular line in place.**

5. **Press (esc) to exit the Perpendicular tool.**

Steps 2 and 3 can be reversed if you have an existing point through which you want your perpendicular line to pass.

Parallel lines

The steps for constructing a parallel line are identical to those steps used to construct a perpendicular line. Just follow the same steps in the previous section, taking out the word *Perpendicular* and using the word *Parallel*.

Sometimes you want to construct perpendicular or parallel segments or rays, not lines. To accomplish this task, construct the perpendicular or parallel line. Then invoke the Segment (or Ray) tool as you normally do. As you move the cursor to the perpendicular or parallel line, the words `Point On` appear, telling you that the segment will be associated with the line. This happens again as you locate the endpoint of your segment (or specify the direction of the ray). After you draw the segment or ray, use the Hide/Show tool to hide the line, and you are all set.

Perpendicular bisector

To use the Perpendicular Bisector tool you must have a segment or an *implied segment* (two points). Then follow these steps:

1. Press (menu)⇨Construction⇨Perpendicular Bisector to invoke the Perpendicular Bisector tool (notice the icon located in the top-left corner of the screen).

2. Click the segment through which you want your perpendicular bisector to pass. Or, click the endpoints of the *implied segment* through which you want your perpendicular bisector to pass.

3. Press (esc) to exit the Perpendicular Bisector tool.

Angle bisectors

To use the Angle Bisector tool you must have three points. Then follow these steps:

1. Press (menu)⇨Construction⇨Angle Bisector to invoke the Angle Bisector tool (notice the icon located in the top-left corner of the screen).

2. Click the three points that form your angle, making sure that the second point you select is the vertex of the angle to be bisected.

3. Press (esc) to exit the Angle Bisector tool.

As with the other tools described in this section, the Angle Bisector tool creates a line rather than a segment or ray.

Although it's nice to "see" the angle that you are bisecting, all you need to use this tool are three points.

Midpoints

To use the Midpoint tool, you must have a segment or an *implied segment* (two points). Then follow these steps:

1. Press (menu)⇨Construction⇨Midpoint to invoke the Midpoint tool (notice the icon located in the top-left corner of the screen).

2. Click the segment to construct the midpoint, or click the endpoints of the *implied segment*.

3. Press (esc) to exit the Midpoint tool.

Figure 10-8 shows some examples of how the Construction tools can be used.

Figure 10-8:
Using the
Construction
tools menu.

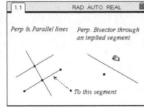
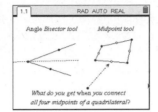

Other constructions — Using the Hide/Show tool

The Construction tools menu is packed with power. Sometimes, however, you have compelling reasons to create constructions using alternative methods. Other more complicated constructions require using a combination of construction tools.

Consider for example that you want to construct the perpendicular bisector to a segment using an alternative method. As shown in the first screen in Figure 10-9, start by drawing two circles, both of which use the segment to define the radius (although in opposite order).

In the second screen, use the Intersection Point(s) tool to construct the points of intersection of the two circles. Then construct a line through these two points of intersection. This line represents the perpendicular bisector of the segment.

The circles themselves are there strictly to support the construct, and they can be hidden from view. Keep in mind that hidden objects continue to work as if they are in full view. To quickly hide an object, move the cursor to the object and press (ctrl)(menu)⇨Hide/Show.

The result of hiding the circles is shown in the third screen in Figure 10-9. Notice that you are moving the endpoint of the segment to manipulate the construction. This demonstrates that you have, in fact, constructed the perpendicular bisector.

Figure 10-9:
Using the
Hide/Show
tool with
more com-
plicated
construc-
tions.

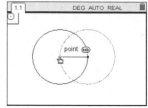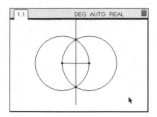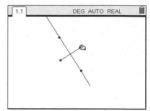

To reveal a hidden object, you must press (menu)⇨Actions⇨Hide/Show to invoke the Hide/Show tool. The Hide/Show icon (an eye) is displayed in the top-left corner of the screen, indicating that this tool is currently active. Additionally, ghosted images of all hidden objects appear, including your hidden graph. Move your cursor to the object until the *∅* icon appears and press (?) once. Press (esc) to exit the Hide/Show tool.

Using the Measurement Tool

Press (menu)⇨Measurement to access the Measurement menu. In Chapter 9 I talk about the Slope and Integral tools. In this section, I feature the Length, Area, and Angle tools.

Measuring angles

Referring back to the perpendicular bisector construction, perhaps you want to verify that the angles formed by the perpendicular bisector and the segment are in fact 90 degrees. To measure one of these angles, follow these steps:

1. **Press (menu)⇨Measurement⇨Angle to invoke the Angle measurement tool.**

2. **Click the three points that form your angle, making sure that the second point you select is the vertex of the angle to be bisected.**

   The vertex of my angle is located at the intersection of the perpendicular bisector and the segment. Although a point does not already exist in this location, TI-Nspire prompts you to select the intersection of the line and the segment. Press (?) to select this point.

3. **Use the NavPad to move the measurement to a desired location and press (?) or (enter) to drop it in place.**

4. **Press (esc) to exit the Angle measurement tool.**

The first screen in Figure 10-10 shows the result of this measurement, given in radians. To convert this measurement to degrees, press ⌂⇨System Info⇨Document Settings and change the Angle field of the dialog box from Radian to Degree.

Figure 10-10:
Measuring
angles and
switching to
degrees.

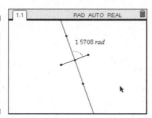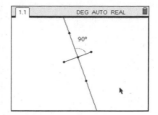

 Using Document Settings to change the angle measurement from radians to degrees will affect all angle measurements within the current document. To change the angle setting for all future documents, use the System Settings option.

Measuring length

Press (menu)⇨Measurement⇨Length to access the Length measurement tool. With this tool you can measure the perimeter of a polygon, the circumference of a circle, the length of a segment, or the distance between any two points.

To find perimeter, circumference, or segment length, follow these steps:

1. **Press (menu)⇨Measurement⇨Length to initiate the Length measurement tool.**

2. **Move your cursor to the object being measured and press ⊚.**

3. **Use the NavPad to move the measurement to a desired location and press ⊚ or (enter) to drop it in place.**

4. **Press (esc) to exit the Length measurement tool.**

The process of finding the distance between two points is almost identical, with one slight change. In Step 2, click each point once and the measurement pops up.

 When finding the perimeter of a polygon, notice the word describing the polygon (triangle, rectangle, polygon) appears along with the (tab) symbol. Press (tab) to switch to finding the length of the side of the polygon corresponding to the current cursor location. Press (tab) again to switch back to finding the perimeter of the polygon.

Creating an 8.5 in. × 11 in. piece of paper

Referring to Figure 10-11, I've measured one side of my rectangle to 5.25 inches. To create an exact model of an 8.5 in. × 11 in. sheet of paper, I start by forcing this measurement to 8.5 inches. Follow these steps:

1. Click the scale and delete the number 1.

2. Type 8.5, ⊕, type the current length measurement (in this case, 5.25), and press ⬡.

3. Lock the measurement.

4. Use the Length measurement tool to find the length of the other dimension of the

rectangle. This measurement will likely not be 11 inches.

5. To change this measurement to 11 inches, click the measurement to allow for editing and change it 11.

6. Press ⬡ and watch the rectangle change in size. Notice the rectangle's shape changes so that it is in exact proportion with a standard 8.5 in. × 11 in. sheet of paper.

The results of these steps are shown here.

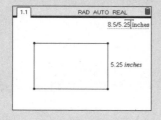 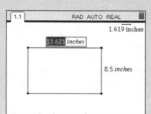 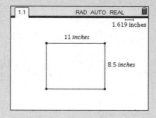

Measuring area

The area measurement tool allows you to measure the area of a circle or polygon. Here are the steps to follow:

1. **Press (menu)⇨Measurement⇨Area to initiate the Area measurement tool.**

2. **Move your cursor to the object being measured and press ⓧ.**

3. **Use the NavPad to move the measurement to a desired location and press ⓧ or ⬡ to drop it in place.**

4. **Press (esc) to exit the Area measurement tool.**

Customizing the scale

To this point, I haven't said much about the scale. By default, the scale is given in centimeters and is located in the top-right corner of the screen.

The scale behaves much like a text box. To change units, click the scale once and use the (clear) key to delete the current unit. Type a new unit using the green alpha keys and press (enter) to complete the task. All existing length and area measurements are automatically updated to reflect this change.

Figure 10-11 shows the result of changing the scale from centimeters to inches.

Figure 10-11:
Customizing
the scale
units.

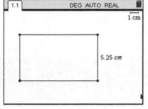
A centimeter measurement

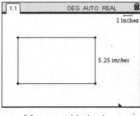
Editing the scale

Measured in inches

Performing Calculations

Inevitably, you will want to perform a variety of calculations on your drawings and constructions. Refer to Chapter 9 for the steps used to perform a calculation.

In Figure 10-12, you see a circle with two chords. I've constructed the intersection point of these chords and found the measure of each of the four segments created by these two intersecting chords.

Figure 10-12:
Exploring
the products
of segments
created by
intersecting
chords.

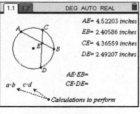
Set up the diagram

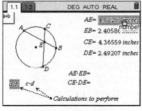
Finding the product
of AE and EB

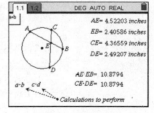
Equal products

You can perform calculations on any measured or entered value.

Exploring Constructions Dynamically

Remember, one of TI-Nspire's most powerful features is its capability to grab and move objects and enable you to observe changes happening dynamically in real time. This is especially true of constructions, including those containing measurements and calculations.

Using the intersecting chord problem from the previous section, grab the edge of the circle and change its size. You see very compelling evidence that the products of the pairs segments formed by two intersecting chords are equal. The high-resolution screen and corresponding precision used by TI-Nspire allow this to happen.

Investigating Transformations

The Transformation menu provides for five different transformations: Symmetry, Reflection, Translation, Rotation, and Dilation. Here's a brief description of what each of these transformations can do and what you do to perform the transformation:

- ✔ **Symmetry:** This transformation gives the image of an object (requirement #1) with a 180-degree rotation about a point (requirement #2).

- ✔ **Reflection:** This transformation gives the image of an object (requirement #1) reflected over a line or segment (requirement #2).

- ✔ **Translation:** This transformation gives the image of an object (requirement #1) translated by a distance and direction given by a vector or two points (requirement #2).

- ✔ **Rotation:** This transformation gives the image of an object (requirement #1) rotated about a point (requirement #2) by an angle (requirement #3).

  The angle of rotation can be defined by three points or by a number.

- ✔ **Dilation:** This transformation gives the image of an object (requirement #1) with a point that is the center of dilation (requirement #2) and a number specifying the dilation factor (requirement #3).

The first two transformations, symmetry and reflection, are accomplished using similar steps. Here, I show you the steps to reflect a polygon over a line.

1. **Draw a polygon.**

2. **Draw a segment or line.**

3. **Press** (menu)➪**Transformation➪Reflection to initiate the Reflection tool.**

4. **Click the polygon.**

5. **Click the segment or line.**

    When using the Symmetry tool, click a point.

6. **Press (esc) to exit the Reflection tool.**

Here are the steps for using the Translation tool:

1. **Draw an object.**

2. **Draw a vector (or two points) that gives the direction and length of the translation.**

3. **Press (menu)⇨Transformation⇨Translation to initiate the Translation tool.**

4. **Click the object.**

5. **Click the vector (or each of the two points).**

6. **Press (esc) to exit the Translation tool.**

The first screen in Figure 10-13 shows the results of using the Symmetry, Reflection, and Translation tools. I started by drawing polygon *A*. I then used the Symmetry tool to complete a 180-degree rotation of polygon *A* about point *p*. This gave me polygon *B*.

I then used the Translation tool to translate polygon *A* to polygon *C*. To complete this step, I clicked polygon *A* and then the translation vector located at the bottom of the screen (to draw a vector, press (menu)⇨Points & Lines⇨Vector). Notice that the corresponding points on polygons *A* and *C* are located at a distance and direction equal to the translation vector.

Finally, I used the Reflection tool to complete the reflection of polygon *C* over line *l*. Don't forget to drag objects and observe the corresponding changes.

To perform a rotation, follow these steps:

1. **Draw an object.**

2. **Draw three points or type a number for the angle of rotation.**

3. **Press (menu)⇨Transformation⇨Rotation to initiate the Translation tool.**

4. **Click the object.**

5. **Click the point about which you wish to rotate.**

6. **Click the three points that define the angle of rotation (with the vertex being the second point) or click the number.**

7. **Press (esc) to exit the Rotation tool.**

The second screen in Figure 10-13 shows the result of using the Rotation tool. On the left, I show the image (polygon *B*) of the pre-image (polygon *A*) using the three-point method to define my angle. I put my angle on the circle for the purpose of animating point *a* (see next section). Notice that the point of rotation (point *p*) is a point on the object itself. The point of rotation can be on the object, inside the object, or outside the object.

On the right side of this screen, I use the numeric method to define my angle of rotation. This provides the advantage of being precise, with the drawback that it's a bit more static (although I can certainly edit this numerical value).

TIP

Positive rotations are in the counterclockwise direction and negative rotations are in the clockwise direction.

To perform a dilation follow these steps:

1. **Draw an object.**

2. **Draw a point (or use an existing point).**

3. **Type a number to give the scale or dilation factor.**

4. **Press** (menu)⇨**Transformation**⇨**Dilation to initiate the Dilation tool.**

5. **Click the object.**

6. **Click the point which defines the center of dilation.**

7. **Click the number which defines the scale factor.**

8. **Press** (esc) **to exit the Dilation tool.**

The third screen in Figure 10-13 shows the result of using the Dilation tool. On the left, I show a dilation that results in an enlargement with a scale factor of 2 and center of dilation at point *p*. Here the image is shown with dashed lines and the pre-image is shown with solid lines.

On the right, I show a dilation that results in a reduction with a scale factor of 2/3 and center of dilation at point *p*.

Figure 10-13:
Using the
Transfor-
mation
menu.

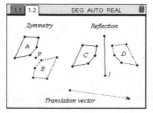
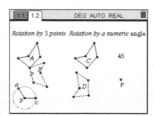
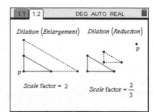

Try using the Reflection tool (with the *x*- or *y*-axis as the line of reflection) or Symmetry tool (with the origin as the center of symmetry) on a graphed function in the Analytic view. Either of these choices transforms a single point on the function. Then, use the Locus tool (click the image point first and the pre-image point second) to see the complete transformation of your function.

Animating Objects

You can animate a point (or multiple points) on a line, ray, axis, vector, graph, segment, or circle. Referring to the second screen in Figure 10-13, assume you want to animate point *a*. As you do so, point *a* rotates in a counterclockwise direction about the circle and, as a consequence, polygon *B* rotates about point *p*.

Here's the easiest way to perform this animation:

1. **Move the cursor to point *a* and press ⌃ ⌨ ⇨ Attributes.**

2. **Press ▾ to select the animation attribute.**

   Notice the words "Unidirectional animation speed." This indicates that the point will move in only one direction, counterclockwise. This is the only option associated with this attribute when animating a point on a circle, line, or ray. If you animate a point on a segment, you have the option of specifying "Alternating animation speed." In this scenario, the point moves to one endpoint, switches direction, and moves back to the other endpoint.

3. **Type a number from 1 to 9, where 1 is slow and 9 is fast.**

   The animation automatically begins. Press ⊕ or ⊖ to speed up or slow down the animation, respectively.

4. **Press ◂▸ to change the direction of the animation.**

   This feature is not available when you animate a point on a circle.

5. **Press ⏎ to close the attributes bar and open the animation control panel.**

The first screen in Figure 10-14 shows the animation attribute. The second screen shows the animation control panel. The object can be moved to any location on the screen. The leftmost button on the animation control panel is used to reset the animation. Move the cursor over this button and press ⊗ to stop the animation and return the animated point to its original location.

The rightmost button toggles between *pause animation* (second screen) and *start animation* (third screen).

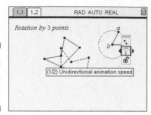 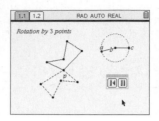 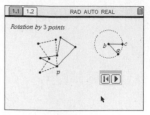

Figure 10-14:
Animating
points.

To stop an animation and remove the control panel, follow these steps:

1. **Stop the animation using the animation control panel.**

2. **Move the cursor back to the animated point and press** (ctrl)(menu)⇨ **Attributes.**

3. **Press ▼ to select the animation attribute.**

4. **Type 0 and** (enter).

Taking It to the Next Level

As I mention in the beginning of this chapter, I cannot possibly cover everything you can accomplish in the Plane Geometry view. I suggest you try incorporating a variety of tools in a single, more complex sketch. You may also want to explore some of the more advanced functions that TI-Nspire has to offer. Chances are, if you can think it, TI-Nspire can do it!

Chapter 11

Working in Both Views Simultaneously

. . . .

In This Chapter

▶ Working with Analytic and Plane Geometry views simultaneously

▶ Investigating an optimization problem

▶ Using the combined view to discover a geometric formula

▶ Taking a look at some other examples

. . . .

*T*here are many reasons for working strictly in the Analytic view or the Plane Geometry view. Sometimes, however, it's to your advantage to work in both of these views simultaneously. In this chapter I show you how to set up such an arrangement. I then provide you with some examples that give compelling reasons for why this is such a good option.

Adding an Analytic Window to the Plane Geometry View

Here are the steps to follow to set up a Plane Geometry view with an Analytic Window:

1. **Open a new Graphs & Geometry page.**

2. **Press (menu)⇨View⇨Plane Geometry View.**

3. **Press (menu)⇨View⇨Show Analytic Window.**

The first screen in Figure 11-1 shows that these steps place a small Analytic Window near the bottom-left corner of the screen. You will also notice (as indicated by the ✍ symbol) that the Analytic Window can be translated by grabbing the origin. In the second screen, I show that the boundaries of the Analytic Window can be expanded by grabbing the end of an axis.

Figure 11-1:
Setting up
a combined
Plane
Geometry
and Analytic
Window.

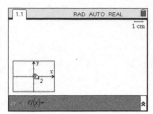 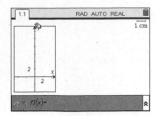

Press (menu)⇨Window⇨Window Settings to adjust the minimum and maximum *x*- and *y*-end values.

How Geometric Objects Behave in Each View

Figure 11-2 does a nice job explaining how objects behave in each of these different views. It shows two identical circles. The circle on the left was drawn in the Analytic Window, whereas the circle on the right was drawn in the Plane Geometry view.

I pressed (menu)⇨Actions⇨Coordinates and Equations to find the equation of the analytic circle on the left. You can use this tool to find the equations of circles, lines, and tangents as long as they are drawn in the Analytic Window. If these same objects are drawn in the Plane Geometry view, this option does not work.

Likewise, I've used the Measurement (length) tool to find the circumference of both circles. Notice that the circumference measurement for the circle on the left is "unitless" (as indicated by the letter *u*) whereas the units for the circle on the right are given in centimeters. Keep in mind that all measurements found in an Analytic Window are unitless; the scale displayed in the top-right corner of the screen applies only to Plane Geometry objects.

Finally, if I change the scale in an Analytic Window, geometric objects change accordingly. Keep in mind that two-dimensional objects become distorted if you adjust the scale on only one axis.

Figure 11-2:
Observing the difference between Analytic and Plane Geometry objects.

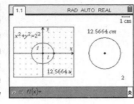

If you move an object that has been drawn in the Plane Geometry view to the Analytic Window, it continues to behave as if it were drawn in the Plane Geometry view.

Press (menu)⇨View⇨Show Grid to reveal a grid in the Analytic Window. The grid corresponds to the tick marks located on each axis. A grid enables you to draw objects with more precision. That's how you can obtain a radius of exactly 2 units. If you resize the circle, it will jump to other grid locations.

Use the Compass tool to draw the circle on the right with a radius of exactly 2 centimeters. To accomplish this task, use the Text tool to type your radius. Then, press (menu)⇨Construction⇨Compass to invoke the Compass tool, click once to define the center of the circle, and click the text to define the radius.

The Power of Multiple Representations

Many geometric properties can be modeled algebraically. For example, the sum, S, of the interior angles of an n-sided convex polygon can be represented by the algebraic formula $S = 180(n - 2)$.

By working in a combined view, TI-Nspire provides the opportunity to explore these geometric and algebraic relationships. Furthermore, the dynamic, click-and-drag technology inherent to TI-Nspire makes these relationships even more evident.

Optimization

To illustrate optimization, cut four equal-size squares from the corners of a standard 8.5 in. × 11 in. piece of paper. By folding the resulting flaps up, you form an open-topped box. What size squares must be cut from this piece of paper to maximize the volume of this open-topped box?

This classic optimization problem can be modeled geometrically and analytically quite nicely using TI-Nspire.

In Chapter 10, I show you how to construct a model of an 8.5 in. × 11 in. piece of paper. In Figure 11-2, I take this model one step further by constructing four equal and resizable squares in each corner of this rectangle. I you drag point c, each of the four squares resize in exactly the same way.

This construction is fairly sophisticated. However, all the tools used to complete this construction are detailed in Chapter 10. Here's a general description as to how to build this sketch:

1. **Construct a square in the top-left corner of the rectangle.**

   I did not use the Regular Polygon tool to construct the square. Rather, I constructed the midpoint of the left side of the rectangle and used the Point On tool to draw point c. This ensures that, when I drag point c, its movement is restricted to only half of the side of the rectangle. Point c and the top-left corner of the large rectangle define one side of the square.

   I then use the Rotation tool to rotate point c 90 degrees in a counterclockwise direction to locate the bottom-right corner of the square. I repeated this rotation to locate the top-right corner of the square. I now have the four corners of a square.

   Finally, I use the Polygon tool, clicking each of the vertices that define the square, to draw it.

   Refer to the first two screens in Figure 11-3 to see these steps.

2. **Translate the square to the other three locations.**

   Using the Translate tool, I translate the square to each of the three remaining corners of the 8.5 in. × 11 in. rectangle. You see this in the third screen in Figure 11-3.

   Incidentally, I used the top-right corner of my first square and the top-right corner of the large rectangle to define the translation vector. I used a similar method to create the bottom two squares.

3. **Use the Hide/Show tool to clean up the drawing.**

You can hide the vertices of the original rectangle, the midpoint, segment, and any other objects that are no longer needed. Notice that I have not hidden the top-left vertex of the large triangle. I use this point and point *c* to determine the length of the side of the squares.

4. Use the Attributes tool to enhance the drawing.

I used dashed lines for my squares to give the impression that they are being cut. I also shaded these squares to differentiate them from the 8.5 in. × 11 in. rectangle.

You see the results of using the Hide/Show and Attributes tools in the last screen in Figure 11-3.

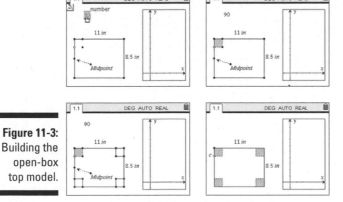

Figure 11-3:
Building the open-box top model.

Now that the drawing is complete, it's time to set up the problem for analysis. In the following steps, I measure the size of the cut (the length of the side of a square), calculate the corresponding volume, transfer these measurements to the Analytic Window, and construct a point in the Analytic Window whose *x*-value represents the cut size and whose *y*-value represents the corresponding volume.

1. Use the Measurement (length) tool to measure the length of the side of the squares.

Measure this distance using point *c* and the top-left point on the rectangle. Hide the top-left point from view because it's no longer needed.

2. Calculate the volume that corresponds to the cut length from Step 1 by following these steps.

a. Use the Text tool to type the expression $x \cdot (11 - 2x) \cdot (8.5 - 2x)$.

   b. Press ⓜ⇨Actions⇨Calculate to invoke the Calculate tool. Click
      the expression $x \cdot (11 - 2x) \cdot (8.5 - 2x)$, click the *cut length* measure-
      ment, move the measurement to a desired location on the screen,
      and press ⓔ to exit the Calculate tool.

   c. Use the Hide/Show tool to hide the expression $x \cdot (11 - 2x) \cdot (8.5 -
      2x)$.

**3. Use the Measurement Transfer tool to transfer *Cut length* to the *x*-axis
   and *Volume* to the *y*-axis. Here are the steps:**

   a. Press ⓜ⇨Construction⇨Measurement Transfer to invoke
      Measurement Transfer tool.

   b. Click the *cut length* measurement.

   c. Click the *x*-axis (notice a point appears on the *x*-axis).

   d. Repeat Steps 2 and 3 to transfer *Volume* to the *y*-axis (notice a
      point appears on the *y*-axis).

   e. Press ⓔ to exit the Measurement Transfer tool.

Adjust your window settings (press ⓜ⇨Window⇨Window Settings) if
the transferred points are not visible on either axis. A good choice for
XMin and XMax are –1 and 5, respectively. A good choice for YMin and
YMax are –6 and 80, respectively.

**4. Through each transferred point construct a perpendicular line (press
   ⓜ⇨Construction⇨Perpendicular) through the corresponding axis.**

**5. Press ⓜ⇨Points & Lines⇨Intersection Point(s) and construct the
   intersection of these two perpendicular lines.**

The first screen in Figure 11-4 shows the result of these steps. The second
and third screens show that, as you drag point *c*, the squares, measurements,
and (x, y) point all update accordingly.

Figure 11-4:
Creating the
geometric
and analytic
connection.

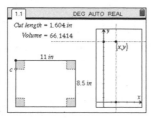
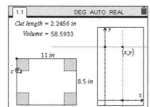
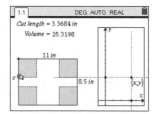

As you can see, this construction is fairly complicated. If you are not up to the
task, consider going to education.ti.com, clicking the Activities Exchange
link, and searching with a keyword such as *optimization*. This searchable data-
base is full of premade TI-Nspire files. You can be assured that this construction and a variety of other terrific activities are available to be downloaded

directly to your computer. These downloaded TI-Nspire files can be quickly transferred to your device using TI-Nspire Computer Link software (see Chapter 24).

At this point, you can observe the path of the point (x, y) in several ways. Here's a brief description of three options:

- Use Geometry Trace to trace the path of (x, y) as point c is dragged.
- Use the Locus tool to create the locus of (x, y) as it relates to the driver point c.
- Use the Data Capture feature to store the *cut length* and *volume* values to a spreadsheet. Plot this data as a scatter plot in the Analytic Window. See Chapter 16 for more information on how to use Data Capture.

Here's a description of how you might use Geometry Trace to explore this relationship.

1. **Press ⒨ ⇨ Trace ⇨ Geometry Trace to access the Geometry Trace tool.**

2. **Move the cursor on the intersection point and press x.**

3. **Move to point c and press ⒸⓉⓇⓁ Ⓖ to grab the point.**

4. **Use the NavPad keys to drag point c and watch the trace appear in the Analytic Window.**

5. **Press ⒺⓈⒸ to exit the Geometry Trace tool.**

The first screen in Figure 11-5 shows the result of using Geometry Trace. In the second screen, I pressed ⒸⓉⓇⓁ Ⓖ to reveal the Entry Line and typed the equation that models this situation. In the last screen, I've put a point on the graph and dragged it to reveal the maximum value (1.59, 66.15). This point suggests that a cut size of approximately 1.59 inches produces a maximum volume of 66.16 cubic inches.

Figure 11-5:
Analyzing
the open-
topped box
problem.

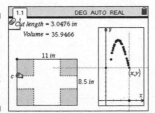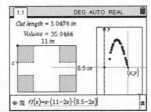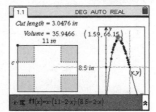

To clear the trace, perhaps to perform this experiment again, press ⒨ ⇨ Trace ⇨ Erase Geometry Trace.

Discovering an area formula

I can use a combined Analytic and Plane Geometry view to explore the formula for the area of a circle.

I've also decided to use the Automatic Data Capture feature to generate a scatter plot of the radius versus area data. This is a slightly more complicated approach than the one that I used with the open-topped box problem. However, this option has the benefit of adding numeric data to a Lists & Spreadsheet page.

Here's a brief description of how I accomplish this task (see Figure 11-5). For more information about configuring TI-Nspire for Data Capture, refer to Chapter 16.

1. **Click each measurement once and press ⟨₅ᵗᵒᵛᵃʳ⟩⇨Store Var. Type a descriptive name for each variable (such as *radius* and *area*). Notice that variable names appear in bold font. See the first and second screens in Figure 11-6.**

2. **Configure a Lists & Spreadsheet page for Automatic Data Capture.**

3. **Configure the Entry Line to draw a scatter plot of the *radius* versus *area* data.**

4. **Drag the edge of the circle and watch the scatter plot appear in the Analytic Window. See the last screen in Figure 11-6.**

Figure 11-6:
Performing
a Data
Capture
on Radius
versus Area
data.

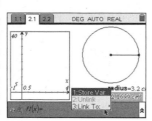 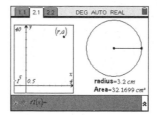 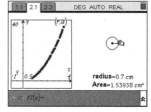

The scatter plot in this exploration is tied to the Analytic Window. That means if I adjust the window settings, the scatter plot adjusts accordingly. On the other hand, the Geometry Trace from the open-topped box problem is not tied into the Analytic Window. Rather, think of it as a geometric object overlaid on the Analytic Window. If you move or adjust the coordinate plane, the Geometry Trace does not move with it.

It would appear that the scatter plot is quadratic — but what is the equation that models this data? Configure the Entry Line for function graphing and graph the function $y = x^2$.

As shown in the first screen in Figure 11-7, move the cursor to the graph until the ⚡ appears and press (ctrl)(✋) to grab the edge of the graph. As you see in the second screen in Figure 11-7, use the NavPad keys to manipulate the graph to pass through the scatter plot and watch the equation update accordingly. It seems pretty clear that the equation $y = \pi x^2$ (better known as $A = \pi r^2$) is the formula that relates the area of a circle to its radius.

Figure 11-7:
Finding the formula for the area of a circle.

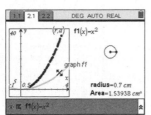 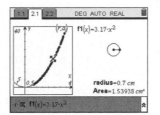

Other examples

I think the two examples included in this chapter do a nice job illustrating the benefits of using the Plane Geometry view and an Analytic Window together. Don't forget to use the Activities Exchange at education.ti.com to find some more ideas that utilize this same environment. The following is a brief description of a couple more explorations that work quite nicely in the simultaneous environment of the Analytic and Plane Geometry views.

✔ **Finding the maximum area of a rectangular fenced in area that uses a barn as one side.**

This problem represents a variation of a problem I feature in Chapter 16. I use the Manual Data Capture feature to draw the scatter plot. See the first screen in Figure 11-8 to see how this problem looks.

✔ **Finding the minimum surface area of a cylinder with fixed volume.**

This is another classic optimization problem in which a quantity must be minimized. To get really fancy, construct a model with a fixed volume of 355 milliliters (the volume of a standard soda can) and use Geometry Trace, the Locus tool, or Data Capture to form an analytic representation. Or, search for optimization in TI's Activities Exchange to find a previously made, and editable, version of this problem. See the second and third screens in Figure 11-8.

Figure 11-8:
A couple
more opti-
mization
problems.

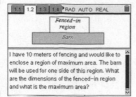
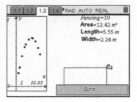
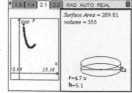

✓ **Finding the formulas for the area and volume of geometric objects.**

As with the area of the circle problem in this chapter, a geometric model of virtually any two- or three-dimensional object can be explored analytically.

In Figure 11-9, I constructed a model of a cone whose height and radius can be varied (by dragging on their respective points). The first two screens show the corresponding scatter plot of the radius versus volume for a constant height. The third screen shows the graph of the function that models this scatter plot.

Using similar methods you can also explore the relationship between height and volume for a constant radius.

Figure 11-9:
Exploring
the volume
of a cone.

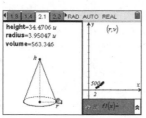
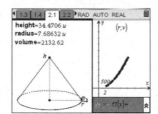
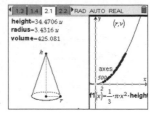

This construction contains a few tricks. For example, I drew the circle on a coordinate grid and adjusted the *y*-axis scale to squish the circle and make it look more like an ellipse. I then used the Segment tool to draw the sides of the cone that meet at the vertex (located on the *y*-axis). Finally, I hid the axes. Because I can only use one analytic view per page, I split the page in two and added an analytic view on the right. This is where I graphed the scatter plot using the Automatic Data Capture feature.

Chapter 12

Using the Graphs & Geometry Application with TI-Nspire CAS

In This Chapter

▶ Understanding which CAS features can be used in the Graphs & Geometry application

▶ Using TI-Nspire CAS tools to explore Calculus

*1*n Chapter 8 I talk about the differences between the numeric TI-Nspire and TI-Nspire CAS. In Chapter 8, I also mentioned that TI-Nspire CAS has the capability to perform symbolic manipulation of mathematical expressions and equations.

In that chapter I also discuss that the TI-Nspire CAS application menu differs slightly from the TI-Nspire application menu. And although these application menu items reside in the Calculator application menu, they can also be accessed via the Math Template or the Catalog. Furthermore, the Math Template and the Catalog can be accessed from any TI-Nspire application, including the Graphs & Geometry application, the focus of this chapter.

In this chapter, I talk about some of the CAS-specific features that can be called into play in the Graphs & Geometry application and how you might want to use them to get the most out of your TI-Nspire CAS device. I focus primarily on exploring calculus concepts because the CAS-specific tools of TI-Nspire CAS lend themselves so well to this subject area.

The Calculate Tool and Approximate Results

In Chapter 8, I show you how TI-Nspire CAS displays results in the Calculator application in symbolic form. It turns out that this feature is not always available in other applications. For example, TI-Nspire and TI-Nspire CAS both display results from using the Calculate tool (see Chapter 9) in decimal form. When it comes to this feature, there is no distinction between these two devices.

To make this point clear, I use the Calculate tool to find the length of the hypotenuse of a right triangle drawn in the Graphs & Geometry application. You see that hypotenuse values that are irrational are given as decimal approximations rather than in simplified radical form.

Take a look at Figure 12-1. Here, I am working in the Analytic Window with the grid in view (press (menu)⇨View⇨Show Grid) and the axes hidden (press (menu)⇨View⇨Hide Axes). By carefully drawing the legs of the triangle to the grid points, I can be assured that subsequent movements of the segments snap from one grid point to another. This is a quick way to work with a right triangle whose legs have whole number lengths.

Keep in mind, however, that this triangle is drawn as a right triangle, not *constructed* as a right triangle. I can easily manipulate the figure so that angle *C* is no longer a right angle.

Before hiding the axes, I adjusted the XScale and YScale to 1. This ensures that the lengths of segments are strictly whole numbers.

Measurements are unitless in the Analytic view.

After drawing the triangle, I used the Calculate tool to find the length of the hypotenuse. Here's a quick review of the steps to accomplish this task:

1. **Press (menu)⇨Measurement⇨Length to invoke the Length Measurement tool.**

2. **Click segment *AC* once, move the cursor to a location where you want this measurement to reside, and press (⊙) or (enter) to drop it in place.**

3. **With the Length Measurement tool still active, measure *BC*.**

4. **Press (esc) to exit the Length Measurement tool.**

5. **Use the Text tool to type the expression $\sqrt{a^2 + b^2}$**

6. **Press (menu)⇨Actions⇨Calculate to invoke the Calculate tool.**

7. **Click the text expression from Step 5, the measurement of *AC*, and the measurement of *BC*.**

8. **Move the cursor to a desired location and press (⊙) or (enter) to drop the calculation in place.**

9. **Press (esc) to exit the Calculate tool.**

I used the Text tool to add *Segment AC =*, *Segment BC =*, and the = symbol located on the third line.

In the first two screens in Figure 12-1, I show you examples in which the hypotenuse has a whole-number length. In the third screen, I have manipulated the triangle so that the hypotenuse is an irrational number. Notice that the result of the calculation is given as a decimal approximation, rather than in its symbolic form. $2\sqrt{13}$

Figure 12-1:
Using the
Calculate
tool with
TI-Nspire
CAS.

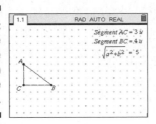 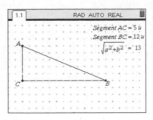 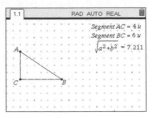

So what does this all mean? The results of TI-Nspire CAS calculations performed in the Graphs & Geometry application are not given in symbolic form. In such instances, no distinction is made between TI-Nspire and TI-Nspire CAS.

However, as you see in the next section, several CAS-specific features are available with TI-Nspire CAS that can be used in the Graphs & Geometry application.

Doing Calculus

The study of calculus should include a focus on the four key mathematical representations: algebraic, geometric, numeric, and verbal. The Calculator application takes care of the algebraic piece, the Lists & Spreadsheet application takes care of the numeric piece, and the Notes application can take care of the verbal piece. The Graphs & Geometry application stands ready to take care of the geometric representation of calculus concepts.

Graphing derivatives with and without CAS

To graph the function $y = x^4 - 8x^2 + 5$ and its derivative on the same screen, follow these steps:

1. **If you haven't already done so, open a new Graphs & Geometry page.**

2. **Graph $y = x4 - 8x2 + 5$ using the first available function on the Entry Line.**

3. **Press (ctrl)(x) to open the Math Template, highlight the derivative template, and press (enter).**

   See the first screen in Figure 12-2.

4. **The derivative template is pasted to the Entry Line. Type x for the first field, and press (tab) to move to the second field of the derivative template.**

5. **Press (var) to see a list of available variables and select f1 from the list.**

   You can also type f1 using the keypad.

6. **Type x to complete the expression f1(x) and press ⊜ to graph the derivative.**

7. **Move the cursor to the graph of the derivative and press ⌃ ⊙⇨Attributes. Change the line style to dotted or dashed to provide some visual clarity between the two graphs.**

See the second and third screens in Figure 12-2.

TIP

Try changing the rule for **f1**(x). The graph of **f1**(x) and its derivative updates accordingly.

You can also graph derivatives using the numeric TI-Nspire. Here are the steps for graphing the derivative of $y = x^4 - 8x^2 + 5$:

1. **Graph $y = x^4 - 8x^2 + 5$ using the first available function on the Entry Line.**

2. **Move to the next available function on the Entry Line, press ⊛ to open the Catalog, and press ① to access the alphabetical list of available commands.**

3. **Press Ⓝ to access those commands that begin with N, use the NavPad to highlight nDeriv, and press ⊜ to paste the command to the Entry Line.**

   The nDeriv command stands for *numerical derivative*.

4. **Configure the nDeriv command as shown in the first screen in Figure 12-3.**

   You can press ⊙ to access the variable **f1** or type it using the keypad.

5. **Press ⊜ to graph the derivative as shown in the second screen in Figure 12-3.**

Graphing anti-derivatives with and without CAS

In this section, I reverse the process and look at graphing anti-derivatives.

Keep in mind that a function has an infinite number of anti-derivatives. In the example given in this section, I look at a particular anti-derivative. I then show you how to use a slider to investigate an entire family of curves defined by an anti-derivative.

To graph the anti-derivative of $y = x^3 - 3x^2 - 2x + 6$ using TI-Nspire CAS, follow these steps:

1. **Graph $y = x^3 - 3x^2 - 2x + 6$ using the first available function on the Entry Line.**

Figure 12-2:
Graphing derivatives with TI-Nspire CAS.

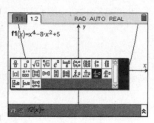
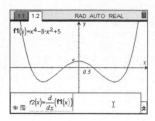
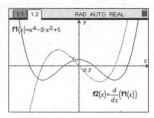

Figure 12-3:
Graphing derivatives with the numeric TI-Nspire device.

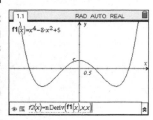
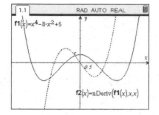

2. **Press** ⌃ ◻ **to open the Math Template, highlight the indefinite integral template, and press** ⏎.

   See the first screen in Figure 12-4.

3. **The indefinite integral template is pasted to the Entry Line. Type f1(*x*) (or press** var **and select f1 from the list of variables) and then close the parenthesis for the first field and press** tab **to move to the second field of the indefinite integral template.**

4. **Type *x* in the second field and press** ⏎ **to graph the anti-derivative.**
   The anti-derivative that is graphed in Figure 12-4 is defined by the equation

   $$y = \frac{1}{4}x^4 - x^3 - x^2 + 6x$$

Figure 12-4:
Graphing anti-derivatives with TI-Nspire CAS using the indefinite integral template.

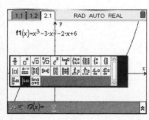
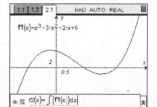
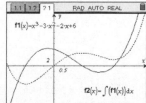

Adding a dynamic element to graphs of derivatives and anti-derivatives

The derivative and integral templates produce graphs of derivatives and anti-derivatives in such a way that you are instantly gratified. That is, the entire graph pops up automatically after you configure the Entry Line and press (enter). However, sometimes it's helpful to slow down an activity and watch these graphs *evolve* at a pace you can control.

The figure below shows how Geometry Trace can be used to trace the derivative of $y = x^4 - 8x^2 + 5$ as you drag the indicated point on the x-axis. If you add a tangent line to the problem, it's a bit clearer how the tangent to a graph relates to the graph of a function — the derivative is a graph of all points so that the y-coordinate is the slope of the original function for each corresponding x-value.

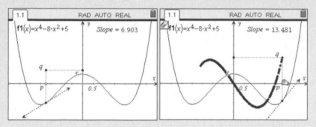

The basic steps behind this construction include measuring the slope of the tangent line and using measurement transfer to transfer this measurement to the y-axis. Next, you construct perpendicular lines through the transferred point and point p and construct the point of intersection of these two lines. To trace the graph of $y = x^4 - 8x^2 + 5$, press (menu)⇨Trace⇨Geometry Trace, click point q, and drag point p.

The figure shown below uses Automatic Data Capture with the Measure (Integral) tool to investigate an anti-derivative. This sketch really helps promote the relationship between the graph of an anti-derivative and the concept of an area function.

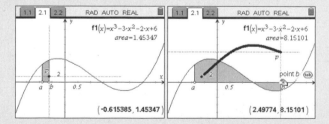

The basic steps behind this sketch include using the Integral tool (press (menu)⇨Measurement⇨Integral) to find the area under the curve on the interval from point a to point b. Transfer this measurement to the y-axis and construct perpendiculars through this transferred point and point b to their respective axes. Construct the point of intersection of these two lines and store the coordinates as variables (I use *xval* and *yval*). Set up automatic data to capture the coordinates of point p and configure a scatter plot to display this data.

This equation is based on the general solution $y = \frac{1}{4}x^4 - x^3 - x^2 + 6x + C$ with $C = 0$.

TIP

You can also graph this anti-derivative using the definite integral template, also found in the Math Template accessed by pressing (ctrl)(math). Figure 12-5 shows the results of using this alternative method.

Figure 12-5:
Graphing anti-derivatives with TI-Nspire CAS using the definite integral template.

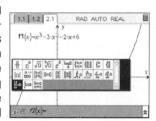 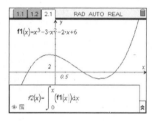 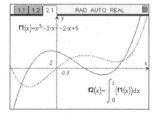

To add a dynamic element, try inserting a slider (see Chapter 9) defined by the variable **c**. As shown in the first screen in Figure 12-6, use the indefinite integral template to graph the anti-derivative as before. Then add + **c** in the equation for the purpose of investigating the family of curves given by the anti-derivative of $y = x^3 - 3x^2 - 2x + 6$. As you see in the last two screens in Figure 12-6, you can drag the slider and watch the graph of the derivative translate vertically.

Figure 12-6:
Using a slider to investigate the general anti-derivative of a function.

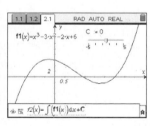 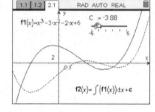 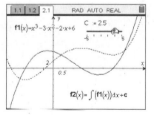

You can also graph anti-derivatives using the numeric TI-Nspire device. Here are the steps for graphing the anti-derivative of $y = x^3 - 3x^2 - 2x + 6$:

1. **Graph $y = x^3 - 3x^2 - 2x + 6$ using the first available function on the Entry Line.**

2. **Move to the next available function on the Entry Line, press (catalog) to open the Catalog, and press (1) to access the alphabetical list of available commands.**

3. **Press ⓝ to access those commands that begin with *N*, use the NavPad to highlight nInt, and press ⓔⁿᵗᵉʳ to paste the command to the Entry Line.**

   The nInt command stands for *numerical integral*.

4. **Configure the nInt command as shown in the first screen in Figure 12-7.**

   You can press ⓥᵃʳ to access the variable **f1** or type it using the keypad.

5. **Press ⓔⁿᵗᵉʳ to graph the anti-derivative as shown in the second screen in Figure 12-7.**

   This graph represents the particular anti-derivative defined by a definite integral with lower limit of integration of 0 and an upper limit of *x*.

As with TI-Nspire CAS, you can include a slider to investigate the general anti-derivative.

Figure 12-7:
Graphing anti-derivatives with the numeric TI-Nspire device.

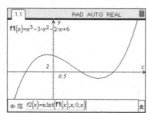 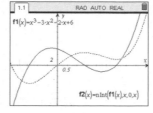 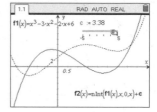

Finding arc length

You can find the length of the curve $y = \sin x$ for a given interval in the Graphs & Geometry application. Although you may be tempted to use the Arclen command in the Catalog menu with the Calculate tool, this approach does not work in the Graphs & Geometry application.

You can definitely split the screen and add a Calculator page to investigate arc length. However, I think that the method outlined in the following list makes this investigation a bit more dynamic.

Here is a general description of how I built this activity:

1. **Graph $y = \sin x$ using the first available function on the Entry Line.**

2. **Construct two segments drawn from the *x*-axis to the graph of $y = \sin x$, perpendicular to the *x*-axis.**

   The segments are drawn on top of perpendicular lines, which are hidden. Here are the steps to follow to accomplish this task:

   a. Press (menu)⇨Construction⇨Perpendicular to access the Perpendicular tool.

b. Move the cursor to the *x*-axis (but not on a tick mark) until the ⬧ symbol appears and press ⊙ twice to construct a perpendicular line.

c. With the Perpendicular tool still active, repeat Step 2 to draw another perpendicular line.

d. Press (menu)⇨Points & Lines⇨Intersection Point(s) to invoke the Intersection Point(s) tool.

e. Click the graph of *y* = sin *x* and then click the first perpendicular line to construct the intersection point with these two objects.

f. With the Intersection Point(s) tool still active, repeat Step 5 to construct the intersection point with the second perpendicular line and the graph of *y* = sin *x*.

g. Press (menu)⇨Points & Lines⇨Segment to invoke the Segment tool and draw the two segments from the *x*-axis to the graph of *y* = sin *x*, perpendicular to the *x*-axis.

These segments are not visible because they are drawn on top of the perpendicular lines.

h. Move to each perpendicular line (but not the segments) and press (ctrl)(menu)⇨Hide/Show to hide the perpendicular lines.

i. Change the attributes of each segment and add labels as shown in the first screen in Figure 12-8.

3. **Press (menu)⇨Actions⇨Coordinates & Equations and display the coordinates of point *a* and point *b*.**

The results of the first three steps are shown in the first screen in Figure 12-8. I also added some text for clarification.

4. **Store the *x*-coordinates of these two points as the variables *a* and *b*, respectively.**

To accomplish this task, click once on the *x*-coordinate and press (var)⇨Store Var. Type the variable name and press (enter). Remember, stored values appear bold.

5. **Type the expression arclen(f1(*x*), *x*, a, b) on the Entry Line and press (enter) to graph the function.**

This expression gives the arc length of *y* = sin *x* for the current values of the defined variables **a** and **b**. Because this is a numerical result, the corresponding graph is a horizontal line.

6. **Construct the intersection point of the horizontal line with the *y*-axis and display its coordinates.**

Here are the steps I use to accomplish this task.

a. Press (menu)⇨Points & Lines⇨Intersection Point(s) to invoke the Intersection Point(s) tool.

b. Click the horizontal line and then click the *y*-axis.

   c. Press (menu)⇨Actions⇨Coordinates and Equations and click the intersection point created in Step 2.

   The *y*-value of this ordered pair represents the arc length of *y* = sin *x* for the current values of the defined variables *a* and *b*. The second screen in Figure 12-8 shows the result of Steps 1 – 6. As you can see, the arc length of *y* = sin *x* from *x* = 1.333 to *x* = 4.754 is approximately 4.1011.

7. Use the Calculate tool to display the *y*-value of the ordered pair from Step 6 as a single number. Add text as needed.

Here are the steps:

   a. Use the Text tool to place any letter on the screen (I used *c*).

   b. Press (menu)⇨Actions⇨Calculate to invoke the Calculate tool.

   c. Click on the letter from Step 1.

   d. Click on the *y*-coordinate of the order pair located on the *y*-axis.

   e. Use the NavPad to move the measurement anywhere on the screen and press ⓧ to drop it on place.

   I added the text Arc Length = and used the Hide/Show command to clean up my sketch.

The last screen in Figure 12-8 shows the final result. Drag either point *a* or point *b* and observe the corresponding change in the arc length value.

Figure 12-8: Using the Arclen command to explore arc length.

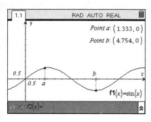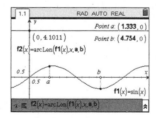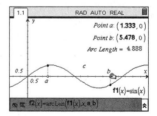

You have the option to change *y* = sin *x* to a different function.

This construction is obviously more complicated than those explored in the previous examples found in this chapter. My intent is to show you that TI-Nspire CAS tools can be used to create just about any construction you want. Perhaps you can find a more efficient way to accomplish this task.

If you are not up to creating such complicated sketches, consider going to TI's Web site, searching for an activity, and downloading it to your computer. There's a good chance a pre-made activity already exists that suits your needs.

Part IV
The Lists & Spreadsheet Application

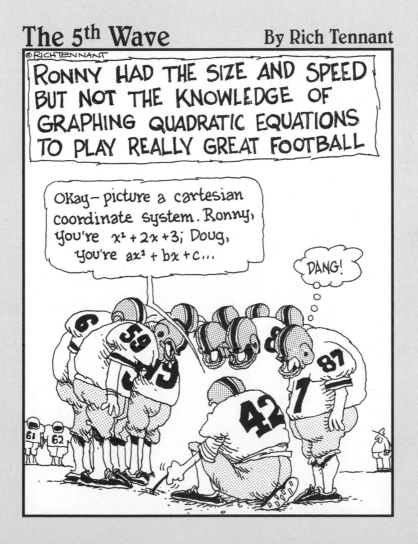

In this part . . .

This part deals with the numeric side of mathematics. I cover the tools and methods that are commonly used with most generic computer spreadsheet applications. I then get into some of the more TI-Nspire-specific tasks related to this application such as constructing scatter plots, performing regressions, and using Data Capture. These tasks will convince you that the Lists & Spreadsheet application forms a great partnership with the Graphs & Geometry application.

Again, I dedicate the last chapter in this part to highlight some of the ways the computer algebra system functionality of TI-Nspire CAS can be used with the Lists & Spreadsheet application.

Chapter 13

Applying What You Already Know About Spreadsheets

*I*f you have some familiarity with computer spreadsheets, you'll feel right at home with the Lists & Spreadsheet application. Regardless of your comfort level with spreadsheets, this chapter offers you an overview that is sure to orient you to the basic structure of the Lists & Spreadsheet application.

In Chapters 14 through 18, I address more advanced features of the Lists & Spreadsheet application, including those features that are unique to TI-Nspire technology.

Understanding Row, Column, and Cell References

To open a new Lists & Spreadsheet page, press (ctrl)(I) and select **Add Lists & Spreadsheet** from the list. Alternatively, press (⌂) and select **Lists & Spreadsheet** from available options. Figure 13-1 shows a blank Lists & Spreadsheet page as well as a description of its various components.

Each Lists & Spreadsheet page contains a total of 26 columns. Each column is labeled with a letter, starting with A and ending with Z.

Each Lists & Spreadsheet page has a total of 2500 rows. Each row is labeled with a number, starting with 1 and ending with 2500.

Column reference

Column/list name area

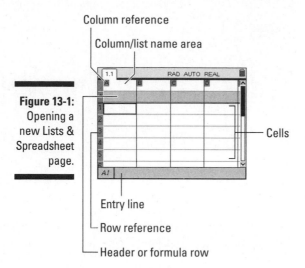

Figure 13-1:
Opening a
new Lists &
Spreadsheet
page.

Cells

Entry line

Row reference

Header or formula row

In Figure 13-1, notice that a dark border surrounds the cell A1. This name is given to the cell because it is located in column A, row 1. When naming cells, make sure you start with the column reference (a letter) followed by the row reference (a number). The cell reference for a highlighted cell is located in the bottom-left corner of the screen. Sometimes you have a rectangular block of cells highlighted. In this case, you see the cell reference associated with the top-left corner of the rectangle, followed by a colon, followed by the cell reference associated with the bottom-right corner of the rectangle. See Figure 13-2.

To highlight a rectangular block of cells, move to any corner of the rectangular block, press and hold the ⟨⟩ key, use the Navpad keys to move to the corner diagonally opposite your starting point, and then release the ⟨⟩ key.

Don't forget this convention of naming a rectangular block of cells. It is used over and over again in a variety of different contexts.

Figure 13-2:
Naming a
rectangular
block of
cells.

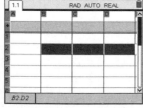

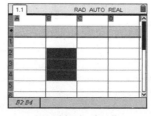

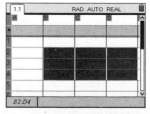

1 × 3 block of cells   3 × 1 block of cells   3 × 4 block of cells

Naming Columns

Each column already has a letter reference. Furthermore, this reference can be used to perform mathematical computations on columns of data. To reference a column in a formula, simply type the letter of the column followed by a set of brackets (⌃⌥). I show you an example of how to use this type of reference in Chapter 14.

Additionally, TI-Nspire offers you a way to name your columns with a word that helps to convey what the data represents. Consider, for example, that you want to analyze data on cellular telephone subscriptions for a range of years. Here are the steps to follow to give your data a descriptive name:

1. **Move the cursor to the column list name area.**

   This is the white box located at the top of a column.

2. **Using the green alpha keys, type the name of your list.**

   As you can see in the first screen in Figure 13-3, I use the word *year* as the list name for column A.

   List names follow the same rules as variable names. Refer to Chapter 6 for a description of how to name variables.

3. **Press ⟨tab⟩ to move the next column and type its name.**

   I've typed the name *subscriptions* to remind me that the data in the second list refers to the number of cellular telephone subscriptions (in millions) for each specified year. See the second and third screens in Figure 13-3.

4. **Continue to press ⟨tab⟩ to name additional columns. Press ⟨enter⟩ after you have named your last column of data.**

Don't worry that you cannot see the full list name. I'll tell you how to widen these columns later in the chapter.

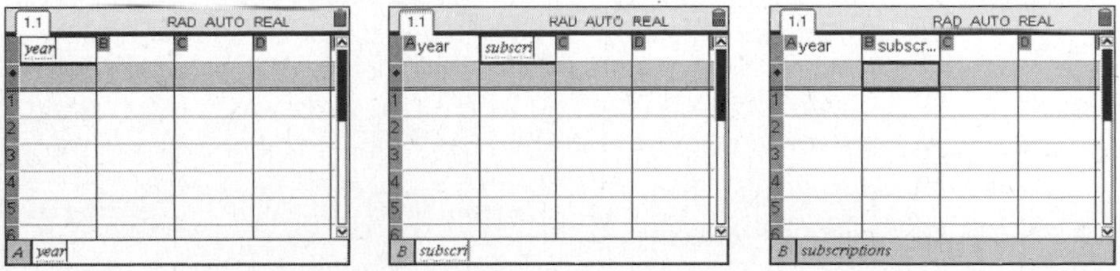

Figure 13-3: Naming columns.

Moving Around in Lists & Spreadsheets

Recall that a dark box designates your current location in a spreadsheet. To enter data or a formula, simply start typing and press the ⊙ key when you have finished. This moves you to the cell beneath the one where you are currently located.

Alternatively, press the ⊙ key after entering data or a formula in a cell. This moves you to the cell immediately to the right of the cell where you are currently located.

In Figure 13-4, I have entered the data, using the methods just described, that represents the number of cell phone subscriptions (in millions) for years since 1985.

Figure 13-4:
Entering
data.

1.1		RAD AUTO REAL		
A year	B subscr...	C	D	
•				
1	0	0.34		
2	1	0.68		
3	2	1.23		
4	3	2.07		
5	4	3.51		
6	5	5.02		
A1	0			

1.1		RAD AUTO REAL		
A year	B subscr...	C	D	
•				
7	6	7.56		
8	7	11.03		
9	8	16.01		
10	9	24.13		
11	10	33.76		
B11	33.76			

In general, you can move around the spreadsheet by pressing the arrow keys on the NavPad. Here are some other tricks that will help you move around a spreadsheet more efficiently.

✔ **Press (menu)⇨Actions⇨Go To.** After you select this command, a dialog box appears. Simply type the reference for the cell that you want to go to and press ⊙ to "jump" to this new location.

Use the shortcut key sequence (ctrl) + (G) to initiate the Go To command.

✔ **Press (ctrl) + (1), the equivalent to the End key on a computer.**

This is a very handy key sequence that works in all applications. In the Lists & Spreadsheets application, you automatically move to the last filled cell in a column of data. If you are in an empty column, this feature moves you to the last row (row 2500) of the column.

I often use this feature when I realize that I need to add new values to a current data set.

✔ **Press (ctrl) + (7), the equivalent to the Home key on a computer.**

Pressing this key sequence automatically moves you to row 1 of the current column.

✔ **Press ⒸⓉⓇⓁ + ③, the equivalent to the Page Down key on a computer.**

The TI-Nspire handheld allows you to view five spreadsheet rows at a time. Therefore, the Page Down key sequence moves you down five rows every time you press these keys.

✔ **Press ⒸⓉⓇⓁ + ⑨, the equivalent to the Page Up key on a computer.**

Pressing these keys moves you up five rows at a time.

Manipulating Rows and Columns

In this section, I talk about some of the things you can do to entire rows of columns contained within a spreadsheet.

Resizing columns

In Figure 13-4, notice that the list name *subscription* is truncated. TI-Nspire offers three different options for changing the width of a column:

✔ Move your cursor to the appropriate column and press (menu)⇨Actions⇨ Resize⇨Resize Column Width.

After you activate this command, press the ◆ keys to set the desired column width and press (enter) or ⓔ to lock it in place. See Figure 13-5.

✔ **Move your cursor to the appropriate column and press (menu)⇨Actions⇨ Resize⇨Maximum Column Width.** This action creates a column size that takes up approximately two-thirds of the entire screen.

✔ **Move your cursor to the appropriate column and press (menu)⇨Actions⇨ Resize⇨Minimum Column Width.** This action reduces the column width to its original size. This feature is not available if you have not resized a column.

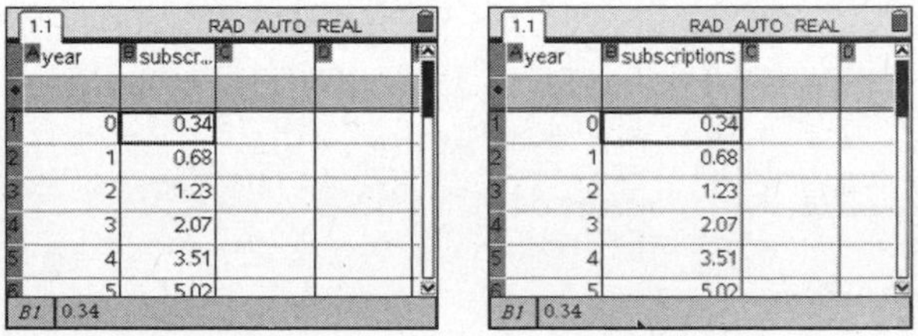

Figure 13-5: Resizing columns.

Resize Column A   Resize Column B

Moving columns

Consider that you want to move an entire column. To accomplish this task, simply position the cursor in the column you wish to move and press (menu)⇨Actions⇨Move Column. This highlights the column (see the first screen in Figure 13-6). Press the ◀▶ keys to move to the desired location as indicated by the dark vertical line shown in the second screen in Figure 13-6. Press (enter) or ⊛ to set the new position as indicated by the third screen in Figure 13-6.

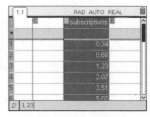

Figure 13-6:
Moving
columns.

Highlight Column B   Move to a new location   Activate the change

Selecting rows and columns

You can perform a variety of editing tasks — such as cutting, copying, or pasting — on entire rows or columns. To do so, you must first highlight the rows or columns you want to work with. Here's how.

- ✓ **Select column.** You have two choices to select an entire column.
    - • Move the cursor to the column/list name area located at the top of the column and press the ▲ key one more time to select the column.
    - • Position the cursor anywhere in the desired column and press (menu)⇨Actions⇨Select⇨Select Column.

- ✓ **Select row.** You have two choices to select an entire row.
    - • Move the cursor to any cell in Column A and press the ◀ key one more time to select the row.
    - • Position the cursor anywhere in the desired row and press (menu)⇨Actions⇨Select⇨Select Row.

- ✓ **Select multiple rows or columns.** After selecting a row or column, press and hold the ⊛ key. While holding this key, press the NavPad keys to select additional rows or columns.

A row must be selected to resize its height. Select the row using the procedures described previously and press (menu)⇨Actions⇨Resize⇨Row Height. Use the ▾ key to increase the height and the ▴ key to decrease the height. Each key press changes the row height by an amount equal to the standard row height.

Using Cut, Copy, and Paste

As mentioned in the last section, highlighted rows and columns can be cut, copied, and pasted. To do this, highlight a row or column and press (ctrl) + (x) for Cut or (ctrl) + (c) for Copy, just as you would on a computer. These two actions place the contents of a row or column in temporary memory. Move to an open row or column and press (ctrl) + (v) to Paste these contents elsewhere.

Deleting and inserting rows and columns

Deleting rows or columns? Nothing could be easier. Just select the row(s) or column(s) to be deleted and press the (clear) key.

Inserting rows and columns? Nothing could be easier, part 2. Press (menu)⇨Insert⇨ Insert Row to insert a row and (menu)⇨Insert⇨Insert Column to insert a column. Of course, give some consideration to your current cell location. For example, the first screen in Figure 13-7 shows that cell B2 is currently selected. The second screen shows what happens after the Insert Row command is used. The third screen shows what happens after the Insert Column command is used.

Figure 13-7: Inserting a row or column.

1.1	RAD AUTO REAL
▣year	▣subscriptions	C	D
1	0	0.34
2	1	0.68
3	2	1.23
4	3	2.07
5	4	3.51
	5	5.02
B2	0.68

1.1	RAD AUTO REAL
▣year		▣subscriptions	C
1	0		0.34
2	1		0.68
3	2		1.23
4	3		2.07
5	4		3.51
	5		5.02
B2	

1.1	RAD AUTO REAL
▣year	▣subscriptions	C	D
1	0	0.34
2	0	0
3	1	0.68
4	2	1.23
5	3	2.07
	4	3.51
B2	0

Using Right-Click

Once again, this miraculous short-cut can be a real time-saver. The first screen in Figure 13-8 shows the available options when a single cell is selected. The second screen shows the available options when a single row is selected. Finally, the third screen shows the available options when a single column is selected.

Press (ctrl)(menu) to access the "right-click" context menu.

I encourage you to investigate the options available when a rectangular block of cells is selected as well as when multiple rows and multiple columns are selected.

Figure 13-8:
Using the
"right-click"
option in
Lists &
Spread-
sheets.

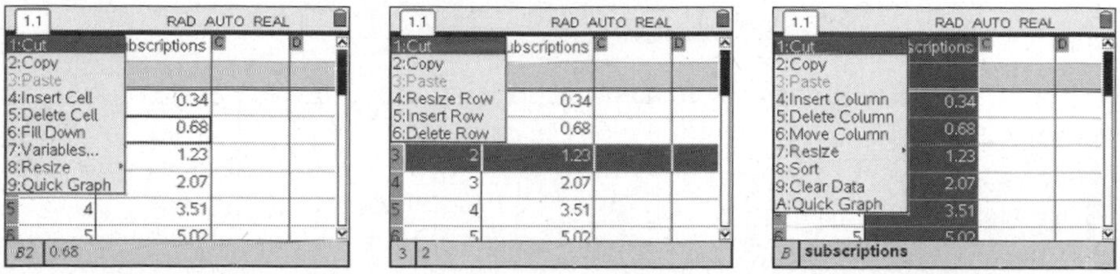

"Right-clicking"   "Right-clicking"   "Right-clicking"
a single cell   a selected row   a selected column

Working with Individual Cells

You have the option of entering numbers, text, and mathematical expressions into a cell. You can also access a variety of formulas and commands from the Catalog menu. The next few sections discuss how to perform these actions.

Entering numbers and typing text

To enter a number in a cell, simply select the cell, type the number, and press (enter) to move to the next cell in the column. Notice that the information you are entering in the cell also appears in the entry line at the bottom of the screen. This is particularly helpful if you are entering numbers with several digits.

TI-Nspire deals with text in the very same way. Using the green alpha keys, type your text and press (enter).

To enter text as a string, press the (") key and then type your text.

When you enclose text in quotes, your text is effectively *grouped*, allowing for words to be referenced elsewhere from within the Lists & Spreadsheet application.

Evaluating mathematical expressions

You can evaluate simple or complex mathematical expressions in the Lists & Spreadsheet application. Just make sure you press the [=] key before typing the expression. In Figure 13-9, I show you how to enter an expression (first screen) and the resulting value of the expression after you press the [enter] key (second screen).

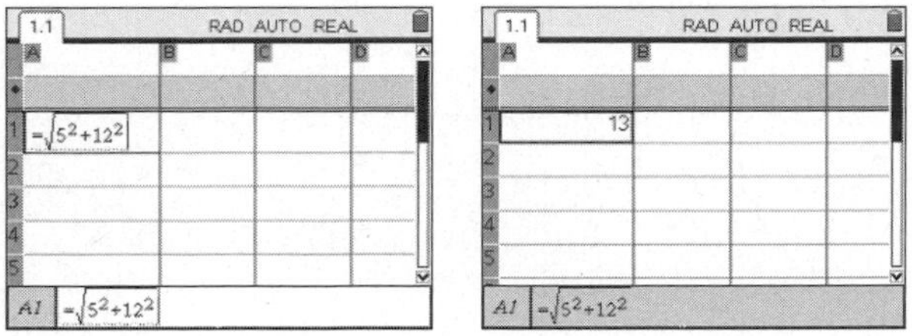

Figure 13-9: Evaluating an expression.

Notice in the second screen of Figure 13-9, I've moved back to cell A1. This reveals the mathematical expression in the entry line at the bottom of the screen.

Using the Catalog

To evaluate more sophisticated expressions, press [catalog] to access the Catalog. You can also press the [ctrl] + [template] to access the math template directly. Figure 13-10 shows an example that finds the determinant of a random 3 × 3 matrix.

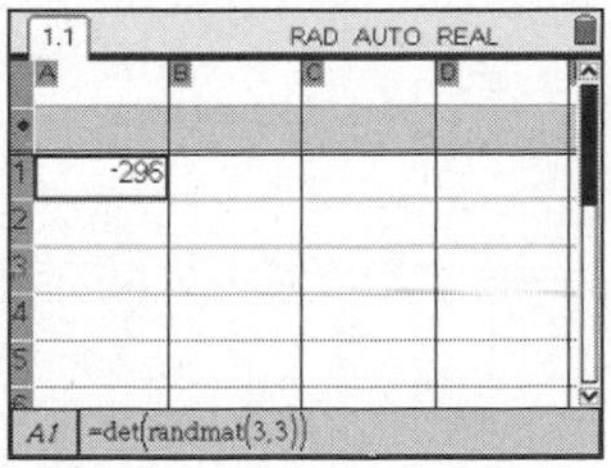

Figure 13-10: Evaluating an expression.

REMEMBER

Don't forget to press the [=] key before entering an expression to be evaluated.

Chapter 14

Working with Data

· ·

In This Chapter

▶ Using cell references to do math

▶ Understanding the difference between relative and absolute cell references

▶ Referencing individual cells and blocks of cells

▶ Creating lists of data using the Fill Down command

▶ Creating lists of data from the header row

▶ Sorting data

▶ Performing statistical analysis on one-variable data

· ·

1n this chapter, I get into some of the features of the Lists & Spreadsheet application that are quite similar to those found in other computer-based spreadsheet applications. You see how cell references can be used to quickly perform calculations on a single cell or a rectangular array of cells. You also gain an appreciation of the fact that cell references allow you to make changes to an existing data set without the need to retype a given formula.

Using Formulas

Imagine that I am interested in converting my height from a value expressed in feet and inches to one expressed in just inches. In the first screen in Figure 14-1, in cells A1 and B1 I have typed my height in feet and inches, respectively.

To convert this measurement to just inches I can move the cursor to cell C1, type =6*12+3, and press ⏎.

Recall from Chapter 13, if you want to perform any calculation in Lists & Spreadsheet, you must first press the ⊜ key.

However, instead of typing the number located in a given cell, type the *location* of the number. This location is what I will refer to as a *cell reference*. This first screen in Figure 14-1 shows that I have typed =A1*12+B1 in cell C1. Pressing ⏎ performs this calculation and displays the result as shown in the second screen in Figure 14-1.

As for my height, I lied. I'm really only 6 feet 1 inch tall. Because I have used a cell reference, I simply go back to cell B1 and change the 3 to a 1. Notice in the third screen in Figure 14-1 that the calculation in cell C1 updates automatically. This is where cell references really come in handy, especially if you are referencing the contents of a cell several times.

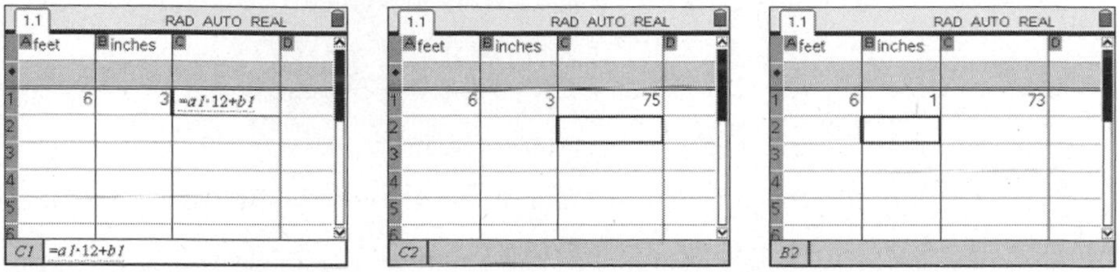

Figure 14-1: Performing a calculation using cell references.

Using relative cell references

Consider now that I want to take the heights of the other members of my family and perform the same type of conversion. Here's how.

1. **Type the heights (in feet and inches) in rows 2 through 4.**

2. **Go to cell C1 and press** ctrl ⌖ **.**

   This action selects the cell and allows for copying as indicated by the dashed box. See the first screen in Figure 14-2.

3. **Use the ▾ key to extend the dashed box to cell C5 and press** enter **.**

   See the second and third screens in Figure 14-2.

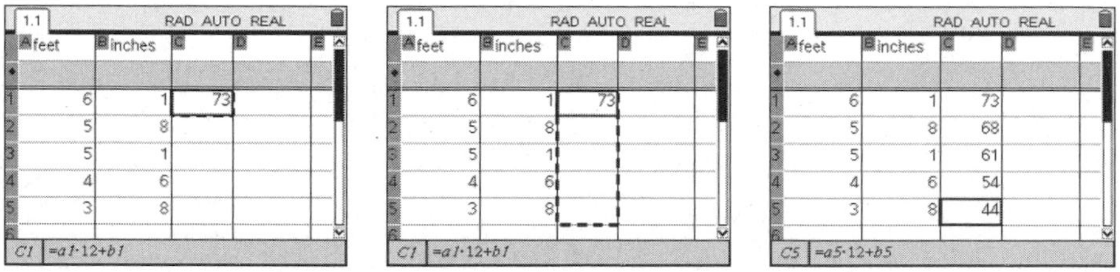

Figure 14-2: Copying a formula.

Notice that cell C5 is highlighted in the third screen in Figure 14-2 and that the formula is located in the entry line at the bottom of the screen. Recall that the original formula that I typed was =a1*12+b1. The formula has changed to =a5*12+b5. This is because I have used *relative cell references*.

When you copy a relative cell reference, the cell references automatically update. If I were to copy this same formula to cell F7, it would reference the cells immediately to the left of this cell and display the formula =d7*12+f7 on the entry line.

Using absolute cell references

Sometimes you want to reference the same cell in a formula, even if you copy the formula to other cells. This is an example of using an *absolute* cell reference. For example, imagine that I want to convert these five heights to centimeters. Follow these steps:

1. **Type the conversion factor for inches to centimeters, 2.54, in cell E1.**

2. **Type the formula =c1*e$1 in cell D1 and press ⬿.**

   The $ symbol, which precedes the row reference, locks the row so that I am always referencing row 1. For example, if I were to copy this formula to cell F7, it would read =e7*g$1. The column is relative and updates accordingly; however, row 1 remains locked. The result of this action is shown in the first two screens in Figure 14-3.

   To access the $ symbol, press ⬚⬚ to open the symbol template. Scroll down and highlight the $ symbol and press ⬿ to paste this symbol into the formula. You can also press the shortcut key sequence, ⬚⬚, to access the $ symbol.

3. **Copy the formula to cells D2 through D5.**

   Use Steps 2 and 3 from the preceding section to accomplish this task. The last screen in Figure 14-3 shows the result of copying this formula to cells D2 through D5. Notice the formula for cell D5 is shown on the entry line. Cell C5 is a relative cell reference and was updated when copied. Cell E1 has not been updated because I locked the row reference.

The conversion factor that I typed in cell E1 converts inches to centimeters. If I want to perform a different conversion, I can simply change this conversion factor and everything in Column D automatically updates. For example, to convert everyone's height to fathoms (for what reason, I'm not sure!), type 0.0139 in cell E1, press ⬿, and watch the change.

Figure 14-3:
Using an
absolute
row
reference.

	feet	inches			
1	6	1	73	=c1·e$1	2.54
2	5	8	68		
3	5	1	61		
4	4	6	54		
5	3	8	44		

D1 | =c1·e$1

	feet	inches			
1	6	1	73	185.42	2.54
2	5	8	68		
3	5	1	61		
4	4	6	54		
5	3	8	44		

D2 |

	feet	inches			
1	6	1	73	185.42	2.54
2	5	8	68	172.72	
3	5	1	61	154.94	
4	4	6	54	137.16	
5	3	8	44	111.76	

D5 | =c5·e$1

Using an absolute column reference

In the preceding example, I used an absolute cell reference to lock a row. I can also lock a column.

In Figure 14-4, I've entered salary information that gives the gross weekly earnings for three people in row 2 and then calculates the taxes (row 3) and net pay (row 4) for these individuals. I am using a tax rate of 25% by typing 0.25 in cell E1.

Notice in the first screen in Figure 14-4, cell B3 is highlighted and the formula that I typed is displayed in the entry line. I placed the $ symbol before the column reference because I always want to reference column E. Note that cell B2 is a relative cell reference.

I then copied this formula to cells C3 and D3. The second screen in Figure 14-4 shows the copied formula (displayed in the entry line). Again, note that the reference for D2 has been updated (because it's relative) and the reference to cell E1 has not changed (because it's absolute).

The values in row 4 were obtained by using relative cell references. I typed =b2-b3 in cell B4 and copied this formula to cells C4 and D4.

The third screen in Figure 14-4 shows that I can change the tax rate in cell E1 and all calculations automatically update.

In the height example, I copied a formula by pressing (ctrl)(⌃) to select a cell and then pressing ▼ key repeatedly, followed by the (enter) key. Recall that this action creates a dashed box. This is actually a shortcut method for the Fill Down command, a feature I describe later in this chapter. However, this option is not available if I want to copy a formula to the right. Rather, I highlight cell B3, press (ctrl)(C) to copy the formula, move to cell C3, and then press (ctrl)(V) to paste the formula. Next, I move to cell D3 and press (ctrl)(V) to paste the formula again.

Using an absolute row and column reference

In the previous two examples, I locked a row and then a column. I also have the option of locking both a row and a column. To do so, simply include the $ symbol before both the column reference and the row reference.

In fact, I could have used an absolute row and column reference in both of these examples and accomplished the same result. In the example related to Figure 14-3, the command =c1*e1 references cell E1 no matter where you copy the formula.

Referencing a rectangular block of cells

So far, I have shown you how to reference individual cells. I can also reference rectangular blocks of cells. To do this, type the cell reference for the top-left corner of the rectangular block of cells, press the ⊙ key, and type the cell reference for the bottom-right corner of the rectangular block of cells.

For example, I have two classes of Algebra 2, one that meets during Period 2 and one that meets during Period 3. I'd like to calculate the mean (average) for each class as well as the combined mean for both classes. The grades for Period 2 are located in Column A and the grades for Period 3 are located in Column B.

There are two ways to accomplish this task:

✓ **Place the cursor in cell E2 and type** =mean(a1:a5).

This gives mean for Period 2. See the first screen in Figure 14-5.

✓ **Place the cursor in cell E3 and type** =mean(b1:b5)*1.0.

This gives mean for Period 3. See the second screen in Figure 14-5.

I forced the result in cell E2 to be displayed as a decimal (rather than a fraction) by multiplying by 1.0. Any time you include a decimal in a calculation, the result is displayed in decimal form.

✓ **Place the cursor in cell E4 and type** mean(a1:b5)*1.0.

This gives the mean for both classes. See the third screen in Figure 14-5.

You can also access the mean command from the Catalog (📖).

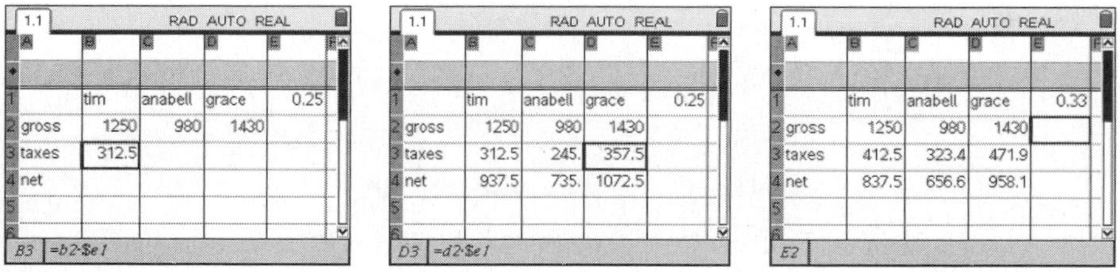

Figure 14-4: Using an absolute column reference.

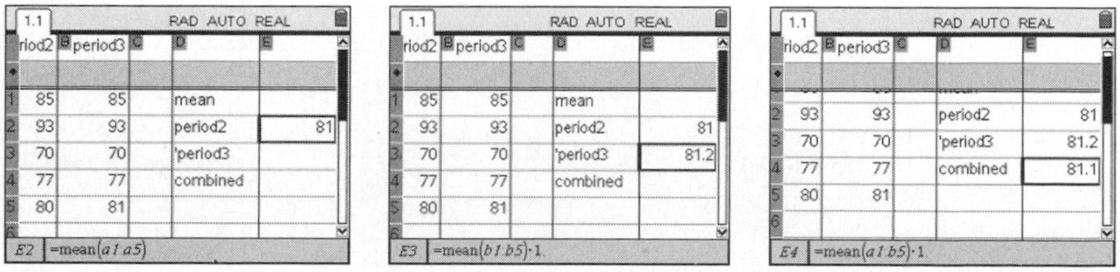

Figure 14-5: Referencing a rectangular block of cells.

Working with Data

TI-Nspire allows you to generate lists of sequential data very quickly. And the analysis of these data sets can be performed quickly and efficiently as well. Again, if you are familiar with spreadsheets, you can draw on this past experience. If you are not, I've got you covered.

Using Fill Down

A *recursive formula* is a formula that is used to determine the next term in a sequence by using one or more of the preceding terms. The Fill Down command can be used to generate a recursive sequence in the case where you always use the previous term to obtain the next term.

Consider that you want to explore the future value of a $1000 deposit under two different scenarios. Under the first scenario, you earn 5% annual interest. Under the second scenario, you simply add $100 each year to the account. Here's how it's done.

1. **Type the initial deposit, 1000, in cells A1 and B1.**

2. **Type** =a1*1.05 **in cell A2 and** =b1+100 **in cell B2.**

3. **Move the cursor to cell A2 and press** (menu)⟹**Data**⟹**Fill Down to grab the cell as indicated by the dashed box.**

   Here are two other options for accessing the Fill Down command.

   • Move the cursor to cell A2 and press (ctrl)(⌂).

   • Move the cursor to cell A2 and (ctrl)(menu)⟹Fill Down.

     This is the *right-click* approach.

4. **Press the ▾ key repeatedly to expand the dashed box to the desired row and press** (enter).

5. **Repeat Steps 3 and 4 for cell B2.**

In Figure 14-6, I have used Fill Down to copy my formulas to row 10.

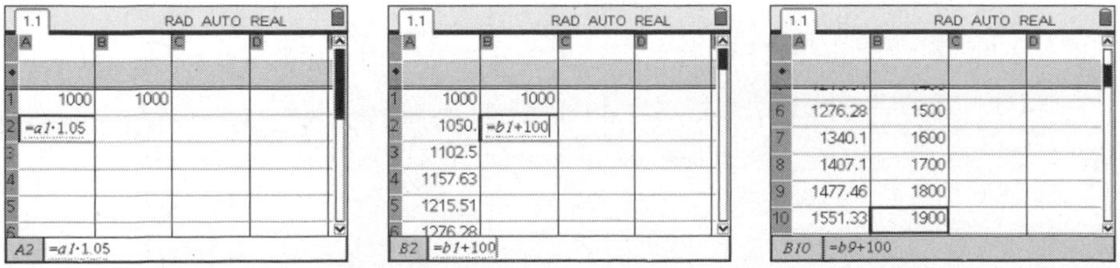

Figure 14-6:
Using the
Fill Down
command.

Notice that the value of the account in column B is higher than the account value in column A. Of course, I'd like to find out when the first investment scenario exceeds the second.

To use Fill Down on both columns simultaneously, move to cell A10, press and hold the ⬡ key, and press the ▶ key once to highlight cells A10 and B10. Now access the Fill Down command as before and copy both formulas to several more rows (I've filled down to row 40). Scroll down to see that the 5% investment strategy surpasses the other investment strategy in row 28!

Using the header row

The header row is the row that is located just above row 1. It is denoted by the w located on the left side of the row. In this section, I show how the header row can be used to manage large data sets without the need to work within the cells themselves.

Generating sequential data

One of my favorite sequences is the famous Fibonacci sequence. The first two values of this sequence are both 1. The remaining values are found by adding the two previous values. To create this sequence, move the cursor to the header row for Column A and follow these steps:

1. **Press (menu)⇨Data⇨Generate Sequence.**

2. **Configure the dialog box to match the one shown in Figure 14-7 and press ⬡ when this is complete.**

Notice that I have two options for controlling the number of terms in my sequence — by maximum number of terms and ceiling value. If you want to specify the maximum number of terms, say 20, just type the number in the Max No. Terms field and leave Ceiling Value blank. If you type a maximum value in the Ceiling Value field, TI-Nspire defaults to this value and ignores any value that is in the Max No. Terms field.

Figure 14-7: Using the Generate Sequence command.

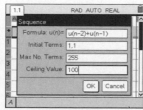

Perhaps I want to edit the sequence command to include more terms. Just move to the header row and press ⊙ or ⊙ to enter edit mode. Then move the cursor to the end of the command by pressing the ▶ key repeatedly (or press ⊙⊙, the equivalent of the End key on a computer). Delete the last number and type a new number.

Working with random numbers

I find that the random numbers and the Lists & Spreadsheet application are a perfect match.

Consider that I want to simulate rolling two dice 50 times using the random integer command. Here's how.

1. Move to the header row, type =randint(1,6,50), **and press** ⊙.

You can type the randint command using the green alpha keys or access the randint command from the Catalog by pressing the ⊙ key.

2. Repeat Step 1 for Column B.

Notice that columns A and B are populated with 50 random integers from 1 to 6.

The syntax for the random integer command is

randInt(*lower bound*, *upper bound*[, *number of trials*]).

Creating column data based on another column

Now I'm interested in finding the sum of the dice for each trial. I can use the header row to accomplish this task.

Just move to the header row for Column C and type =a[]+b[] and press ⊙. The first screen in Figure 14-8 shows the results of this action.

When referencing a column in the header row, you must include an empty set of brackets, accessed by pressing ⊙⊙ after the column letter.

Perhaps I chose to name the first three columns *firstdie, seconddie,* and *total,* respectively. Rather than use a letter reference for a column, I can reference these list names. After naming the first two columns (see Chapter 13), follow these steps:

1. Move the cursor to the header row for Column C and press the ⊙ key.

Notice total:= automatically appears in the header row.

2. Press ⊙, highlight *firstdie,* **and press** ⊙.

3. Press ⊙.

4. **Press ⌨, highlight *seconddie*, and press ⏎.**

   See second screen in Figure 14-8.

5. **Press ⏎ to complete the command.**

   See third screen in Figure 14-8.

Figure 14-8:
Creating
column data
based on
other
columns.

Two-dice sum   Accessing a list name   Two-dice sum

If you are following along with me, your screen may differ from the screen shown in Figure 14-8. That's okay. Remember, these are random integers and it's to be expected that they will differ each time.

Recalculating cell references and formulas

You can update all cell references and formulas by pressing ⌨⇨Actions⇨ Recalculate. Alternatively, press ⌨⒭, the shortcut method for accessing the Recalculate command.

The Recalculate command is particularly handy when working with random numbers. Each time you press ⌨⒭, you get an entirely new set of random numbers. In the case of the two-dice experiment, it's like rolling two dice another 50 times each time you use this command.

Sorting data

Perhaps you want to sort the data contained in Column C from the two-dice experiment to see how the sums are distributed. Follow these steps and refer to the screen images in Figure 14-9.

1. **Select columns A, B, and C.**

2. **Press ⌨⇨Actions⇨Sort (alternatively, press ⌨⌨⇨Sort).**

   At the warning prompt, press ⏎.

3. **Press ⒭ to see the choices for Sort By and select *c*.**

4. **Press ⏎ to sort by Ascending or highlight this field and change it to Descending and press ⏎.**

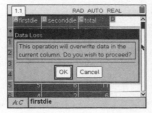

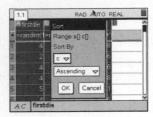

Figure 14-9:
Sorting
data.

Notice in the third screen in Figure 14-9, the formulas in the header row have been deleted. This happens any time you do a sort on a column containing a formula in the header row. Your random numbers are now static and `recalculate` no longer gives you a new set of random numbers. Pressing (ctrl)(esc) undoes the sort and restores the header row formulas.

If you select only Column C and do a sort, the relationship between Columns A, B, and C is lost. Each value in Column C is likely not to equal the sum of the two numbers to its left.

Basic Statistical Analysis

In this section, I show you some basic statistical functions that can be performed on a single data set. In Chapter 15, I show you how to perform statistical analyses on two-variable data sets.

Using one-variable statistics

I've entered the first semester averages for my two Algebra 2 classes in a column titled *algebra2,* and I'm interested in performing a one-variable statistical analysis on this data. Here are the steps:

1. **Press (menu)⇨Statistics⇨Stat Calculations⇨One-Variable Statistics.**

2. **Press (enter) to indicate that you want to analyze one list.**

   If you have additional lists, change **Num of Lists** to match the number of lists you are interested in analyzing.

3. **Configure the dialog box as shown in Figure 14-10.**

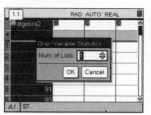 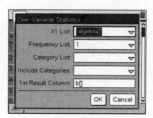

Figure 14-10:
Performing
one-variable
statistical
analysis.

Select number   Configure   One-variable
of lists   dialog box   statistical results

Scroll down column C to review the statistical results that are generated by this action. The following list contains a description of what each result means.

- ✔ ⁻x: Sample mean

- ✔ Σx: Sum of the data

- ✔ Σx2: Sum of the squared data

- ✔ sx: Sample standard deviation

- ✔ σx: Population standard deviation

- ✔ n: Sample size

- ✔ MinX: Minimum value

- ✔ Q1X: First quartile

- ✔ MedianX: Median

- ✔ Q3X: Third quartile

- ✔ MaxX: Maximum value

- ✔ SSX: Sum of squared deviations

I also could have created a separate list for each Algebra 2 class, one in Column A and one in Column B. To do this, press ⓜ⇨Statistics⇨Stat Calculations…⇨Two-Variable Statistics to obtain the single-variable statistics for both classes simultaneously.

Statistical analysis using the Catalog

You also have the option of finding individual statistics on a data set by accessing commands from the Catalog ().

In the first screen in Figure 14-11, I've accessed the Mean function from the Catalog. The second screen in Figure 14-11 shows that I've also accessed the Sum function. Notice that I must press ⊜ before inserting a command. I also pressed ⬚⊏⟩Link To: ⟩Algebra2 to paste my list name within each of these commands.

I can type a function using the green alpha keys rather than access it via the Catalog.

Figure 14-11:
Using the
Catalog
to find
statistical
results.

Chapter 15

Constructing Scatterplots and Performing Regressions

*F*inding a mathematical model for a data set is a common application found in a typical algebra or higher-level math course. Mathematical models are very important because they enable us to create an analytical representation of numerical data. In turn, this mathematical model (or equation) can be used to make predictions for values of the input variable for which data is not available.

In this chapter, I focus on how to input data into the Lists & Spreadsheet application, inspect the corresponding scatter plot in the Graphs & Geometry application, and find an appropriate model to fit the data using TI-Nspire's regression capabilities. I then show you how to graph your regression equation along with the scatter plot. Finally, I talk about the dynamic capability of TI-Nspire to update results from a regression without performing the regression a second time.

Constructing a Scatter Plot in the Graphs & Geometry Application

The phrase "a picture is worth a thousand words" rings quite true when you are trying to find a mathematical equation to model a data set. In fact, before you perform a regression, it's almost imperative that you view a scatter plot of the data to assist you in deciding on an appropriate model. Yes, there are ways to look at the numerical data to determine a good model (such as finding first and second differences); however, an inspection of a scatter plot can often reveal this information much more efficiently.

Consider that you are interested in looking at the following relationship:

- ✔ Years after 1900 versus United States Immigrant Population (in millions)
- ✔ Years after 1900 versus total United States Population (in millions)

Table 15-1 gives the numerical data for both these relationships.

Table 15-1	United States Immigrant Population since 1900	
Years Since 1900	**Immigrant Population (in millions)**	**US Population (in millions)**
0	10.3	76.2
10	13.5	92.2
20	13.9	106
30	14.2	123.2
40	11.6	132.2
50	10.3	151.3
60	9.7	179.3
70	9.6	203.2
80	14.1	226.5
90	19.8	248.7
100	31.1	281.4

In the next section, I tell you how to enter this data in the Lists & Spreadsheet application.

Entering the data

Here are the steps to enter the data in a Lists & Spreadsheets page:

1. **To start with a new document, press (ctrl)(N) (a shortcut key) or press (⌂) ➪ New Document.**

   If you currently have an open document, you are prompted to save the document. Press (enter) for Yes or press (tab)(enter) for No.

2. On the next screen, select Add Lists & Spreadsheets and press ⏎.

Figure 15-1 shows this sequence of screens.

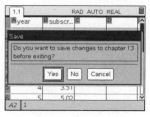 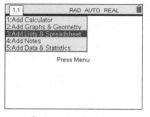 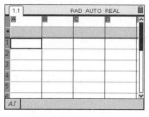

Save file prompt   Select application   Blank L&S screen

Before entering your data, it's a good idea to name your lists.

The name given to the list contained in Column A shows up as the *x*-variable of the scatter plot of the data. The name given to the list in Column B shows up as the *y*-variable of the scatter plot. This is assuming that you specify that Column A represents the X List and Column B represents the Y List. Consequently, it's a good idea to choose names that convey the meaning of the data they represent.

3. Press the ▲ key repeatedly until the small white box located next to the column reference letter is highlighted.

4. Next, type your list name using the green alpha keys and press (tab) to move to the white box in Column B.

Again, type a name that describes the immigrant data and then move to Column C and choose a meaningful name for the US population data. Figure 15-2 shows the names that I chose for each column of data.

5. **Now enter the data in Column A.**

Notice that the data for *years* forms the arithmetic sequence 0, 10, 20, . . . 100. Here are three options for entering this data that eliminate the need to actually type each number.

- **Use Fill Down.** Type the number 0 in cell A1. Next, type the command =A1+10 in cell A2 and press ⟨enter⟩. Position the cursor back in cell A2 and press ⟨menu⟩▷ **Data** ▷ **Fill Down**. Notice that the box around cell A2 becomes dashed indicating that it has been selected. Press the ▾ key repeatedly until the dashed box reaches row 11 and press ⟨enter⟩. The second screen in Figure 15-3 shows that the sequence is complete.

Figure 15-3: Using Fill Down to generate a sequence.

Type formula in A2   Grab cell A2   Fill down

- **Use Fill Down without a formula.** Type **0** in cell A1 and **10** in cell A2. Next, position the cursor in cell A1, hold down the ⟨shift⟩ key, and press ▾ once to highlight cells A1 and A2, as shown in the first screen in Figure 15-4. Press ⟨ctrl⟩⟨shift⟩ to grab both cells, press the ▾ key repeatedly until the dashed box reaches row 11, and press ⟨enter⟩. The second screen in Figure 15-3 shows that the sequence is complete.

This method of highlighting two cells to generate a sequence works only for a sequence that is arithmetic, meaning each term is generated by adding or subtracting the same value from the previous term. If you want to create a different sequence, such as the geometric sequence 1, 2, 4, 8, . . . 128, use Fill Down with a formula or the method shown in the next bullet.

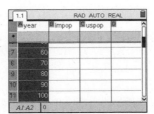

Figure 15-4: Generating an arithmetic sequence.

Grab A1 and A2   Fill down

- **Use the Sequence command.** Position the cursor in the Column A header (the gray box located above Row 1) and press (menu)⇨**Data**⇨**Generate Sequence**. Configure the dialog box as shown in the first screen of Figure 15-5. Press (enter) to execute the command and populate cells A1 through A11 with the values 0, 10, 20, . . . 100.

Figure 15-5: Generating a sequence using the Generate Sequence command.

Referring back to Figure 15-5, the first line of the Generate Sequence dialog box enables you to write the sequence using a recursive definition that calculates each term, u(n), by adding 10 to the previous value, u(n-1). By pressing the (tab), you can move to the next line of the dialog box and specify that the first term is 0. In the last line of the dialog box, specify that the last term is 100. To accomplish the same result, you can also type 11 for Max No. Terms.

Any time you are happy with the contents of an open dialog box, just press (enter) for the configuration to take effect. If you want to go back to a previous field in a dialog box, press (caps)(tab), just as you do on a computer.

6. **Enter the data for Columns B and C.**

The data for Column B, U.S. Immigrant Population (in millions), and that of Column C, U.S. Population (in millions), must be entered manually. Refer back to Table 15-1 and enter the data one value at a time.

Insert a Graphs & Geometry page

You are now ready to view the scatter plot of *year* versus *U.S. Immigrant* population. Here's what you do:

1. **Press (ctrl)(I) and select Add Graphs & Geometry from the options listed. Alternatively, press (on) and select Graphs & Geometry from the choices given.**

Notice that the cursor is located in the entry line located at the bottom of the screen indicating that the entry line is currently active. Also note that the entry line is set by default for graphing functions.

2. **Press (menu) ⇨Graph Type⇨Scatter Plot to switch the entry line to scatter plot. Alternatively, press (ctrl)(menu)⇨Scatter Plot while the cursor is located in the entry line. Remember, this second option is the equivalent of doing a right-click on a computer.**

In the first screen in Figure 15-6, you have pressed ⓘ to view a list of choices for the *x*-variable.

3. **Press ⓘ to view a list of choices for the *y*-variable.**

4. **Using the ▲▼ keys, highlight *year* and press ⓘ or (enter).**

5. **Next, press (tab) to move to the *y*-variable, press ⓘ to view a list of choices for the *y*-variable, highlight *impop*, and press ⓘ or (enter).**

Figure 15-6:
Configuring
Graphs &
Geometry
to display a
scatter plot.

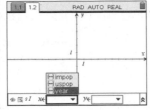
Select *x*-variable

Select *y*-variable

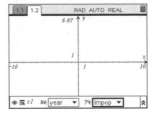
Graph scatter plot

If you configured your scatter plot with incorrect list names you can press (tab) to move from the work area back to the entry line. Notice that the next available unused scatter plot (probably *s2*) is ready to be configured. To edit the previous scatter plot, press ▲ and change the settings as needed.

Notice in the last screen of Figure 15-6 that the current window settings do not provide a good view of the scatter plot. In fact, there are no visible points.

To improve the view of the scatter plot, press (menu)⇨Window⇨Zoom – Data. This sets your window settings to match those in Figure 15-7. Hide the entry line by pressing (menu)⇨View⇨Hide Entry Line to reveal the complete scatter plot.

Figure 15-7:
Using
Zoom – Data
to set an
appropriate
viewing
window.

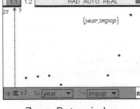
Zoom-Data window

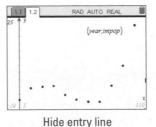
Hide entry line

The shortcut key sequence ⌃G toggles between Hide Entry Line and Show Entry Line.

If you inspect the scatter plot, it appears that a cubic polynomial is a good fit for the data. In this next section, I tell you how to perform this type of regression.

Performing a Regression

To perform a regression, follow these steps:

1. **Press ⌃◄ to move back to the Lists & Spreadsheet page containing the data for *year* versus *US immigrant population*.**

2. **Press ⒨⇨Statistics⇨Stat Calculations…⇨Cubic Regression.**

   A dialog box opens as shown in Figure 15-8. As with any dialog box, you can press ⭾ to move from one field to the next or ⇧⭾ to move backwards through a field.

   Notice in the first screen in Figure 15-8 you have pressed Ⓣ and selected *year* to specify the location of the X List. You could also specify the column by its letter reference, which is exactly what you did for Y List (by pressing Ⓑ⌃⏏). In the second screen in Figure 15-8, you have pressed Ⓓ⌃⏏ to indicate where you want the results to be stored. You selected Column D because it is the first available empty column.

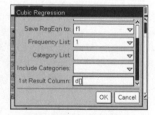

Configuring the cubic regression dialog box

Figure 15-8: Performing a cubic regression.

Cubic regression results

The third and fourth screens in Figure 15-8 (with Columns D and E widened) show that the results of the regression are pasted directly into the spreadsheet. Notice that the *Coefficient of Determination*, R^2, is very close to 1. This suggests that the choice of doing a cubic regression was a good one.

A cubic regression can be done with a minimum of four points. Under this scenario, TI-Nspire finds a third-degree polynomial fit by solving a system of four equations determined by using the *xy*-values of the four points. With five or more points, TI-Nspire performs a cubic regression.

Understanding the results of a regression

A variety of variables are stored by TI-Nspire after a regression. To view this list, add a Calculator page and press ⬚. See the first screen in Figure 15-9. Using the ▲▼ keys, you can scroll through this list and paste a variable to the entry line in the Calculator page.

For example, I've pasted the variable `stat.resid` to the entry line (see the second screen in Figure 15-9) and pressed ⬚ to view a list of *residuals*. This list represents the difference between the *y*-value of each data point and the corresponding *y*-value associated with the regression equation.

It might be interesting to inspect a scatter plot of the residuals as a function of the year. This plot shows, visually, the difference between the *y*-value of each data point and the corresponding *y*-value associated with the regression equation. To construct this scatter plot, use the same methods just described. Let *year* be the variable used for X List and `stat.resid` be the variable used for Y List. The graph of this scatter plot is shown in the third screen of Figure 15-9. A perfect fit regression places the residuals directly on the *x*-axis because there is no variation between the regression model and the data points.

Figure 15-9:
Viewing
residuals on
a calculator
page and
the related
scatter plot.

Regression variables

Residuals list

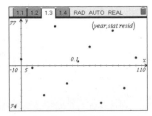

Year vs. Residuals

Referring back to the first screen of Figure 15-9, you see several other statistical variables generated from this cubic regression. For example, the variable `stat.results`, when executed on a Calculator page, displays a list of all the regression results pasted into Columns D and E when the cubic regression was first performed in the Lists & Spreadsheets page.

Graphing your regression equation

To view the graph of your regression equation, follow these steps:

1. **Move back to the Graphs & Geometry page. If you hid the entry line earlier, press** (ctrl)(G) **to bring it back into view. Also, change the entry line to** Function **by pressing** (ctrl)(menu)(1) **or** (menu)⇨Graph Type⇨Function.

    Recall that you configured the regression dialog box to save the regression equation to f1.

2. **Press ▲ until your regression equation appears as shown in the first screen in Figure 15-10.**

3. **Next, press** (enter) **to activate the graph of the regression equation as shown in the second screen in Figure 15-10.**

Figure 15-10:
Graphing a
regression
equation.

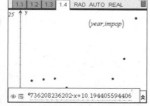

Locate regression equation

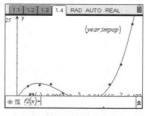

Activate the graph

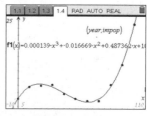

Hide entry line

Updating your regression equation

The data contained in Table 15-1 gives population data for the years 1900 through 2000. Imagine that you want to add more recent data. For example, the U.S. immigrant population in the year 2006 was approximately 37.5 million. TI-Nspire allows you to add or revise data and then update the regression automatically. Here is what you do:

1. **Move your cursor to Column A and press** (ctrl)(1) **to jump down to the bottom of the list.**

2. **Type** 106 **in cell A12 and** 37.5 **in cell B12.**

3. **Move back to the** Graphs & Geometry **page and compare the results shown in Figure 15-11 with those from the original regression in Figure 15-10.**

   Although the change is subtle, you can clearly see that the scatter plot and regression equation have changed. Also, take a look at the regression results located in Columns D and E of the Lists & Spreadsheets page. The regression results have been updated there as well.

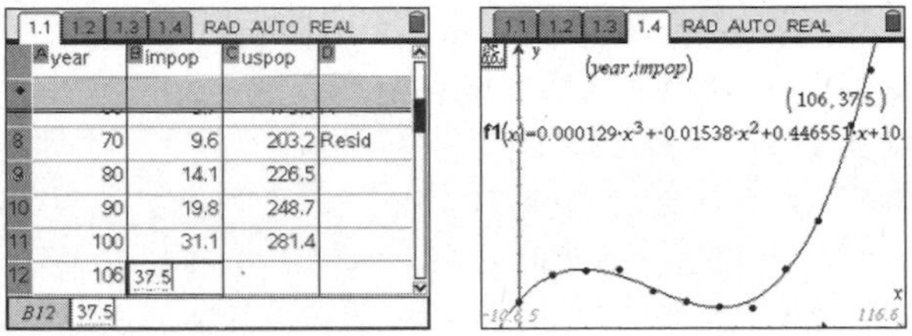

Figure 15-11: Updating a regression.

Update data

Updated regression!

If you use the Generate Sequence command in the Column A header to generate the X list data and then try to add data at the bottom of the list, you see the following warning:

"This operation will overwrite data in the current column. Do you wish to proceed?"

Pressing ⊙ (indicating yes) deletes the existing column data and replaces it with zeros.

Performing a Second Regression

Perhaps you want to construct a scatter plot and associated regression for *year* versus *Total U.S. Population*. Nothing could be easier! Just follow these steps, which also serve as a nice summary for this chapter.

1. **Enter the data.**

   If you haven't already done so, refer to Table 15-1 and enter the data for US Population in Column C.

2. Configure a second scatter plot.

On the Graphs & Geometry page, configure a second scatter plot (*s2* in this case) to plot *year* for *x* and *uspop* for *y*.

Because you are viewing a new scatter plot, the window settings must be adjusted.

3. Change the window settings. Press (menu)⇨**Window**⇨**Zoom – Data. Press** (ctrl)(G) **to hide the entry line. See the first screen in Figure 15-12.**

4. Decide on a regression model.

Although the scatter plot might suggest a linear model, what you know about population growth also suggests that an exponential model might be a better fit.

5. Perform an exponential regression.

    a. Go back to the Lists & Spreadsheets page and press (menu)⇨Statistics⇨Stat Calculations…⇨Exponential Regression.

    b. Configure the dialog box as shown in the second screen in Figure 15-12 and press (enter) to view the results of the regression as shown in the third screen in Figure 15-12.

6. Graph the regression equation. Go back to the Graphs & Geometry page and plot your regression equation (stored in *f2*) as shown in the last screen in Figure 15-12.

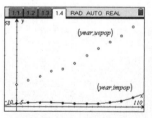

Year vs. U.S. population   Configure dialog box

Figure 15-12: Performing a second regression.

Perform regression   Graph regression equation

Notice that in Figure 15-12 the value of the correlation coefficient, r, is 0.9975. . . . Had you performed a linear regression, the value of r would have been slightly lower (0.9906. . .). This confirms that the exponential regression provides a better fit than a linear regression.

You may have also noticed that the second scatter plot consists of hollow points to offset them from the first scatter plot. You can change the attributes of a scatter plot by moving the cursor on the scatter plot and pressing (ctrl)(menu)⇨Attributes. In total, there are seven different scatter plot styles to choose from as shown in Figure 15-13.

Figure 15-13:
Scatter
plot style
choices.

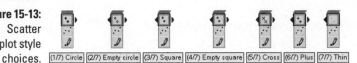

(1/7) Circle (2/7) Empty circle (3/7) Square (4/7) Empty square (5/7) Cross (6/7) Plus (7/7) Thin

Chapter 16

Manual and Automatic Data Capture

*I*n case you haven't already noticed, TI-Nspire is unique in its capability to show multiple representations of mathematical concepts. Furthermore, TI-Nspire's grab-and-move functionality allows you to view these representations dynamically. If I had to choose one aspect of TI-Nspire that embodies these features, it would be the data capture feature.

In this chapter, I show you a classic math problem that can be analyzed using manual and automatic data capture. You will also learn how data capture is a perfect fit for use with both the Graphs & Geometry application and the Lists & Spreadsheet application.

Storing Variables in Graphs & Geometry

Many situations arise in mathematics that require you to investigate a geometric object numerically and algebraically. Take, for example, the situation in which you want to determine the maximum area enclosed by a rectangle with fixed perimeter.

To analyze this situation, open a Graphs & Geometry window and press (menu)⇨View⇨Plane Geometry View. Then press (menu)⇨View⇨Show Analytic Window. Add a separate page with a Lists & Spreadsheet application. See Figure 16-1.

Figure 16-1:
Adding a
Graphs &
Geometry
and Lists &
Spread-
sheet page.

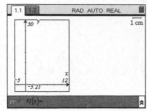 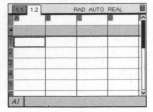

Set your Analytic Window to have the same window settings as those shown in the first screen in Figure 16-1. See Part III for more information about adjusting the settings for your Analytic Window.

You are now ready to construct a rectangle and obtain some measurements. Here are the steps to follow:

1. **Press (menu)⇨Shapes⇨Rectangle to access the Rectangle tool.**

   a. Move the cursor to the top-left corner of the rectangle and press ⓧ.

   b. Move the cursor to the top-right corner of the rectangle and press ⓧ.

   c. Move the cursor to the bottom-right corner of the rectangle and press ⓧ.

2. **Press (menu)⇨Measurement⇨Length to access the Length tool.**

   a. To measure the perimeter of the rectangle, move the cursor to the rectangle until you see `rectangle` (tab) appear. This tells you that you are about to measure the perimeter of the rectangle. Press ⓧ to measure the perimeter of the rectangle. Move the measurement using the NavPad keys and press ⓧ to drop the measure in place.

   b. Move the cursor to the side that represents the length of the rectangle (I chose the bottom) until you see rectangle (tab) again. Press (tab) to reveal `side` (tab). This tells you that you are about to find the length of just one side, rather than the perimeter of the rectangle. Press ⓧ to measure the length of this side of the rectangle. Move the measurement using the NavPad keys and press ⓧ to drop the length measurement in place.

3. **Press (menu)⇨Measurement⇨Area to access the Area tool.**

   Move the cursor to any side of the rectangle and press ⓧ to measure the area of the rectangle. Move the measurement using the NavPad keys and press ⓧ to drop the measurement in place.

Two of your measurements should be in centimeters (*cm*), the larger of which represents the perimeter. The area measurement is units of square centimeters (*cm²*). Your diagram should resemble the first screen in Figure 16-2.

The next step is to lock the perimeter. This allows you to manipulate the rectangle while maintaining a fixed perimeter. To accomplish this task, move the cursor to the perimeter measurement and select (ctrl)(menu)⇨Attributes to open the Attribute control panel. Press ▾ to highlight the lock icon and then press ▸ (enter) to lock the perimeter. See the second and third screens in Figure 16-2.

Figure 16-2: Configuring the maximum area activity.

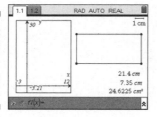 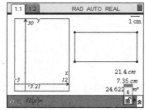 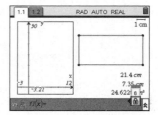

Recall that you want to analyze the relationship between the length of the rectangle and its area for a fixed perimeter. To explore this relationship, you must store these values as variables. Refer to Figure 16-3 and follow the steps that follow.

1. **Move your cursor to the length measurement from Step 2 above and press ⊛ to highlight the measurement (as indicated by the gray box).**

2. **Press (stoVar)⇨Store Var and type (L)(enter).**

   This stores the length measurement as the variable *l*.

   A stored variable is always displayed in a bold font.

3. **Repeat Steps 1 and 2 and store the area measurement to the variable *a*.**

TIP

Figure 16-3: Storing variables.

 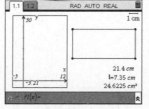 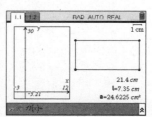

Storing a variable   Bold variable label   Storing *a* for area

Configuring Lists & Spreadsheet for Data Capture

Your stored variables are now available for use in any application that is part of the same problem. In this section, I show you how to use these variables to set up the Lists & Spreadsheet page for data capture.

Before doing so, move to the Lists & Spreadsheet page and name Column A *Length* and Column B *Area*. See Chapter 13 for more information about naming lists.

Automatic data capture

The automatic data capture command collects the length and area data automatically when you move the rectangle in the Graphs & Geometry application.

To configure the automatic data capture command, move your cursor to the header row of Column A and follow these steps.

1. **Press (menu)⇨Data⇨Data Capture⇨Automated Data Capture.**

   This action pastes the automatic data capture command in the header row. The cursor is positioned in the place where you input the variable name to be captured.

2. **Specify the variable by pressing (var), highlighting *l*, and pressing (enter) twice.**

   Recall in the previous section that I named the length using the variable *l*. After you press (enter) for the last time, notice that the current length measurement is automatically placed in cell A1.

3. **Move the cursor to the header row for Column B and repeat Steps 1 and 2. Select *a* as the variable to link to.**

   Notice that the current area measurement is automatically placed in cell B1.

The first screen in Figure 16-4 shows the automatic data capture command in the entry line for Column A. The second screen shows the command for Column B.

Manual data capture

With manual data capture, data is only captured each time you press (ctrl)(.) from within the Graphs & Geometry application. This is helpful if you want to limit the amount of data that is captured. At times, the current activity lends itself to using manual data capture.

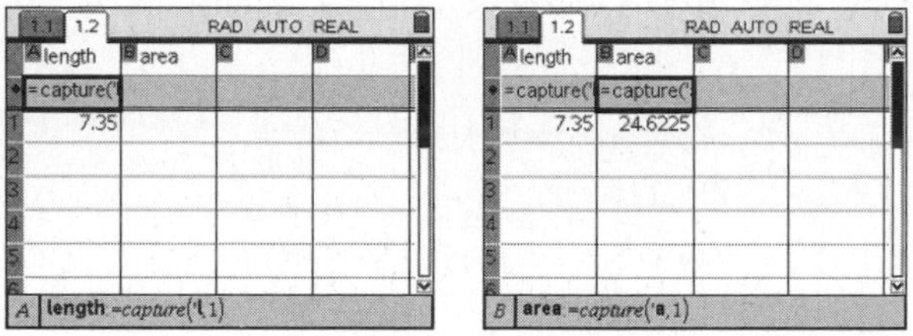

Figure 16-4:
Configuring
Lists &
Spread-
sheet for
automatic
data
capture.

The steps for configuring TI-Nspire for manual data capture are identical to those described in the preceding section with one small exception. Press (menu)⇨Data⇨Data Capture and select Manual Data Capture rather than Automated Data Capture.

After configuring Lists & Spreadsheets for manual data capture, notice that the current length and area values do not appear in cells A1 and B1, respectively. That's because you must capture the data manually! I show you how to do this a little later in the chapter.

Referring back to Figure 16-4, notice that the entire data capture command is revealed in the entry line. The 1 following the variables l and a indicates automatic data capture. A 0 indicates manual data capture.

Setting up Graphs & Geometry to Display Your Data

You are now ready to configure a scatter plot of the *length* versus *area* data. Here's what you need to do:

1. **Move back to the Graphs & Geometry page and press e to activate the entry line (as indicated by a blinking cursor located next to the first available function).**

2. **Press** (menu) **⇨Graph Type⇨Scatter Plot to switch the entry line to scatter plot. Alternatively, press** (ctrl)(menu)**⇨Scatter Plot while the cursor is located in the entry line. Remember, this second option is the equivalent of doing a right-click on a computer.**

   In Figure 16-5, I have pressed (▣) to view a list of choices for the *x*-variable.

3. **Using the ▲▼ keys, highlight *length* and press (▣) or (enter).**

4. **Next, press (tab) to move to the *y*-variable, press (▣) to view a list of choices for the *y*-variable, highlight *area*, and press (▣) or (enter).**

You should see a single point appear on the graph, with an ordered pair label, corresponding to the single data point located in the Lists & Spreadsheet application.

You may need to adjust your window settings (press (menu)⇨Window⇨Window Settings) to view the captured data.

Figure 16-5: Configuring Graphs & Geometry to display a scatter plot.

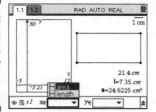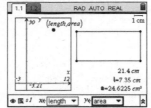

Capturing Data

If you've been following this discussion, your TI-Nspire should be all set for data capture. Yes, a bit of work is involved, but I think you'll appreciate the payoff.

Automatic data capture

Capturing data automatically is as easy as dragging the object that changes the values of your stored variables. In the case of this activity, manipulating the rectangle changes the length and area measurements. Consequently, these updated measurements are periodically dropped into the Lists & Spreadsheet application and plotted in the coordinate plane at the same time.

Recall that when you constructed the rectangle, you defined three corners. You can drag the third corner of the rectangle (or the fourth corner that was never defined) to change the size of the rectangle. Remember that the perimeter has been locked. This adds the constraint that the perimeter must remain fixed at all times.

Move the cursor to an appropriate corner of the rectangle and press (ctrl)(🖰) to grab the corner. Resize the rectangle using the arrow keys on the NavPad. As shown in the first two screens in Figure 16-6, a scatter plot of the length versus area data automatically appears. The third screen in Figure 16-6 shows the corresponding numerical data in the Lists & Spreadsheet page.

You may find that you need to adjust your window settings to fit your data. Press (menu)⟹Window⟹Zoom – Data to quickly set a window that fits the data.

You may be tempted to drag the rectangle back and forth many, many times. Remember, each time you manipulate the rectangle you are adding more points to the lists. It is possible to collect too much data.

Figure 16-6:
Results of the auto-mated data capture activity.

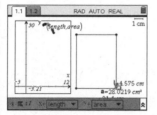
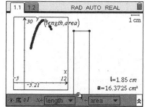

Manual data capture

I mention earlier in this chapter that you must press (ctrl)(.) from within the Graphs & Geometry application each time you want to manually capture a data point. Assuming you have configured the Lists & Spreadsheet page for manual data capture and configured your scatter plot to graph the *Length* and *Area* data, move to the Graphs & Geometry page and press (ctrl)(.) once. You see a single point appear on the coordinate grid with an ordered pair label that represents the current length and area measurements.

Now start dragging the rectangle (see the previous section for instructions for how to do this). Periodically, press (ctrl)(.) to capture another point. Figure 16-7 shows a typical sequence of results from using the manual data capture feature. You can capture as many points as you want. Just make sure that you capture enough to reveal the general shape of the graph as well as the location of the length value that produces a maximum area.

Figure 16-7:
Results of the manual data cap-ture activity.

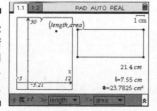
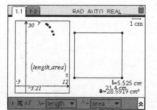
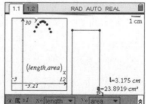

Repeating a data capture

Sometimes you want to repeat an experiment. To do this, just move to the Lists & Spreadsheet page and highlight the header row for Column A. Press ⏎ twice to clear the data in the first column while preserving the data capture command you spent so much time configuring. Repeat this procedure to clear the data in Column B. Now you are ready to go to Graphs & Geometry and repeat the experiment.

Analyzing Captured Data

As a result of this activity, you now have graphical and numerical results that can be analyzed. Here are two possibilities that come to mind.

✔ **Find and graph an equation to model the scatter plot.** An inspection of the scatter plot suggests that a quadratic equation can be used to model the data. In fact, if you let x represent the length of the parabola, you can find an expression for the area in terms of x knowing that the perimeter has a fixed value.

In my example, I have a fixed perimeter of 21.4 centimeters. Therefore, the height of the rectangle must be $10.7 - x$. The formula for the area is the product of length and width, or $area(x) = x(10.7 - x)$. Type this equation into $f1(x)$ on the entry line to verify that it goes through the scatter plot. See the first screen in Figure 16-8.

✔ **Sort the data to find the length that produces a maximum area.** For those of you that are more into the numbers, move to the Lists & Spreadsheet application, highlight Columns A and B, and perform a descending sort by Column B (see Chapter 14 for details as to how to sort data). The second screen in Figure 16-8 shows how to configure the Sort dialog box. The third screen in Figure 16-8 shows that, for my example, the area is maximized for a length of approximately 5.525 centimeters.

Figure 16-8:
Analyzing
captured
data.

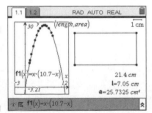

Formulas contained in a header row are deleted any time you do a sort on that column. Press ⌃ esc to undo the sort and restore the header row formulas.

Chapter 17

Using the Lists & Spreadsheet Application with TI-Nspire CAS

*I*n this chapter, I talk about how the Computer Algebra System functionality associated with the TI-Nspire CAS can be used with the Lists & Spreadsheet application. Specifically, I focus on using the tools found in the Calculator application Algebra submenu to do algebra and the tools found in the Calculator application Calculus submenu to do calculus.

I also make sure to show you how TI-Nspire CAS defaults to the symbolic manipulation of expressions and equations and how this feature can also enhance your mathematical investigations.

Doing Algebra

Whether you are using a specific algebra tool (such as the Expand command) or simply taking advantage of the symbolic manipulation feature of TI-Nspire CAS, the Lists & Spreadsheet application offers a variety of options when it comes to investigating algebra concepts using the Computer Algebra System functionality of TI-Nspire CAS.

In this section, I highlight a couple ways you can use the Lists & Spreadsheet application to do algebra. Clearly, there is no substitute for doing algebra using traditional paper-and-pencil methods. However, the TI-Nspire CAS Lists & Spreadsheet application offers an alternative approach that may suit your needs quite nicely.

Solving equations

Solving equations involves a multistep process that is perfectly suited to TI-Nspire CAS. For example, if you want to solve the equation $2x - 5 = 5x + 1$, step by step, using the Lists & Spreadsheet application, here are the steps to follow:

1. **Type** $2x - 5 = 5x + 1$ **in cell A1 and press** ⏎.

2. **Type** =A1+5 **in cell A2 and press** ⏎.

   The = symbol that precedes the expression typed in cell A2 tells TI-Nspire CAS to perform a mathematical operation. Notice that TI-Nspire performs symbolic manipulation of the equation in cell A1 and displays this result in cell A2.

3. **Type** =A2–5x **in cell A3 and press** ⏎.

4. **Type** =A3/-3 **in cell A4 and press** ⏎.

Figure 17-1 shows the result of this sequence of steps.

In the last screen in Figure 17-1, I have used the Solve command in cell B4 to check my answer. I've highlighted this cell so you can see the syntax associated with this command at the bottom of the screen.

You can also use the tools found in the Algebra submenu of the Calculator application to solve more complicated equations such as $(x - 3)^2 = 3x^2 - x + 6$.

As you see in Figure 17-2, I use the Expand command to expand the expression $(x - 3)^2$ on the left side of the equation. I also solved the left side for zero using one step. Finally, I use the Factor command to factor the resulting quadratic expression on the right side of the equation.

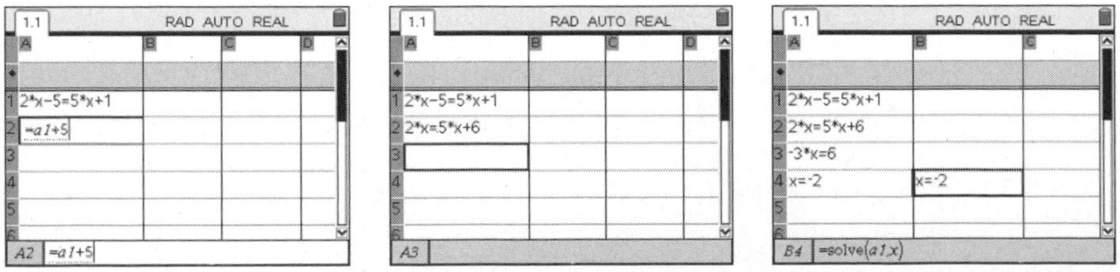

Figure 17-1:
Using the
Lists &
Spread-
sheet
application
to solve a
multistep-
problem.

Figure 17-2:
Using
algebra
tools with
the Lists
& Spread-
sheet
application
to solve
equations.

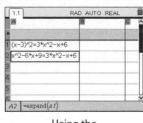
Using the
Expand command

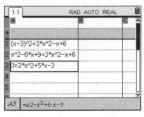
Solve the left side
for zero in one step

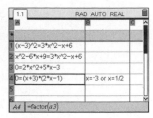
Using the Factor command
to factor the right side

You can readily find the solution to this equation using the linear factors shown in cell A4. I used the Solve command in cell B4 to confirm my answer.

You can type commands (such as Solve) using the green alpha keys. Alternatively, press ⌨① to access the alphabetical lists of functions in the Catalog.

Solving systems of equations

The Lists & Spreadsheet application can also be used to solve systems of equations. Consider that you want to solve the following system of equations using the elimination method.

$$\begin{cases} 3x + 5y = 6 \\ -4x + 2y = 5 \end{cases}$$

Here are the steps to follow to solve this equation using the Lists & Spreadsheet application:

1. **Enter the equations in cells A1 and A2**

2. **Enter the expression** =expand(4•*a1*) **in cell B1.**

    This operation multiplies the first equation by –4 and displays the result in cell B1. I use the Expand command; otherwise, the resulting equation will be displayed as –4(3x + 5y) = –24.

3. **Enter the expression** =expand(3•*a2*) **in cell B2.**

    The first screen in Figure 17-3 shows the result of the first three steps.

4. **Enter the expression** =*b1* + *b2* **in cell B3.**

    This adds the equations $12x + 20y = 24$ and $-12x + 6y = 15$ and displays the result in cell B3. Notice that the variable x is eliminated.

5. **Enter the expression** =*b3*/26 **in cell B4.**

    This step solves for the variable y. The results of Steps 4 and 5 are shown in the second screen in Figure 17-3.

6. **Enter the expression** =*b1*|*b4* **in cell C4.**

    Press ⓘ to access the | (with) operator. This expression takes the equation located in cell B1 and replaces the variable y with its numerical value located in cell B4. You now have an equation strictly in terms of x.

7. **Enter the expression** =(*c4* – 30)/12 **in cell C5.**

    This expression solves the equation in cell C4 for the variable x. The results of Steps 6 and 7 are shown in the third screen in Figure 17-3.

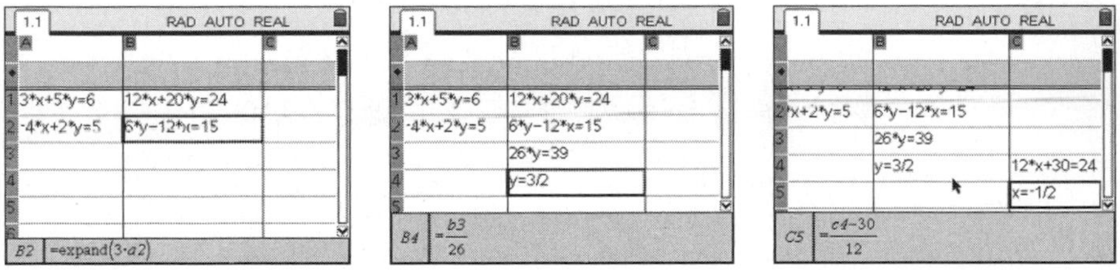

Figure 17-3:
Using the
Lists &
Spread-
sheet
application
to solve a
system of
equations.

Exploring binomials

The Lists & Spreadsheet application offers a nice opportunity to use patterns to explore the product of two binomials as well as the factorization of quadratic expressions.

In the first two screens in Figure 17-4, I have configured the Lists & Spreadsheet application to explore the square of a binomial. Here are the steps to accomplish this task:

1. **Generate the sequence 1, 2, 3, ..., 10 in cells A1 through A10.**

    I accomplish this by typing 1 in cell A1 and =*a1* + 1 in cell A2. I then used Fill Down to copy the formula in cell A2 down to cell A10.

2. **Type** =(*x* + *a1*)² **in cell B1.**

    This formula displays a binomial squared in cell B1 of the form $(x + k)^2$ where k is the value in the adjacent cell, A1. See the first screen in Figure 17-4.

3. **Use Fill Down to copy the formula in B1 down to B10.**

4. **Type the formula** =expand(*b1*) **in cell C1.**

   This formula expands the expression contained in cell B1.

5. **Use Fill Down to copy the formula in cell C1 to cell C10.**

   The result of this last step is shown in the second screen in Figure 17-4. By observing this pattern, students can generalize that $(x + k)^2$ has an expansion equal to $x^2 + 2kx + k^2$.

The last screen in Figure 17-4 shows that this process can be reversed. That is, patterns can be used to observe the relationship between expressions given in expanded form and expressions given in factored form. Specifically, I used the Lists & Spreadsheet application to demonstrate that a quadratic expression of the form $x^2 - k^2$ can be factored as $(x - k)(x + k)$.

Here are the steps that I used to accomplish this task:

1. **Generate the sequence 1, 2, 3, ..., 10 in cells A1 through A10.**

   See Step 1 from the previous example.

2. **Type** =*a1*^{2} **in cell B1 and then fill this formula down to cell B10.**

   This step takes the square of the values in cells A1 through A10.

3. **Type** =x^2 – *b1* **in cell C1 and then fill this formula down to cell C10.**

   This step displays expressions of the form $x^2 - k^2$ where k is the value in the adjacent cell.

4. **Type** =factor(*c1*) **in cell D1 and then fill this formula down to cell D10.**

   This step displays the factored form of the expressions found in column C.

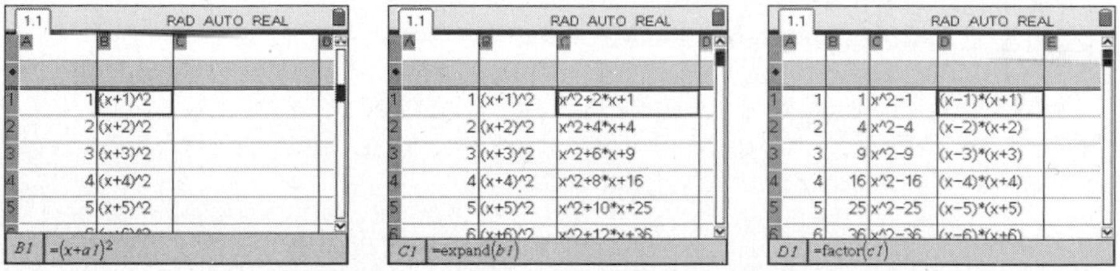

Figure 17-4:
Using the Lists & Spreadsheet application to explore the square of a binomial and the difference of squares.

Exploring powers of binomials

You can take the ideas from the last section one step further to explore the expansion of binomials to higher powers. As you see in Figure 17-5, In Column B, I've generated the list $x + k$, $(x + k)^2$, $(x + k)^3$, ..., $(x + k)^{10}$. I then used the Expand command in Column C to expand the expressions contained in Column B.

Here are the specific steps:

1. **Generate the sequence 1, 2, 3, ..., 10 in cells A1 through A10.**

2. **Type** $=(x + k)a1$ **in cell B1 and then fill this formula down to cell B10.**

   This step takes the binomial $(x + k)$ and raises it to the power equal to the values in cells A1 through A10. See the first screen in Figure 17-5.

3. **Type** $=$expand($b1$) **in cell C1 and then fill this formula down to cell C10.**

   This step expands the expressions contained in cells B1 through B10 as shown in the second screen in Figure 17-5.

As you can see, these expansions get quite long and cumbersome. Referring to the last screen in Figure 17-5, if you highlight a cell where the entire expression does not fit, TI-Nspire reveals the entire expansion.

Figure 17-5:
Investigating
binomial
expansions.

1.1		RAD AUTO REAL	
▲	B	C	D
1	x+k		
2	(x+k)^2		
3	(x+k)^3		
4	(x+k)^4		
5	(x+k)^5		
B1	=(x+k)^a1		

1.1		RAD AUTO REAL	
▲	B	C	
1	x+k	x+k	
2	(x+k)^2	x^2+2*k*x+k^2	
3	(x+k)^3	x^3+3*k*x^2+3*k^2*...	
4	(x+k)^4	x^4+4*k*x^3+6*k^2*...	
5	(x+k)^5	x^5+5*k*x^4+10*k^...	
	6 (x+k)^6	x^6+6*k*x^5+15*k^	
C1	=expand(b1)		

1.1		RAD AUTO REAL	
▲	B	C	
1	x+k	x+k	
2	(x+k)^2	x^2+2*k*x+k^2	
3	(x+k)^3	x^3+3*k*x^2+3*k^2*...	
4	x^5+5*k*x^4+10*x^2..^3+10*k^3*x^2+5*k^4*x+k^5		
5	(x+k)^5	x^5+5*k*x^4+10*k^...	
	6 (x+k)^6	x^6+6*k*x^5+15*k^	
C5	=expand(b5)		

I used the binomial expansion of the expression $(x + k)$ to help generalize the patterns associated with this concept. I could have used any variable or value for k and achieved similar results.

Using Calculus Tools in Lists & Spreadsheets

The symbolic manipulation feature of TI-Nspire CAS and the built-in calculus tools commonly used in the Calculator application offer a variety of options when it comes to investigating calculus concepts.

Investigating derivatives

As with algebra, the use of patterns to explore calculus concepts can be a powerful learning tool. Take, for example, a simple experiment in which the derivatives of x, x^2, x^3, ..., x^{10} are calculated.

Here are the steps to this exploration:

1. **Generate the sequence 1, 2, 3, ..., 10 in cells A1 through A10.**

2. **Type *xa1* in cell B1 and then fill this formula down to cell B10.**

   The result of the first two steps is shown in the first screen in Figure 17-6.

3. **Move the cursor to cell C1, type =, and press ⬡ ⬡ to open the Math Template.**

4. **Highlight the Derivative template (shown in the second screen in Figure 17-6) and press ⬡ to paste it to the current cursor location.**

5. **Type *x* in the first field of the Derivative template and *b1* in the second field of the Derivative template and press ⬡.**

   Press ⬡ to move from one field to the next.

6. **Use the Fill Down command to copy the formula contained in cell C1 down to cell C10.**

The third screen in Figure 17-6 shows the results of this quick investigation.

Figure 17-6:
Using the
Derivative
template
with the
Lists &
Spreadsheet
application.

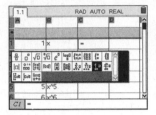

Notice in the third screen, I have used the Derivative template in cell D1 to evaluate the derivative of xn. I added this generalization to support the particular results shown in cells C1 through C10.

I can also use the Nth Derivative template to investigate higher-order derivatives. In Figure 17-7, I have found the 1st through 10th derivatives of the expression $x^2\sin(x)$. The steps to accomplish this task are listed here:

1. **Generate the sequence 1, 2, 3, ..., 10 in cells A1 through A10.**

2. **Move the cursor to cell B1, type =, and press (ctrl)(≈×) to open the Math Template.**

3. **Highlight the Nth Derivative template (shown in the first screen in Figure 17-6) and press (enter) to paste it to the current cursor location.**

4. **Type *x* in the first field of the Derivative template, *a1* in the second field, $x^2\sin(x)$ in the third field, and press (enter).**

   Press (tab) to move from one field to the next. This formula takes *n*th derivative of the expression $x^2\sin(x)$ where *n* is the value located in the adjacent cell.

5. **Use the Fill Down command to copy the formula contained in cell B1 down to cell B10.**

The following generalizations can be made as a result of this activity:

✔ Derivative order 1, 5, 9, ..., *n*: $[x^2 - (n^2 - n)]\cos(x) + 2n\,x\sin(x)$

✔ Derivative order 2, 6, 10, ..., *n*: $[(n^2 - n) - x^2)]\sin(x) + 2n\,x\cos(x)$

✔ Derivative order 3, 7, 11, ..., *n*: $[(n^2 - n) - x^2)]\cos(x) - 2n\,x\sin(x)$

✔ Derivative order 4, 8, 12, ..., *n*: $[x^2 - (n^2 - n)]\sin(x) - 2n\,x\cos(x)$

Figure 17-7:
Using
the Nth
Derivative
template
with the
Lists &
Spreadsheet
application.

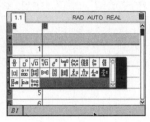
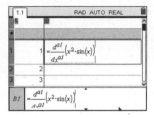

Investigating integrals

You can also evaluate definite and indefinite integrals using the Lists & Spreadsheet application. Both of these items can be accessed from the Math template by pressing ⟨ctrl⟩⟨ₓ⟩.

Figure 17-8 shows how to use cell references with these templates to generate patterns of definite and indefinite integrals. The first screen shows the syntax used to find the value of the definite integral of $f(x) = x^n$ on the interval $[0, 1]$ for the corresponding values of n found in Column A. The second screen shows the syntax used to find the indefinite integral $f(x) = x^n$ for the corresponding values of n found in Column A.

You can also use cell references in limits of integration fields of the Definite Integral template.

Figure 17-8:
Using the
Integral
templates
with the
Lists &
Spreadsheet
application.

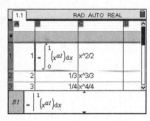

Working with sequences and series

The TI-Nspire, the Generate Sequence command contained in the Lists & Spreadsheet application enbles you to create numerical sequences. With TI-Nspire CAS, this command can also be used to generate algebraic sequences.

Consider you want to generate the sequence $1, x, \dfrac{x^2}{2!}, \dfrac{x^3}{3!}, \dfrac{x^4}{4!}, ..., + \dfrac{x^{10}}{10!}$

Here are the steps to follow:

1. **Move the cursor to the Header row and choose ⓜ⇨Data⇨Generate Sequence.**

2. **Configure the dialog to match the one shown in the first screen in Figure 17-9.**

3. **Press ⏎ to generate the sequence as shown in the second screen in Figure 17-9.**

As shown in the last screen of Figure 17-9, I've used the Sum template (press ⓒ ⓣⓡⓛ ⧈) to find the infinite sum of the terms of this sequence. You can access the μ symbol using the shortcut key sequence ⓒⓣⓡⓛ ⓘ. Press ⏎ to find that this infinite sum is equal to *ex*.

Figure 17-9:
Working
with alge-
braic series
and sums in
the Lists &
Spreadsheet
application.

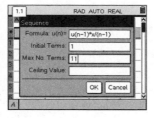
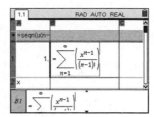

The examples contained in this chapter are intended only to give you a sense of how the computer algebra system of TI-Nspire CAS can be used to explore algebra and calculus concepts. Clearly the sky's the limit when it comes to pushing this functionality. When using TI-Nspire CAS with the Lists & Spreadsheet applications, think about how it can be used to explore patterns or to work through the steps associated with solving algebraic equations or simplifying algebraic expressions.

Part V

The Data & Statistics Application

The 5th Wave

By Rich Tennant

"Okay – let's play the statistical probabilities of this situation. There are 4 of us and 1 of him. Phillip will probably start screaming, Nora will probably faint, you'll probably yell at me for leaving the truck open, and there's a good probability I'll run like a weenie if he comes toward us."

In this part . . .

This part takes you through a tour of the Data & Statistics application. I show you how this application is used to produce graphs of one- and two-variable data sets that reside in the Lists & Spreadsheet application. You also learn about the many tools available within this application to assist you with the analysis of these graphs. And, I show you how the two-way communication between the Lists & Spreadsheet and Data & Statistics applications adds a dynamic element to these analyses.

Finally, I give an overview of the data collection process, a feature of TI-Nspire that uses the Graphs & Geometry, Lists & Spreadsheet, and Data & Statistics applications.

Chapter 18

Constructing Statistical Graphs

· ·

In This Chapter

▶ Creating single-variable and two-variable Quick Graphs from the Lists & Spreadsheet application

▶ Understanding different page layout options

· ·

*T*he Data & Statistics application operates in conjunction with the Lists & Spreadsheet application. It provides a visual representation of numeric or categorical data using a variety of common single-variable and two-variable statistical graphs.

You can also use the Data & Statistics application in conjunction with the Calculator application, although this method is less common.

In this chapter, I show you how to launch the Data & Statistics application directly from the Lists & Spreadsheets application using the Quick Graph feature. I also show you an alternative method of producing graphs in the Data & Statistics application. In Chapters 19 and 20, I discuss the tools available within this application that allow you to get the most out of these statistical graphs.

Launching Data & Statistics from the Lists & Spreadsheet Application

As with any TI-Nspire application, you have the option of launching the Data & Statistics application by inserting a new page and selecting Data & Statistics from the five available choices. However, because the purpose of the Data & Statistics application is graph numerical (and sometime categorical) data, it makes sense to start with the Lists & Spreadsheet application. Then use the Quick Graph feature in the Lists & Spreadsheet application to launch the Data & Statistics application.

Entering data in Lists & Spreadsheet

The rules for using the Lists & Spreadsheet application in conjunction with Data & Statistics are quite straightforward. You must have one or two named lists in the Lists & Spreadsheet application.

For example, look at the lists displayed in Figure 18-1. In the first screen, I've created a list called *dice_sum* and used the command =randint(1,6,50) + randint(1,6,50) to produce a list of 50 numbers. This list represents a simulation of rolling two dice 50 times and recording their sums. I call this a single-variable data set because there is only one list of data to be analyzed.

The second screen shows the *Year* versus *U.S. Immigrant Population* data that I use in Chapter 15. This represents a two-variable data set with the independent variable represented by *Year* and the dependent variable represented by *U.S. Immigrant Population*.

Notice that I have named each list. You must have named lists to use the Data & Statistics application.

TI-Nspire also provides the option of graphing *categorical data*. For example, you can create a two-variable graph representing the results of a survey on favorite ice cream flavors. Perhaps the horizontal axis contains a list of six common ice cream flavors, and the vertical axis represents the corresponding number of times each flavor was considered a favorite. Keep in mind that text entered in the Lists & Spreadsheet application must be included in quotation marks. Categorical data can be displayed as a dot plot (default), a bar chart, or a pie chart. I show you more about graphing categorical data in Chapter 20.

Figure 18-1:
Setting up
Lists &
Spreadsheet
for use with
Data &
Statistics.

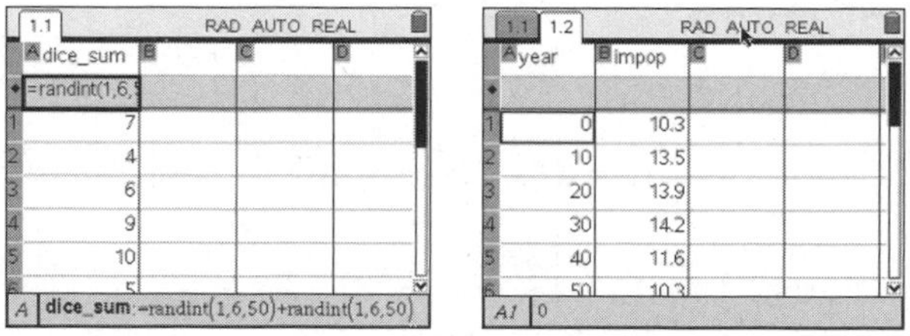

A single-variable data set   A two-variable data set

Using Quick Graph

After your named lists are complete, choose (menu)⇨Data⇨Quick Graph to access the Quick Graph feature. The first screen in Figure 18-2 shows the result of using Quick Graph with the single-variable data set. TI-Nspire automatically splits the screen and opens a Data & Statistics page side-by-side with the existing Lists & Spreadsheet page. By default, single-variable data sets are visually represented by a dot plot. As you see in Chapter 19, TI-Nspire can represent single-variable data sets with a dot plot, box plot, or histogram.

The second screen in Figure 18-2 shows the result of using Quick Graph with the two-variable data set. Again, TI-Nspire automatically splits the screen and opens a Data & Statistics page side-by-side with the existing Lists & Spreadsheet page. Two-variable data sets are always represented by a scatter plot.

Figure 18-2: Using Quick Graph with single-variable and two-variable data sets.

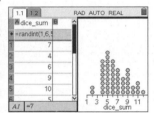 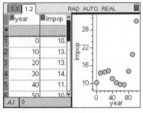

Single-variable data: Two-variable data:
Dot plot   Scatter plot

If you have a page layout with two applications, Quick Graph configures a page layout with three applications. If you have a page layout with three applications, Quick Graph configures a page layout with four applications. If you have a page layout with four applications, Quick Graph runs out of options and must open a new page to display a graph in the Data & Statistics application.

With the Lists & Spreadsheet page active, try pressing (ctrl)(R) to recalculate the values dependent on the formula =randint(1,6,50) + randint(1,6,50). This action generates an entirely new set of values, and the dot plot updates accordingly.

If you have two or more columns of data contained in a Lists & Spreadsheet application, you must select the column or columns of data to be used with Quick Graph. Here's how you accomplish this task:

- **Select column.** You have two ways to select an entire column:
  - Move the cursor to the column/list name area located at the top of the column and press the ▲ key one more time to select the column.
  - Position the cursor anywhere in the desired column and choose (menu)⇨Actions⇨Select⇨Select Column.
- **Select multiple rows or columns.** After selecting a column, press and hold the (shift) key. While holding this key, press the NavPad keys to select additional columns.

Working with Data & Statistics in a Separate Page

As you see in the previous section, Quick Graph reconfigures your page layout to display a Data & Statistics graph on the current screen (unless your current page layout contains four applications).

To view a Data & Statistics graph on a separate page, choose 🏠⇨Data & Statistics (or press ctrl①) and select Data & Statistics from the available choices). The first screen in Figure 18-3 shows the result of this action. By default, the caption located at the top of the screen shows the available list. Move your cursor to the Click to Add Variable region, press ⑨ to view the available lists (as defined in all Lists & Spreadsheet applications within the current problem), highlight your list choice, and press enter.

The second and third screens in Figure 18-3 show the result of selecting the list called *dice-sum*.

Figure 18-3:
Graphing
a single-
variable
data set on
a separate
Data &
Statistics
page.

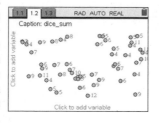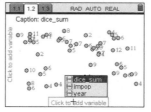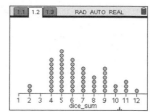

Similarly, you can add a separate Data & Statistics page to view the scatter plot corresponding to a two-variable data set. As can be seen in Figure 18-4, you must select the variable to be represented on both the horizontal and vertical axes.

Figure 18-4:
Graphing a
two-variable
data set on
a separate
Data &
Statistics
page.

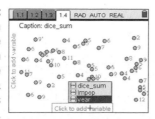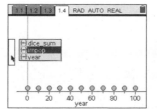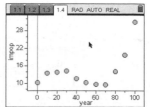

Chapter 19

Working with Single-Variable Data

*1*n this chapter, I show you the choices of graphs available for use with numerical and categorical data contained in a single list and the tools available for use with each of these graphs. I also show you how to manipulate either the data values or the graphs themselves and observe the corresponding effects of such actions.

Selecting a Statistical Graph

Three types of graphs are available when you work with a single list of numerical data: dot plot, box plot, and histogram. When working with categorical data, you have the option of creating a dot plot, bar chart, or pie chart.

To select a chart type, choose (menu)⇨Plot Type and select the Plot Type from the list of available options.

Dot Plots

In the first screen in Figure 19-1, I give a variation of the two-dice sum example from Chapter 18. The first column (called *first_die*) uses the command = randint(1,6,50) to simulate rolling one die 50 times. The second column (labeled *second_die*) represents the outcome of rolling a second die 50 times, and the third column (labeled *total*) represents the sum of the first two columns.

The second screen shows the result of choosing (menu)➪Data➪Quick Graph. The current page layout is configured with a Data & Statistics page, and the default dot plot of the data contained in the *Total* column is graphed automatically.

Changing variables

Perhaps you want to view a dot plot depicting the distribution of the *first_die* data. To accomplish this task, follow these steps:

1. **Move the cursor to the horizontal axis label at the bottom of the screen until the words "Click to change variable" appear.**

2. **Press (⊛) to reveal a list of choices.**

3. **Use the NavPad keys to highlight your choice and press (⏎).**

The third screen in Figure 19-1 shows the result of changing the horizontal axis category from *total* to *first_die*. Notice that the scale on the horizontal axis changes automatically. I also have the option of changing this category to display the *second_die* data.

Figure 19-1: Changing variables on a Data & Statistics graph.

 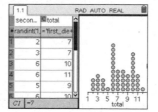 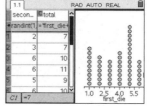

If you press, (menu)➪Plot Properties, you see menu options to add or remove X and Y variables. These options enable you to switch back and forth between one and two-variable data sets. They also allow you to switch your plots from a vertical orientation to a horizontal orientation and vice versa.

Consider, for example, the vertically oriented dot plot shown in the second screen in Figure 19-1. You can choose (menu)➪Plot Properties➪Remove X Variable to effectively remove the graph from the screen. Next, you move the cursor to the left side of the screen until the words "Click to add variable" appear, press (⊛), and select *total* from the list. You see the same Dot Plot as before, but with a horizontal orientation.

Changing your window settings

The first screen in Figure 19-2 shows the results of a two-dice sum experiment in which a sum of 2 and a sum of 12 never occurred. TI-Nspire, therefore, produces a horizontal scale that ranges from 3 to 11. To change these settings to range from 2 to 12, choose (menu)⇨Window/Zoom⇨Window Settings and change the Xmin and XMax values accordingly. The second screen in Figure 19-2 shows the result of changing Xmin to 1.5 and Xmax to 12.5.

In the third screen, the *x*-axis variable is switched back to *first_die*. I then chose (menu)⇨Plot Properties⇨Force Categorical X. This action treats each value in the list as categories, much as it would if this list contained words. This is a nice option that gives a clean-looking graph and is especially well-suited for a discrete variable such as the numerical value on a die. Additionally, switching to categorical data gives the option of choosing (menu)⇨Plot Type and selecting Bar Chart or Pie Chart.

When numerical data are switched to categorical data, TI-Nspire sorts by the first digit it sees. If you switched the dot plot for *total* from numerical to categorical, the values on the horizontal axis would go 10, 11, 12, 2, 3, …, 9 from left to right — probably not a good option.

Choose (menu)⇨Plot Properties⇨Force Numerical X to switch back to numeric values.

Histograms

Choose (menu)⇨Plot Type⇨Histogram to display single-variable data as a histogram. The first screen in Figure 19-3 shows a histogram of the *total* data.

The number of *bins*, the name given for the bars in a histogram, is determined by the number of data sets and the distribution of the data. As shown in the first screen in Figure 19-3, you can click a bin to display the width of the bin and the number of values contained in the bin.

Figure 19-2:
Changing window settings and forcing categorical data.

 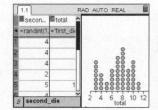 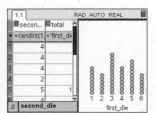

Changing the scale

Choose (menu)⇨Plot Properties⇨Histogram Properties⇨Histogram Scale and select a scale for your histogram, as follows:

- ✔ **Count:** By default, histograms give the *count* of each bin. This scale tells you how many values are contained in each bin. Referring to the first screen in Figure 19-3, eight values are contained in the bin ranging from 6.5 to 7.5.

- ✔ **Percent:** Choose (menu)⇨Plot Properties⇨Histogram Properties⇨Histogram Scale⇨Percent to change the scale to *percent*. This scale tells you the percent of all values that are contained in each bin. The second screen in Figure 19-3 shows that 16 percent of all values fall in the bin from 6.5 to 7.5. This makes sense because the ratio 8 out of 50 is equal to 16%.

- ✔ **Density:** Choose (menu)⇨Plot Properties⇨Histogram Properties⇨Histogram Scale⇨Density to change the scale to *density*. The density is calculated by dividing the relative frequency of a bin by the bin width.

Figure 19-3:
Plotting histograms and adjusting the scale.

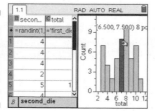 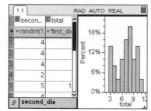 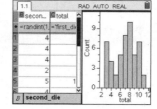

Adjusting the bins

To adjust the bin width, follow these steps:

1. **Move the cursor to the right edge of any bin until the ✛ symbol appears.**

2. **Choose (ctrl)(✋) to grab the bin and use the NavPad keys to adjust the width.**

   Notice the numerical value associated with right edge of the bin is displayed.

3. **Press (esc) when finished.**

To adjust the bin width numerically, follow these steps:

1. **Choose ⓜ⇨Plot Properties⇨Histogram Properties⇨Bin Settings**
2. **Configure the dialog box for a desired bin width and alignment.**

   The bin width is fairly self-explanatory — it sets the width of each bin of your histogram. The alignment is a bit trickier. For example, if you specify a bin width of 2 with an alignment of 5, you can be assured that one of your bins has a right edge located at 5 with a width of 2. All other bins fall into place. A bin width of 2 and an alignment of 7 (or any odd integer) produces the same histogram.

   Perhaps you want your bins to have a width of 1 and be centered on the values represented by the possible two-dice sum outcomes. Use a bin width of 1 and any bin alignment with a decimal portion equal to 0.5. For example, a bin alignment of 7.5 works.

3. **Press ⏎ when finished.**

Changing variables

As with the Dot Plot, you can change variables or use the Add/Remove Variable options located in the ⓜ⇨Plot Properties submenu. Remember to use the Add/Remove tools to change your histogram from a vertical orientation to a horizontal orientation and vice versa.

Inserting a normal curve

The command =sum(randint(0,1,10) can be used to simulate guessing on 10 straight true/false questions. This formula generates a list of 10 integers that are either 0 or 1 and calculates the sum. If you assign a 1 to represent getting a question correct, then a result of 6 means you got 6 out of 10 questions correct.

In the first screen in Figure 19-4, I have used Fill Down to copy this formula to cell A100. I then used Quick Graph to graph a histogram of the data. I clicked the third bin to show that I got 7 questions correct exactly 11 times.

This binomial experiment should have a shape that resembles a normal distribution. Choose ⓜ⇨Analyze⇨Show Normal PDF to overlay a normal curve on your histogram. The normal graph is based on the mean of the data set (in this case, the mean is 4.87) and the standard deviation (1.42 in this case). See the second screen in Figure 19-4.

Plotting a value

I can also plot a value on a histogram which displays as a vertical line perpendicular to the horizontal axis at a point equal to the specified value. In Figure 19-4, I chose (menu)⇨Analyze⇨Plot Value. At the prompt, I typed **mean(correct)** and pressed (enter).

Figure 19-4:
Displaying
a normal
curve and
plotting a
value.

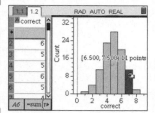 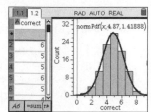 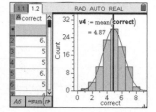

You can plot a single number or an expression that equals a number. Statistical values such as mean or standard deviation are good choices for Plot Value.

The Plot Value feature is also available with dot plots and box plots.

To remove a plotted value, move the cursor over the vertical line and press (ctrl)(menu)⇨Removed Plotted Value. To hide a normal curve, choose (menu)⇨Analyze⇨Hide Normal PDF.

Try moving your cursor to the normal curve and choosing (ctrl)(menu)⇨Shade Under Function. This gives you the option of shading a region under the curve and displaying the corresponding probability associated with this interval.

Box Plots

Consider you want to investigate the Major League home run leaders between the years of 1988–2007. I realize this is somewhat controversial but from a data standpoint, the results are quite interesting!

In the first screen in Figure 19-5, I have entered the data in Column A (named *al* for American League) and Column B (named *nl* for National League). I then chose (menu)⇨Data⇨Quick Graph and, by default, obtained a dot plot for the American League data.

Choose (menu)⇨Plot Type⇨Box Plot to switch from a dot plot to a box plot. See the second screen in Figure 19-5.

As you move the cursor over the box plot, each of the values that comprise the five-number summary are revealed. If you click one of the four regions in a box plot, the individual data points are revealed. Keep in mind that multiple occurrences of the same number are displayed as a single point. Press ⓔsⓒ to hide the points.

Outliers

To graph a second box plot containing the National League data, follow these steps:

1. **Highlight Column B.**

2. **Choose (menu)⇨Data⇨Quick Graph.**

3. **Choose b⇨Plot Type⇨Box Plot to switch from a dot plot to a box plot.**

The third screen in Figure 19-5 shows the second box plot representing the National League results. Notice three outliers appear on this graph.

To hide outliers, select (menu)⇨Plot Properties⇨Extend Box Plot Whiskers. To reveal outliers (if they exist), select (menu)⇨Plot Properties⇨Show Box Plot Outliers.

Figure 19-5: Constructing box plots.

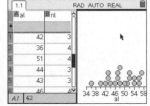
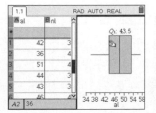
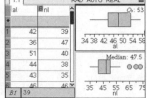

Adjusting your window settings

Notice the scales used for the American League data and the National League data are slightly different. To provide a better comparison of the two leagues, change the window settings so that they are identical. To accomplish this task, choose (menu)⇨Window/Zoom⇨Window Settings and configure the dialog box with appropriate XMin and XMax values.

Figure 19-6 shows the result of changing the XMin and XMax values for both box plots to 30 and 80, respectively.

A short course in box plots

Box plots (sometimes referred to as box-and-whisker plots) consist of four regions. The leftmost region and the rightmost region are aptly named *whiskers*. The box located between the whiskers is divided into two regions. The dividing line in the box corresponds to the median of the data set. To draw these four regions, you need five numbers (called the five-number summary): the minimum value, the median, the maximum value, the lower quartile (the median of the lower half of the data set), and the upper quartile (the median of the upper half of the data set).

The figure below shows two ways to draw a typical box plot. The first figure does not delineate *outliers*, data values that are numerically distanced from other data values. The second figure highlights two values that are outliers. Points that are a distance 1.5 times the Interquartile Range beyond the quartiles are considered outliers and are drawn as distinct points. The Interquartile Range is defined as the difference between the upper quartile and the lower quartile.

Each of the four regions created by a box plot contains 25% of the data values. As a result, box plots are helpful in displaying the spread and skew of the data.

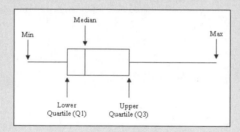
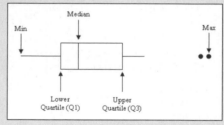

Plotting a value

As with a dot plot or histogram, box plots offer you the option of plotting a value and displaying it as a vertical line through the horizontal axis at a point equal to the value. A plot of the mean of a data set represents a good choice.

Figure 19-6:
Adjusting window settings.

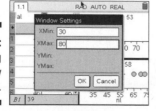
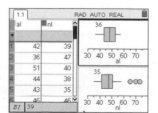

Working with Categorical Data

As I mention earlier in this chapter, TI-Nspire gives you the option of graphing categorical data. You can spot most categorical data by text, such as the list of the favorite ice cream flavors of 20 people shown in Figure 19-7.

Sometimes numerical data is better represented as categorical data. For example, a survey of the number of siblings in 20 families might be better suited for categorical data. Choose (menu)⇨Plot Properties⇨Force Categorical X (or Categorical Y) to switch numerical data to categorical data.

Categorical data can be presented in the following ways:

- ✔ **Dot plots:** The first screen in Figure 19-7 shows that TI-Nspire defaults to categorical data when a *string* values are typed into a column of data. To type a string into a cell, enclose the characters in quotation marks.

- ✔ **Bar charts:** Choose (menu)⇨Plot Type⇨Bar Chart to switch to a bar chart. The second screen in Figure 19-7 shows a bar chart of the ice cream data. Notice that you can click a bar to reveal the number of cases and the corresponding percent for the selected category.

- ✔ **Pie charts:** Choose (menu)⇨Plot Type⇨Pie Chart to switch to a pie chart. The third screen in Figure 19-7 shows the pie chart of my ice cream data. Once again, you can click a sector to reveal the number of cases and the corresponding percent for the selected category.

Perhaps your categorical data is given in categorical split form. That is, one column gives the category name and a second column gives the frequency of occurrence.

To graph categorical data given in this form, follow these steps:

1. **Highlight the column containing the category names.**

2. **Choose (menu)⇨Data⇨Quick Graph (see first screen in Figure 19-8).**

3. **Move the cursor to the left side of the Data & Statistics page until the words "Click to add variable" appear.**

4. **Select the list name containing the frequency values and press (enter) (see the second and third screens in Figure 19-8).**

You cannot graph categorical split data as a bar chart or pie chart.

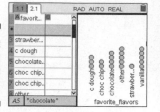
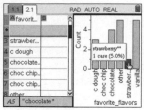
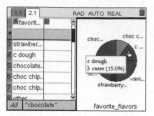

Figure 19-7:
Graphing
categorical
data.

Figure 19-8:
Graphing
data given
in categori-
cal split
form.

Manipulating Single-Variable Data

TI-Nspire allows for two-way manipulation of data. This means that you can
change values in the Lists & Spreadsheet application and watch a Data &
Statistics graph update automatically. Likewise, you can click and drag dot
plot points, histogram bins, and box plots and observe updates in the corresponding numerical data.

Plotted values, such as the mean, update automatically as well.

Manipulating dot plots

The first two screens in Figure 19-9 show the result of moving the point corresponding to a value of 36 to a location with a value of 46. Remember, to grab
a point, move the cursor to the point and press (ctrl)(⊙). Then use the NavPad
keys to move the point and press (enter) to release it.

In the third screen, I selected and moved two points. To select multiple points,
click each point individually. Then press (ctrl)(⊙) to grab and move them as you
wish. To deselect points, move to open space on the screen and press (⊙).

Press (ctrl)(esc) to undo a manipulation.

You can also change numerical values and observe changes to the graph.

Referring back to Figure 19-1, this data is generated by typing commands in the header row (the header row is denoted by the ♦ symbol). You cannot manipulate the graph of a data set that is dependent on a formula located in the header row. However, you can manipulate graphs in which formulas are located directly in the cells of the spreadsheet.

Figure 19-9:
Mani-
pulating a
dot plot.

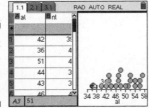
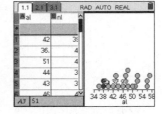

One note of caution: If you manipulate data generated from formulas, the formulas are deleted and replaced with their numerical values.

Manipulating histograms

Figure 19-10 shows the result of grabbing a bin containing one value and dragging it to a bin containing four values. The bin corresponding to values from 38 – 42 is now empty and the bin corresponding to values from 42 – 46 contains five values. You can be assured that the data values contained in the Lists & Spreadsheet application have changed as well.

You may need to change your window settings after manipulating a histogram.

Figure 19-10:
Mani-
pulating a
histogram.

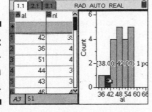
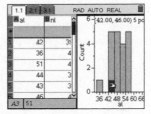

Manipulating box plots

You can grab and move any of the four quartiles contained in a box plot. The first screen in Figure 19-11 shows that I've pressed (ctrl)(☞) and grabbed the second quartile. The number 43.00 displayed on the screen corresponds to the lowest data value contained within this quartile.

In the second screen in Figure 19-11, I used the NavPad keys to translate all the points contained within this quartile 48.94 – 43 = 5.94 units to the right. Press (enter) to complete the translation and release the quartile.

Figure 19-11: Manipulating a box plot.

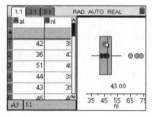 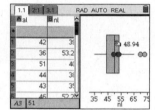

Chapter 20

Working with Two-Variable Data

··

In This Chapter

▶ Graphing scatter plots of two-variable data contained in the Lists & Spreadsheet application

▶ Using a variety of tools to explore scatter plots

▶ Working with dynamic regressions

▶ Understanding the differences between using Graphs & Geometry and Data & Statistics to analyze two-variable data sets

··

*I*n Chapter 19, I talk about single-variable data. In this chapter, I feature two-variable data sets. Two-variable data sets are represented by scatter plots, which are displayed in the Data & Statistics application much the same way as the Graphs & Geometry application does. In addition to graphing scatter plots of two-variable data, I showcase some of the tools available in the Data & Statistics application that help you get the most out of your graphs.

I also discuss some of the pros and cons related to choosing to use the Data & Statistics application rather than the Graphs & Geometry application to represent two-variable data.

Creating an x-y Statistical Plot

Once again, I refer back to the U.S. population data contained in Table 15-1. I have opened a new document and entered the *year* versus *U.S. population* data into the first two columns of a Lists & Spreadsheet page. The first column, titled *year*, represents years after 1900. The second column, titled *uspop*, gives the corresponding U.S. population in millions.

Using Quick Graph

Highlight both columns and choose (menu)⇨Data⇨Quick Graph. This action automatically splits the page and adds a Data & Statistics application with the *x-y* plot of the *year* versus *uspop* data. See the first screen in Figure 20-1.

Graphing on a separate page

To graph this scatter plot to a separate page, follow these steps:

1. **Enter the data on in a Lists & Spreadsheet page.**

2. **Choose (⌂)⇨Data & Statistics (or press (ctrl)(1) and select Data & Statistics from the available choices).**

3. **Move your cursor to the Click to Add Variable region at the bottom of the screen, press (?) to view the available lists, highlight *year*, and press (enter).**

4. **Move your cursor to the Click to Add Variable region at the left side of the screen, press (?) to view the available lists, highlight *uspop*, and press (enter).**

See the second and third screens in Figure 20-1.

Figure 20-1:
Creating an
x-y scatter
plot.

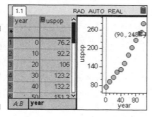 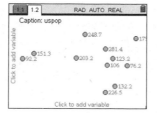 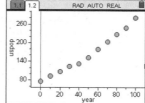

Notice in the first screen in Figure 20-1, I can move the cursor to any point and press (?) to reveal its coordinates.

Exploring x-y Scatter Plots

In this section, I talk about many of the options and tools available for use with an *x-y* scatter plot.

Changing the plot type

The two ways to view a two-variable data in the Data & Statistics application: as an *x-y* scatter plot or as an *x-y* line plot. The *x-y* line plot is identical to the scatter plot except that adjacent points on a scatter plot are joined with a segment.

Choose (menu)⇨Plot Type⇨XY Line Plot to switch to an *x-y* line plot.
Choose (menu)⇨Plot Type⇨Scatter Plot to revert back to an *x-y* scatter plot.
Alternatively, move your cursor to the plot and choose (ctrl)(menu)⇨Connect Data Points or (ctrl)(menu)⇨Hide Connecting Lines.

Adding a movable line

The data in my *x-y* scatter plot looks nearly linear (although an exponential function provides a better fit). To add a movable line to a graph, choose (menu)⇨Analyze⇨Add Movable Line.

Here are three ways to manipulate a movable line:

- ✔ **Perform a translation:** Move the cursor to the center of the line until the ✛ symbol appears. Press (ctrl)(⸱) to grab the line, and use the NavPad keys to translate it. This action changes the *y*-intercept of the line.

- ✔ **Perform a rotation:** Move the cursor away from the center of the line until the ↺ symbol appears. Press (ctrl)(⸱) to grab the line, and use the NavPad keys to rotate it. This action changes the slope of the line.

- ✔ **Lock the *y*-intercept at zero:** Choose (menu)⇨Analyze⇨Lock Intercept at Zero to lock the *y*-intercept at zero. If you choose to lock the *y*-intercept at zero, the movable line can only be rotated. Choose (menu)⇨Analyze⇨Unlock Movable Line Intercept to unlock the *y*-intercept.

Figure 20-2 shows the movable line feature in action.

Figure 20-2:
Manipu-
lating a
movable
line.

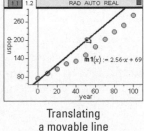

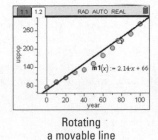

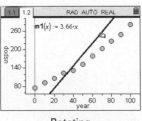

Translating
a movable line

Rotating
a movable line

Rotating
with a locked intercept

TIP

Notice that the movable line is stored to the variable m1(x). This variable is available for analysis anywhere within the same problem.

Showing residual squares

Choose (menu)⇨Analyze⇨Residuals⇨Show Residual Squares to view the residual squares of movable line (see Figure 20-3). Each square has sides whose length equals the difference between the y-value of a given data point and the corresponding y-value on the movable line.

The sum of the areas of the residual squares is also displayed on the screen. The *least squares regression line* is the line for which the sum of the residual squares is minimized. Click and grab the movable line and try to obtain as small a sum as possible.

Try choosing (menu)⇨Analyze⇨Residuals⇨Show Residual Plot. As shown in the last screen in Figure 20-3, this action produces a scatter plot of the residuals. Don't forget to try dragging the movable line to observe the corresponding changes to the residual plot.

Figure 20-3:
Manipu-
lating a
movable
line.

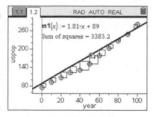
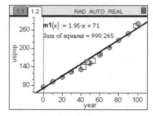
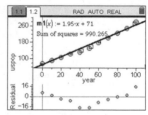

Show Residual Squares   Minimize the sum   Show Residual Plot

TIP

Move your cursor to the movable line and press (ctrl)(menu) to bring up the context menu. This gives you to the choice of removing the movable line and hiding or showing the residual squares and the residual plot.

Performing regressions

Choose (menu)⇨Analyze⇨Regression to view a list of available regressions (the same list that is available in the Lists & Spreadsheet applications). Select Show Linear ($mx + b$) or Show Linear ($a + bx$) to view the least squares regression line for the data set. This is a good feature to use after experimenting with a movable line.

The regression line associated with the U.S. population data is shown in the first screen in Figure 20-4. The second screen shows that I can add residual squares and a residual plot to a regression equation. The third screen shows that I can choose (menu)⇨Analyze⇨Graph Trace to trace along a graph.

Figure 20-4:
Performing
a linear
regression
on the U.S.
population
data.

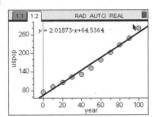 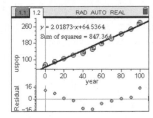 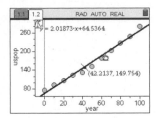

You can have multiple regressions and/or a movable line displayed on the same scatter plot. Click each graph to highlight it and to reveal its equation. Furthermore, if you choose to reveal the residual squares or the residual plot, only the residuals associated with the current selected graph are displayed. Click a different graph to view its residuals.

Plotting a value

As with single-variable data sets, I can plot a value on a scatter plot that is displayed as a vertical line perpendicular to the *x*-axis at a point equal to the specified value. To access the Plot Value feature, choose (menu)⇨Analyze⇨Plot Value. At the prompt, type the value (or expression that yields a numerical value) and press (enter) to draw the vertical line associated with the value.

You can plot a single number or an expression that equals a number. Statistical values such as mean or standard deviation are good choices for the Plot Value feature.

To remove a plotted value, move the cursor over the vertical line and choose (ctrl)(menu)⇨Removed Plotted Value.

Plotting a function

As I mention earlier, the best fit for the U.S. population data is an exponential function. To graph a function, choose (menu)⇨Analyze⇨Plot Function. Enter the function at the prompt, and press (enter) to view the graph.

Adding a slider

To get really fancy, try adding sliders to your graph (choose
(menu)⇨Actions⇨Insert Slider). In the first screen in Figure 20-5, I created two
sliders, one to manipulate the value of *a* in the function *y* = *abx* and one to
manipulate the value of *b* in the function *y* = *abx*. See Chapter 9 for more
information about using sliders.

In the second screen in Figure 20-5, I have invoked the Plot Function tool and
typed the function **a·b***x* at the prompt. The boldface letters indicate that I
am working with the stored variables defined in my sliders. The third screen
in Figure 20-5 shows my attempt to drag these sliders in order to get a nice
match for the data set.

Figure 20-5:
Plotting a
function
with a
slider.

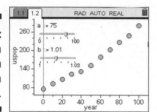 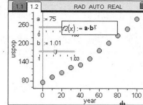 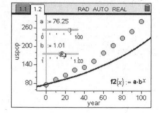

Shading under a function

Choose (menu)⇨Analyze⇨Shade Under Function to shade under a function. Then
follow these steps:

1. **Move the cursor to a desired location and press ⊚ to set the left
   bound of the shaded region.**

   Observe the dotted line and the number indicating the current *x*-value
   location.

2. **Move the cursor to a desired location and press ⊚ to set the right
   bound of the shaded region.**

3. **A shaded region appears along with a number representing the area
   of the region.**

   Click and drag the left or right side of the shaded region to change the
   endpoints. See Figure 20-6.

Figure 20-6: Finding the area under a curve.

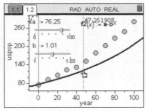
Set the left bound

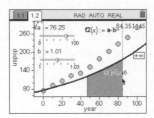
Set the right bound

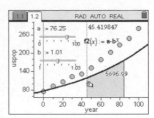
Adjust the region

Adjusting your window settings

Choose (menu)⇨Window/Zoom⇨Window Settings to manually change the XMin, XMax, YMin, and YMax values. Remember to press (tab) to move through each field, and press (enter) at any time to close the dialog box.

Personally, I think TI-Nspire does a great job coming up with a good initial window to fit a data set. However, sometimes the manipulation of a graph or data set results in window settings that are no longer appropriate. Choose (menu)⇨Window/Zoom⇨Data to let TI-Nspire adjust the window settings for you.

Finally, choose (menu)⇨Window/Zoom⇨Zoom @nd In (or Zoom – Out) to access the Zoom – In or Zoom – out tool. Position the cursor on an area of the graph you want to zoom in (or zoom out) and press (⊙). Continue pressing (⊙) to zoom in or out some more. When finished, press (esc) to exit the zoom tool.

Move your cursor to some open space on a graph, and choose (ctrl)(⊙)⇨Zoom for quick access to the Window/Zoom menu.

Try moving your cursor to the horizontal or vertical axis. Press (ctrl)(⊙) to grab an axis, and use the NavPad keys to change the scale. Only the selected axis changes.

Manipulating Two-Variable Data

As with single-variable data, you have the option of changing data values in the Lists & Spreadsheets application and dragging points directly on a scatter plot. Keep in mind that the two-way communication established between these two applications allows for changes in one environment to be reflected in the other.

Changing list values

If you decide to change or add a value(s) to your spreadsheet, go right ahead. Your Data & Statistics graph updates automatically. Just highlight a cell, type a new value, and press ⏎ to put the change into effect.

You can also add data to the end of a list. For example, the U.S. population data from this U.S. population example goes up to the year 2000 ($x = 100$). The total U.S. population in the year 2007 was approximately 301 million. To add this data to the existing lists, simply type 107 in cell A12 (the first available cell in Column A) and 301 in cell B12. The scatter plot updates automatically. Don't forget to change your window settings to see this new point.

Dragging points in Data & Statistics

Move your cursor over a scatter plot point until the ﹂ symbol appears and press ⓒⓣⓡⓛ ⓧ to grab the point. Use the NavPad keys to move the point to another location on the screen and press ⓔⓢⓒ to release the point. As you move the point, take note of the changing coordinates.

To move multiple points, click each point individually. Then press ⓒⓣⓡⓛ ⓧ to grab and move them as you wish. To deselect points, move to open space on the screen and press ⓧ.

All changes resulting from dragging points are reflected in the Lists & Spreadsheet applications to which the current Data & Statistics application is linked.

Dynamic regressions

To observe the real power behind manipulating a scatter plot, try moving one or more x-y points while the graph of a regression equation is displayed.

In the first screen in Figure 20-7, I drag a point whose current coordinates are (2.064, 1.551). As this point moves the regression equation automatically updates. That is, the graph moves and the displayed equation changes. The coordinates of this point also change in the corresponding Lists & Spreadsheet application.

To select multiple points, click each point individually. Then press ⓒⓣⓡⓛ ⓧ to grab and move them as you wish (as shown in the second screen in Figure 20-7). To deselect points, move to open space on the screen and press ⓧ.

In the third screen, I choose ⓜⓔⓝⓤ➪Analyze➪Residuals➪Show Residual Squares. This gives me the option of observing changes to the residuals as I move points on the scatter plot.

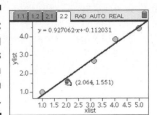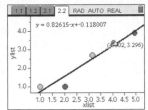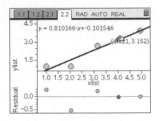

Figure 20-7: Dragging points tied to a regression equation.

By why stop there! Try grabbing and moving a point on the residual plot and watch the corresponding change to the scatter plot as shown in Figure 20-8. This adds another level of interactivity to an already dynamic graph.

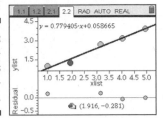

Figure 20-8: Manipulating points on a residual plot.

Choose ⓒⓣⓡ Ⓡ➪Zoom➪Zoom – Data if you need to readjust your window settings.

Investigating Scatter Plots in Graphs & Geometry versus Data & Statistics

As you read this chapter, you may wonder why you would ever use the Graphs & Geometry application to graph and analyze a two-variable data. Here are two reasons why you may choose to use the Graphs & Geometry application over the Data & Statistics application.

✔ **Function graphing and analysis:** Although the Data & Statistics application offers several tools to analyze graphed functions (for example, Graph Trace, Shade Under Function), the Graphs & Geometry offers several additional options not available in Data & Statistics. For example, the Graphs & Geometry application enables you to translate and stretch graphs as well as add a function table, perform calculations, construct a locus, transfer measurements, and so on.

✔ **Geometry tools:** The Graphs & Geometry application allows you to add geometric objects to an Analytic Window including lines, segments, circles, tangents, and so on. For example, perhaps you want to add a tangent to a graph for the purpose of exploring rate of change. This option is only available in the Graphs & Geometry application. The Graphs & Geometry application also gives you the option of working in the combined Plane Geometry View and Analytic View.

The Data & Statistics application also has several advantages over the Graphs & Geometry application, especially if the focus of your work is related primarily to statistical analyses.

I encourage you to give these ideas some consideration. Also, with a bit of practice using both applications, you will surely gain a better understanding of which application best suits your needs.

Chapter 21

Data Collection

・・

In This Chapter

▶ Understanding the data collection process

▶ Conducting experiments automatically or manually

▶ Understanding how the Data Control Console works

▶ Using the Data Control Console application menu to customize experiments

・・

TI-Nspire has the capability of collecting real-time data by attaching a variety of compatible sensors to either the handheld device or directly to a computer running TI-Nspire Computer Software. For example, you can attach a temperature sensor to your device (or computer) and collect time versus temperature data at a rate and duration specified by you.

In this chapter, I focus primarily on the collection of motion data (via a motion detector) but you can be assured that the methods and procedures that I describe for this detector can be easily adapted for use with any sensor. I also tell you about the compatible sensors that work with TI-Nspire and how to customize experiments to suit your specific needs.

An Overview of the Data Collection Process

Data Collection works in conjunction with the Graphs & Geometry, Lists & Spreadsheet, and Data & Statistics applications. That is, if you are working within any one of these three applications, you can launch the Data Collection utility and start collecting data. Here's a brief overview of how to conduct a data collection experiment:

1. Attach a compatible sensor to a TI-Nspire device or a computer running TI-Nspire Computer software.

2. Select an application from which to run the experiment. Or, configure a page with two or more applications.

3. Manually configure the Data Collection Console or choose to work with the default sensor settings.

4. Run the experiment.

5. Analyze the results, which are given graphically (a scatter plot), numerically (lists of data from the experiment), or both.

At the conclusion of an experiment, you have the option of saving the data and running a new experiment or running a new experiment and overwriting the existing data.

Compatible Sensors

At the time of this writing, TI-Nspire is compatible with more than 30 different sensors including sensors that measure electric charge, gas pressure, light intensity, pH, sound, temperature, and voltage. Additionally, the following interface devices work with TI-Nspire:

✔ **Vernier Go!Link:** This device provides an interface between a computer and compatible Vernier sensors.

✔ **Vernier EasyLink:** This device provides an interface between the TI-Nspire handheld device and compatible Vernier sensors.

I focus on the Texas Instruments CBR2 Motion Detector in this chapter. Again, you can be assured that the methods and procedures associated with the use of the other compatible sensors are nearly identical to those described in this chapter.

Conducting Experiments

Consider that you want to collect data on a bouncing ball. Your interest is in observing the successive heights of each bounce of the ball. Figure 21-1 illustrates the setup of this activity.

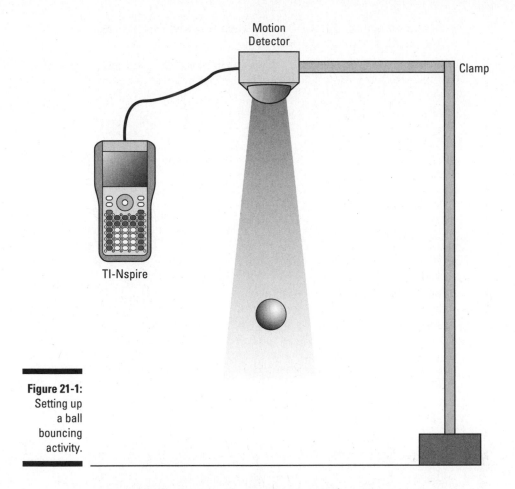

Figure 21-1:
Setting up
a ball
bouncing
activity.

Initiating an experiment using automatic launch

Compatible sensors initiate the data collection process automatically when connected to a TI-Nspire handheld device or a computer running TI-Nspire. After setting up the configuration in Figure 21-1, follow these steps to collect data from the experiment:

1. **Connect the motion detector (or other compatible probe) to the TI-Nspire device using a USB cable.**

   The sensor automatically initiates the data collection process.

2. **Select an application to view the data as shown in the first screen in Figure 21-2.**

   The selected page opens (in this case, a Graphs & Geometry page) with the Data Control Console located on the page as shown in the second screen in Figure 21-2.

By default, the Data Control Console is active. You know this because an inactive Data Control Console appears semitransparent. Press ⓒᵗʳˡ ⓣᵃᵇ to toggle between the current application and the Data Control Console. When the Data Control Console is active, press ⓣᵃᵇ to move around between the various fields.

3. **Press ⏎ to run the experiment.**

   Data is collected at a default interval and duration for the given sensor. The Texas Instruments CBR2 Motion Detector collects data every 0.05 seconds for 5 seconds. This corresponds to 100 data points.

   I chose to view collected data in the Graphs & Geometry application. As the experiment runs, a scatter plot is graphed in real time and the window settings are automatically configured to view the data (see third screen in Figure 21-2). A similar result occurs when you use the Data & Statistics application. With the Lists & Spreadsheet application, data is collected and displayed automatically in four lists: `dc01.time` (time data), `dc01.dist1` (distance), `dc01.vel1` (velocity), and `dc01.acc1` (acceleration).

Figure 21-2:
Results of bouncing ball activity displayed in the Graphs & Geometry application.

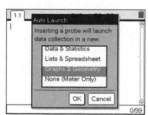 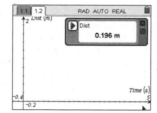 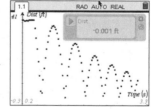

Data is displayed only in real time for sampling rates of 20 samples per second or lower. This experiment collects exactly 20 samples per second (1 ÷ 0.05 = 20), which allows viewing the data in real time. For sampling rates that exceed 20 samples per second, data is collected and displayed at the end of the experiment.

Because of the location of the motion detector, maximum distances are recorded when the ball hits the ground. I used the Zero and Reverse option to give maximum distances when the ball is *closest* to the motion detector.

This gives the same effect it would if the motion detector were on the ground pointing up at the bouncing ball. I discuss the Zero and Reverse features more toward the end of this chapter.

Figure 21-3 shows how this same experiment looks if I choose to view the experimental data in the Lists & Spreadsheet application and the Data & Statistics application.

Figure 21-3:
Results of
bouncing
ball activity
displayed
in the Lists
& Spread-
sheet and
Data &
Statistics
applica-
tions.

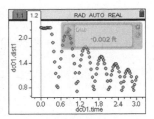

Lists & Spreadsheet   Data & Statistics
application   application

Repeating an experiment

To repeat an experiment, follow these steps:

1. **Activate the Data Control Console (press ⟨ctrl⟩⟨tab⟩) and press ⟨tab⟩ to select the Start/Stop button (if necessary).**

2. **Press ⟨enter⟩ to initiate a new experiment.**

3. **A dialog box opens, prompting you to store the current data, discard the current data, or cancel the operation altogether. Here's what happens when you choose the Store and Discard options.**

   • **Store:** If you select this option, a second dialog box opens indicating the names given to the lists that contain the stored data from the first experiment.

   In Graphs & Geometry, a second scatter plot appears with the original scatter plot when the Store option is selected. The scatter plot attributes are changed to help differentiate between the two scatter plots. In the Data & Statistics application, you must move the cursor to the label for each axis and select the lists associated with the most recent experiment. Finally, a new data set collected in the Lists & Spreadsheet application is stored to the first available columns.

- **Discard:** If you select this option, the original data set is overwritten with the new data set. You cannot retrieve the original data set if you choose to discard data.

4. **Press ⬡ to conduct the new experiment.**

Initiating an experiment manually

If the Data Control Console is closed, you need to initiate data collection manually. The Data Control Console may be closed for a variety of reasons. For example, if you insert a new problem within the same document (see Chapter 2 for more information about inserting problems to your documents), the Data Control Console will not be in view.

To manually insert the Data Control Console, choose ⓒⓣⓡⓛ⬡⇨Insert⇨Data Collection. You can also insert the Data Control Console using the shortcut key sequence ⓒⓣⓡⓛⒹ.

When the Data Control Console is in view, you can run an experiment by following the same steps as outlined in the section "Initiating an experiment using automatic launch" earlier in this chapter.

Working with the Data Control Console

You can press ⓣⓐⓑ to move around the Data Control Console. As you can see, four different areas comprise the Data Control Console (five if you are using Events with Entry or Selected Events).

The first image in Figure 21-4 shows the Data Control Console with the Start/Stop icon highlighted. When an icon is highlighted, you can press ⬡ to activate the icon.

When the measurement display area is highlighted, press ⓒⓣⓡⓛⓜⓔⓝⓤ to access the context menu associated with this region. The context menu associated with the motion detector includes Zero, Reverse, m (change units to meters), and ft (change units to feet). I talk more about the features contained in this context menu later in the chapter.

The third image shows the Change View icon highlighted. When this icon is highlighted, press ⬡ to minimize the Data Control Console as shown in the last image in Figure 17-4. Press ⬡ again to maximize the Data Control Console.

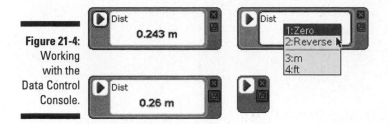

Figure 21-4:
Working with the Data Control Console.

Customizing Your Experiments

In this section I talk about a number of ways you can configure experiments to your specifications.

Working with more than one application on a page

Sometimes, it's nice to view data both graphically and numerically. Here's how to run the bouncing ball experiment on a split page with both a Graphs & Geometry and Lists & Spreadsheet application.

1. **Open a new Graphs & Geometry page.**

2. **Choose** (ctrl)(⌂)⇨**Page Layout**⇨**Select Layout**⇨**Layout 2.**

3. **Press** (ctrl)(tab) **to activate this new application.**

4. **Choose** (menu)⇨**Add Lists & Spreadsheet.**

5. **Press** (ctrl)(D) **to open the Data Control Console.**

6. **With the Data Control Console active, choose**
   (menu)⇨**Experiment**⇨**Display Data In**⇨**App(s) on Current Page.**

   This step ensures that you see the data (both graphically and numerically) as it's being collected.

7. **Press** (enter) **to run the experiment.**

Figure 21-5 shows the results of the ball bounce experiment with this split screen configuration.

You can split the screen even more to display the results of an experiment on three or four applications.

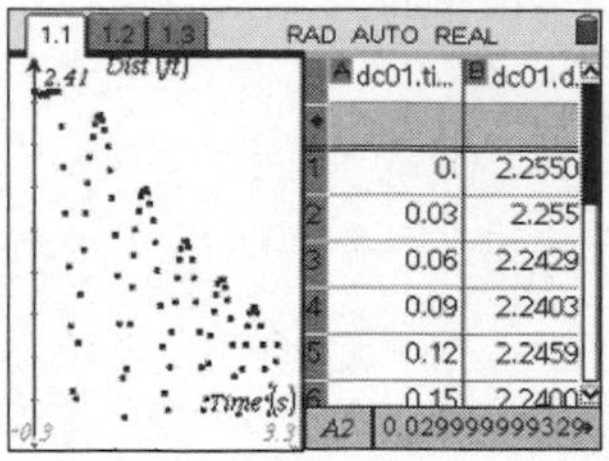

Figure 21-5: Running an experiment with two applications on the same screen.

Choosing (menu)⇨Experiment⇨Display Data⇨App(s) on Current Page allows you to view data in all applications on the current page. The Display Data option also enables you to view data on a new Data & Statistics page, Graphs & Geometry page, or Lists & Spreadsheet page. Select any of these options, and a new page opens in the selected application along with the Data Control Console.

Working with the Data Control Console application menu

You may have noticed in the previous section that the Data Control Console comes with its own application menu. To access this application menu, the Data Control Console must first be active.

The Data Control Console is inactive if it appears semitransparent. Press (ctrl)(tab) to toggle between the current application(s) and the Data Control Console.

Press (menu) to access the Data Control Console application menu.

A variety of options in the Data Control Console application menu allow you to customize your experiments. I talk about some of these features in the next two sections.

Configuring your sensor settings

Each sensor comes with its own default settings. For example, the Texas Instruments CBR2 Motion Detector is configured to collect data every 0.05 seconds for five seconds.

To change these settings, Choose (menu)⇨Experiment⇨Set Up Collection⇨Time Graph. A dialog box opens with two fields: Time Between Sample (s) and Experiment Length (s). The units for each of these values are in seconds. Type your new values and press (enter) to put them into effect.

To determine the number of samples, divide the Experiment Length by the Time Between Samples.

Notice two other options are in the Set Up Collection submenu: Events with Entry and Selected Events. Here are descriptions of each of these options:

- ✔ **Events with Entry:** This option allows you to capture data manually and specify a value for the independent variable. Open the Data Control Console and follow these steps to use this feature:

  1. **Choose (menu)⇨Experiment⇨Set Up Collection⇨Events with Entry.**

  2. **Press (enter) to start the experiment.**

     This activates the Keep icon on the Data Control Console.

  3. **Press (enter) to capture a data point (or choose (menu)⇨Experiment⇨Keep).**

     A dialog box opens with a prompt to enter a value for the independent variable to be associated with this captured data value.

  4. **Enter a value and press (enter) to complete the operation.**

     If you have configured experiment to display the data in the current application, the captured data appears.

  5. **Continue capturing data until finished. Press (tab) until the Start/Stop icon is highlighted and press (enter) to stop the experiment.**

     Figure 21-6 shows the results of using the Events with Entry feature.

Figure 21-6:
Capturing data using the Events with Entry feature.

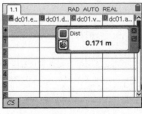

The Data Control Console with the Keep icon

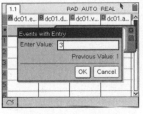

Select a value for the independent variable

Event with Entry results

- ✔ **Selected events:** This option also allows you to capture data manually. Each selected value is automatically paired with a number, starting with one and incrementing by one each time you collect a new data point. Here are the steps to follow:

  1. **Choose (menu)⇨Experiment⇨Set Up Collection⇨Selected Events.**

  2. **Press (enter) to start the experiment.**

     This activates the Keep icon on the Data Control Console.

3. **Press ⊛ to capture a data point (or choose (menu)⇨Experiment⇨Keep).**

   If you have configured the experiment to display the data in the current application, the captured data appears with 1 as the value of the independent variable and the associated data value as the dependent variable.

4. **Continue pressing ⊛ to capture additional data.**

   The independent variable increments by one each time you capture a new data point.

5. **Press (tab) until the Start/Stop icon is highlighted and press ⊛ to stop the experiment.**

Additional feature of the Data Control Console application menu

Here are a few other notable features associated with the Data Control Console application menu:

- ✔ **Choose (menu)⇨Sensors to access the Sensors submenu.** Here are brief descriptions of the features available in this submenu:

  - **Zero:** This feature sets the current sensor measurement to zero. For example, if the motion detector is currently pointing at a wall located 2 meters away from the sensor, this distance is set to zero. All subsequent measurements are exactly 2 meters less than their actual distance.

  - **Reverse:** This setting changes the sign of all measurements. Positive values become negative and negative values become positive.

  - **Change Units:** This setting allows you to change the measurement units. For example, you can use the Change Units menu to change the motion detector units from meters to feet.

- ✔ **Choose (menu)⇨Data to access the Data submenu.** Here are brief descriptions of the features available in this submenu:

  - **Store Run:** This feature stores the data from the current run. When you access this feature, a dialog box opens indicating the names given to the lists that contain the stored data. You observe a similar effect if you choose to run a new experiment and select the Store option.

  - **Clear All Data:** This feature allows you to clear all data from previous experiments. A dialog box opens with a warning prompt. Press (tab)⊛ to clear the data.

- ✔ **Choose (menu)⇨View⇨Small to minimize the Data Control Console. Choose (menu)⇨View⇨Large to maximize the Data Control Console.**

Part VI
The Notes Application

The 5th Wave   By Rich Tennant

"You can sure do a lot with a TI-Nspire, but I never thought dressing up in G.I. Joe clothes and calling it your little desk commander would be one of them."

In this part . . .

This part covers the last, but not least, of TI-Nspire's five core applications. I show you how the Notes application can be used to add continuity to your documents and virtually eliminate the need to include separate paper instructions or questions with your TI-Nspire documents. You see that the TI-Nspire Notes application really does complete the document structure.

I also discuss how the Default, Q & A, and Proof templates contained in the Notes application can take your documents to a whole new level.

Chapter 22

The Why and How of Using Notes

. . . .

In This Chapter

▶ Understanding how the Notes application can enhance your documents

▶ Using the three available Notes templates for greater flexibility

. . . .

*I*n this chapter, I introduce the Notes application. I talk about how Notes comprises an integral component of an entire document, and I give you some suggestions as to how you can use Notes to customize activities to suit your exact needs.

Using Notes to Complete the Document Model

Mathematical concepts can be represented in multiple ways, and TI-Nspire does a great job accommodating these different representations. The Calculator application is well-suited for *algebraic* representations. The Graphs & Geometry and Data & Statistics applications provide *graphical* and *geometric* representations. The Lists & Spreadsheet application specializes in the *numeric* representations.

Finally, the Notes application allows for the *written* or *verbal* representation of mathematical concepts. Taken together, the five core TI-Nspire applications can be used to create dynamically linked documents that allow users to see math in multiple ways.

In many ways, the Notes application is the perfect complement to the other four TI-Nspire applications. For example, if you are a teacher writing an activity for use by students, the Notes application can be used to interject instructions. This eliminates the need for paper notes to accompany activities. The Notes application also provides a place for teachers to pose questions and for students to type their responses.

Here is a summary of three keys ways to use the Notes application:

✔ As the name suggests, the Notes application is a place to interject notes within a document. It can be used to give instructions such as "Advance to the next page and graph a function that …." This is a great way to enhance the continuity of a document. It also eliminates the need for instructions on paper.

✔ The Notes application provides a place to pose and answer questions. In a classroom setting, students can type their responses directly into the Notes application. At the conclusion of an activity, students can save their work and submit it to the teacher. Now the teacher has complete electronic documentation of student work.

✔ Sometimes, teachers use the Notes application in conjunction with a paper worksheet. Students may follow instructions or prompts contained within the Notes application and use a worksheet to provide paper documentation of their thoughts and ideas as well as answers to specific questions. This is a good option for those educators who prefer to keep student work and assessments in paper form. Perhaps the result of an activity may end up in a journal.

As you see in the next section, the Notes application comes with the tools to allow users to use Notes to customize their documents for a variety of purposes.

Finding Out Which Template Is for You

The Notes application includes three templates from which to choose. In this section, I describe each of these templates and give you some reasons why these templates are used.

The Default template

From within an existing document, choose ⌂⇨Notes to open a new Notes page. Alternatively, press ctrl ① and select Add Notes from the list of available options.

The Notes application opens in the Default template as shown in the first screen in Figure 22-1. This is the most commonly used template, and it resembles a blank sheet of paper.

The second screen in Figure 22-1 shows how the default page is typically used to provide instructions and enhance the continuity of a document. The third screen is included for reference.

Figure 22-1:
Using the
Default tem-
plate to built
a complete
document.

 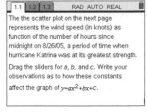 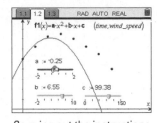

The Default template   Adding instructions   Carrying out the instructions

Notice the italicized font in the second screen in Figure 22-1. I talk about how to customize fonts in Chapter 23.

The Q & A template

Choose (menu)⇨Template⇨Q&A to access the Q&A template. As this name implies, this template is used to pose and answer questions.

The first screen in Figure 22-2 shows the Q&A template with a question contained in the top portion of the screen. To move the cursor to the answer portion of the screen, press (tab) three times. If there is no text in the question area, you only need to press (tab) twice. You can then type your response as shown in the second screen in Figure 22-2.

Notice the symbol located near the middle of the screen. Press (tab) until you move from the question region and activate this control. Press (enter) to collapse the answer region; this is a good option if you want to include the answer but keep it hidden from view. This icon changes to when the answer region is hidden from view. Activate the expand/collapse control and press (enter) again to expand the answer region.

Figure 22-2:
The Q & A
template.

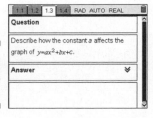 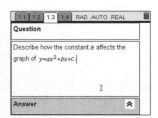

Pressing (tab) moves you from the question region to the Hide/Show tool to the answer region and then back to the question region. Press (shift)(tab) to move in the reverse direction.

The Proof template

Choose (menu)⇨Template⇨Proof to access the Proof template.

In the first screen in Figure 22-3, I configured a page with the Notes application on the left (Default view) and the Graphs & Geometry application on the right (Plane Geometry view). This serves to present the problem, with a related sketch, to be proved.

In the second screen in Figure 22-3, I have opened a Notes page and configured it for the Proof template. As you can see, I've included some statements and reasons.

In the third screen in Figure 22-3, to complete the proof, I've asked a student to fill in the missing statements and reasons.

Figure 22-3:
The Proof A template.

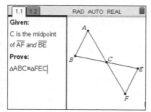

It's okay for the length of a proof to extend beyond the viewable region. If so, a scroll bar appears on the right side of the screen.

As you can see in Figure 22-3, I've included several symbols with my proof. See Chapter 23 to learn more about changing fonts and inserting special symbols.

Chapter 23

Taking Notes to a Whole New Level

In Chapter 22, I used a variety of different fonts. I also included some symbols, particularly with the Proof template.

In this chapter, I show you how to work with special text styles and characters. You also find out about some other tools available in the Notes application, including a tool that allows you to evaluate expressions, as you can do in the Calculator application.

Formatting Text

A range of font styles and symbols can be added to your Notes pages. Many of the symbols that are used in Notes are accessed through the Symbol palette (by pressing (ctrl)(▦)). Other symbols, as well as font choices, are available directly from the application menu associated with the Notes application.

Selecting text

Standard text is the default font used in the Notes application. As you type words, you can be assured that they appear without bold, italics, subscript, or superscript.

Perhaps you have typed some text and you want to go back and change a word or phrase to add emphasis. To accomplish this task you first select the text that you want to reformat. Here are the steps to follow:

1. **Move the cursor to the beginning or end of the word or phrase you want to change.**

2. **Press and hold the ⟨ᴬ⟩ key.**

3. **Press the ◄ or ► keys on the NavPad to drag the highlight over the entire word or phrase.**

Choosing a text format

To change the font of selected text, choose (menu)⇨Format and select the desired text style. Figure 23-1 shows the different text styles available in the Notes application.

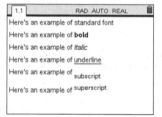

Figure 23-1: Working with different text formats.

1.1	RAD AUTO REAL

Here's an example of standard font
Here's an example of **bold**
Here's an example of *italic*
Here's an example of underline
Here's an example of subscript
Here's an example of superscript

You can change text format as you type. Just choose (menu)⇨Format and select a text style. Text that you type after the current cursor location appears in this new style.

You may have noticed that there is no menu option to revert back to standard font. Instead, you turn off the current style you are working with. Consider, for example, that you have just finished typing a word in **bold** and want to switch back to standard font. Choose (menu)⇨Format⇨Bold to turn off the bold font. This action automatically puts you back in standard font.

Inserting special characters

A variety of geometric shape symbols are located within the Notes application. These shapes are particularly helpful when working with the Proof template.

To access these geometric shapes, choose (menu)⇨Insert⇨Shape and choose the appropriate symbol. The first screen in Figure 23-2 shows each of the symbols available in the Shapes menu.

Each time you access these shapes, a small dashed box appears around the shape. Any text that you type immediately after invoking a shape is contained in this box with the symbol. This is particularly helpful when using the line, segment, ray, and vector shapes because your text appears underneath each of these symbols. Press the ▸ key to move out of the dashed box and resume normal typing.

A multitude of other mathematical symbols are available via the Symbol Palette. As shown in the second screen in Figure 23-2, press (ctrl)(⌂) to access this palette, scroll through and highlight your choice, and press (⏎) to paste it into the Notes application.

Figure 23-2:
Using the
Shapes
menu and
the Symbol
Palette.

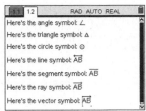 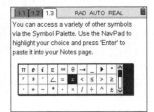

Inserting and Evaluating Expressions

Choose (menu)⇨Insert⇨Math Expression Box to type a mathematical expression in the Notes application. Alternatively, press the shortcut key sequence (ctrl)(M) to access the Math Expression Box option.

When you invoke the Math Expression Box tool, a dashed box opens and you can type your expression within this box. Press the ▸ key to move out of the dashed box and resume normal typing.

 Pressing some keys, such as (⌂), automatically opens a Math Expression Box.

 Text contained in a Math Expression Box is italicized, just as in the Calculator application. However, some text (such as *delvar*) appears non-italicized, indicating that you have typed a system function.

Sometimes it's helpful to evaluate a mathematical expression in the Notes application. In the first two screens in Figure 23-3, I have used the Math Expression Box tool to type an expression that gives the exact value of the golden ratio. I copied and evaluated this expression to give the corresponding decimal approximation.

Here are the steps that I followed to accomplish this task:

1. Type the expression using the Math Expression Box tool.

2. **Select, copy, and paste the expression.**

    You now have two copies of the expression.

3. **Place the cursor anywhere in the copied expression box and choose** (menu)⇨**Actions**⇨**Evaluate.**

Keep in mind that you do not need to make a copy of an expression to evaluate it. However, each time you evaluate an expression, the result replaces the expression.

You can also evaluate a part of an expression. Refer to the second line in the second screen in Figure 23-3, where you see I have typed a numerical expression and highlighted the fractional portion. I then choose (menu)⇨Actions⇨Evaluate Selection. The result is shown in the last screen in Figure 23-3.

Figure 23-3:
Using
the Math
Expression
Box tool and
the Evaluate
tool.

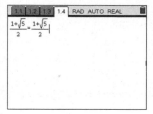 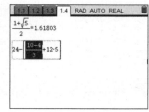 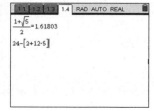

Inserting Comments

To insert a comment, Choose (menu)⇨Insert⇨Comment and select Teacher or Reviewer. This tool offers a nice way to distinguish comments from text within the Notes application.

Figure 23-4 shows an example of how the comment feature can be used in the Q & A template. Notice that I can format text within a comment for added emphasis.

Figure 23-4:
Inserting
comments.

Part VII

TI-Nspire Computer Software

The 5th Wave   By Rich Tennant

I'm mathematically dyslexic. But it's not that unusual — 100 out of every 15 people are.

In this part . . .

This part gets into how TI-Nspire's two software applications are used to support and enhance your TI-Nspire handheld experience. You'll find out how the free TI-Nspire Computer Link software application establishes communication between your handheld and a computer. This connection allows you to manage and transfer files as well as take screen shots of your device, back up files, and upgrade your handheld's operating system.

I also discuss the optional TI-Nspire Computer software application and give plenty of reasons why you might want to consider adding this product to your bag of tricks.

Chapter 24

TI-Nspire Computer Link Software

TI-Nspire Computer Link software establishes a connection between your computer and your TI-Nspire (or TI-Nspire CAS) handheld device. This connection allows you to transfer documents, capture images of your handheld screen, back up files, and update the operation system of your device.

As you read this chapter, you should gain an appreciation for why this software is such an indispensable tool.

Downloading and Installing a TI-Nspire Computer Link

The TI-Nspire Computer Link software can be downloaded for free from TI's Web site. Just go to www.ti-nspire.com and click the link for Connectivity Software. Alternatively, you can install TI-Nspire Computer Link from the product CD that came with your device.

 After you launch the installation file, I recommend that you select the default destination folder for the program. A shortcut is automatically placed on your computer desktop, unless you deselect the check box during the installation process.

 TI-Nspire Computer Link software only works with TI-Nspire and TI-Nspire CAS. Use TI-Connect software to establish computer connectivity with other TI products such as TI-84 and TI-92.

Making the TI-NSpire and Computer Connection

To establish a connection between your computer and TI-Nspire, follow these steps:

1. **Locate the black USB cable that came with the device. Plug the standard USB end into your computer and the small (Mini-B) end into the top of the TI-Nspire handheld. Press firmly.**

2. **Turn on the TI-Nspire handheld device.**

3. **Double-click the TI-Nspire Computer Link software icon.**

4. **A list of all connected TI-Nspire devices appears, as shown in Figure 24-1. Highlight a device and click Select.**

   You can only communicate with one handheld at a time.

Figure 24-1:
Selecting
a handheld
device.

The Explorer Window

By default, TI-Nspire Computer Link opens in the Explorer window as shown in Figure 24-2. The top half of the Explorer window contains the Computer File Browser. On the left, you dig through folders and subfolders using standard browsing techniques. The contents of a selected folder are displayed on the right side of the Computer File Browser.

The bottom half of the Explorer window contains the TI-Nspire File Browser. This window shows the contents of your handheld device. This browser works exactly the same as its computer browser with one notable exception: Folders on your TI-Nspire cannot contain subfolders. Click any folder to display its contents on the right side of the screen.

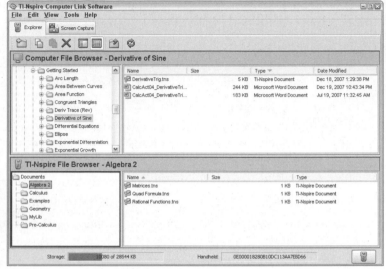

Figure 24-2:
The
TI-Computer
Link
Explorer
window.

 Notice the small icon of a TI-Nspire device located in the bottom-right corner of the Explorer Window. Click this icon to re-open the Select Handheld dialog box. Use this option if you want to switch from one connected handheld to another.

Here are a couple of other features you find in the Explorer view:

✔ Choose View⇨List View (or the associated toolbar button) to view a list of only the filenames.

✔ Choose View⇨Detail View (or the associated toolbar button) to view a list of filenames as well as additional details including Type and Date Modified.

✔ Choose View⇨Hide Folder View to hide the outline view of folders on the left side of the Explorer window.

✔ Choose View⇨Show Folder View to reveal the outline view of folders on the left side of the Explorer window (this is the default view).

Performing .tns file transfers

When you create a file on your TI-Nspire handheld device or via TI-Nspire Computer software, a .tns extension is automatically appended. However, you do not see this extension when viewing documents on your handheld.

Use the Explorer window to transfer .tns files from your computer to your handheld device and from your handheld device to your computer. Simply click a .tns file and drag it from the Computer Browser to the TI-Nspire File Browser or vice-versa.

To copy a document by dragging, follow these steps:

1. **Click the file you want to copy. This file can reside on your computer or handheld device.**

2. **Drag the file to the desired destination.**

   Referring to Figure 24-2, consider that I want to drag the file DerivativeTrig.tns from the Computer File Browser to my handheld device. If I drag this file to the right side of the TI-Nspire File Browser, it is located in the folder called Algebra 2. If I drag this file to the left side of the TI-Nspire File Browser, I have the option of dropping it into one of five folders: Algebra 2, Dummies, Examples, Geometry, or MyLib.

3. **The transfer happens automatically.**

   A dialog box opens on your handheld indicating a file was transferred or received. See the first two screens in Figure 24-3.

   As the third screen in Figure 24-3 suggests, TI-Nspire prompts you when you try to copy a file to a location in which a file with the same name exists.

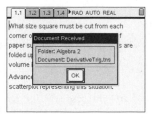
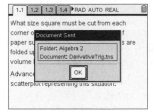

Figure 24-3: Copying files.

Press and hold down the Ctrl key on your computer to select multiple files for copying. To separate .tns files from other files, click the Type heading in the Computer File Browser.

You can also copy a file by highlighting the file and choosing Edit⇨Copy. Move the cursor to the destination area and choose Edit⇨Paste to copy the file.

With the exception of .fig files created with Cabri II Plus, only .tns files can be transferred to your device. If you try to copy an unsupported file, you are greeted by the message "One or more unsupported files were encountered. Only supported files were transferred."

Managing folders and files on your handheld

In addition to copying files, you can also use the Explorer window to manage files and folders.

To rename any file or folder, right-click the file (or folder) and select Rename. Type a new name for the file (or folder) and press Enter.

To create a new folder on your handheld device, highlight the Documents folder in the TI-Nspire File Browser and choose File➪New Folder. Type the name for your new folder and press Enter.

Folders cannot be created within folders on the handheld device.

To delete a file on your handheld, highlight the filename in the TI-Nspire File Browser and choose Edit➪Delete. Click Yes at the warning prompt or No if you decide not to delete the file.

You cannot Undo a file deletion.

Capturing TI-Nspire Screen Images

 Click the Screen Capture tab to switch to the Screen Capture window. This part of the TI-Computer Link software allows you to take pictures of the screen on your handheld device. Captured screens can then be used in a variety of other computer applications such as word processors. I find this feature quite helpful when typing up instructions for students. As you can probably tell from reading this book, I find Screen Capture to be an indispensable tool!

Capturing a screen

To capture a screen, choose Tools⇨Take Screenshot. Alternatively, use Ctrl+G or click the Screen Capture icon located on the toolbar.

Viewing thumbnails

To view thumbnails of all captured screens, choose View⇨Thumbnails or click the Thumbnails icon on the toolbar.

To view one screen at a time, choose View⇨Single Screen or click the Single Screen icon on the toolbar. In this view, click the Previous Screen and Next Screen icons on the toolbar to scroll through your images. See Figure 24-4.

Figure 24-4:
Viewing
images.

 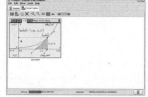

Thumbnail view   Single screen view

Adding and removing borders

By default, screen captures contain a black border around each image. To remove borders, choose Edit⇨Remove Border or click the Remove Border icon located on the toolbar.

To show borders, choose Edit⇨Add Border or click the Add Border icon located on the toolbar.

Copying screen images to other applications

As mentioned earlier, I like to copy screen images for use with a word processor. Here are two ways to copy a screen image to another application.

You can copy by dragging, as follows:

1. **Resize the TI-Computer Link screen and the destination application screen so that both are in view.**

2. **Click the image in the Screen Capture window.**

3. **Drag the image to the destination application.**

Or you can copy by using Ctrl+C, as follows:

1. **Click the image in the Screen Capture window.**

   Selected images are enclosed in a red border.

2. **Choose Edit⇨Copy or press Ctrl+C to copy the image to the clipboard.**

3. **Click the other application and set the cursor to the location where you want to copy the image.**

4. **Click Ctrl+V to paste the image to the application.**

Click the Zoom In and Zoom Out icons to change the size of your screen captures. Copied or saved images retain the current size.

Saving screen images to the computer

Individual screens can be saved in .TIFF, .GIFF, or .JPEG formats. Here are the steps to follow to save a screen image to your computer:

1. **Click a screen image to save.**

2. **Choose File⇨Save Selected Screen(s) if you have not previously saved the screen or File⇨Save Selected Screen(s) As if you want to save a previously saved screen with a different name or location.**

3. **When the Save as dialog box opens, browse to a location to save the image, type a filename, select the appropriate file format, and then click the Save button.**

To save the entire group of screens, each as a single image file, choose File⇨Save All Screens. Each screen is saved with a default filename.

Backing Up Your TI-Nspire Handheld

TI-Nspire Computer Link software makes it easy to back up your handheld device. Knowing that all files contained on your handheld are copied, with a time stamp, to your computer gives you peace of mind.

Using one-click backup

When you install TI-Nspire Computer Link software on your computer, a folder called `TI-Nspire` is saved to your My Documents folder. Within this folder reside several other folders, including a folder called `Backups`. This is the destination folder for your one-click backup files.

To perform a one-click backup, choose Tools⇨One Click Backup. A dialog box opens which displays the progress of the backup. At the conclusion of the backup, the prompt "The backup operation was successful" appears. Click OK to complete the backup procedure.

If you look in your `TI-Nspire/Backups` folder, you find a file such as `TI-Nspire080721065836.tnb`. This filename gives the year, month, day, hour, minute, and second of the backup — talk about precise! So, for this example, I backed up my device on July 21, 2008 at 6:58 (and 36 seconds) in the morning.

Backing up to a specific folder

If you want some control over the destination and filename associated with your backup, choose Tools⇨Backup. When you select this option, a dialog box opens, prompting you for a filename. You can also browse and select a location to save your backup file.

As for the file itself, it contains the exact same information as the one-click backup file.

Using backup to restore your device

To restore your device, choose Tools⇨Restore.

The dialog box shown in Figure 24-5 opens with a warning about losing unsaved data. Click Yes to restore the device or No to cancel the operation. After clicking Yes, a dialog box opens that shows the progress of the backup. When the restoration finishes, you see the message shown in the second screen in Figure 24-5. Click OK to complete the operation.

Figure 24-5:
Restoring
your hand-
held device.

Restoration warning   Restoration complete

Any files that reside on your handheld device that were not present during the last backup are permanently deleted during the backup process. This includes all unsaved files.

Updating Your TI-Nspire Device

Texas Instruments periodically upgrades the operating system associated with your handheld device. These upgrades are free and very much worth installing. For example, the Insert Slider feature contained in the Graphs & Geometry and Data & Statistics application was not available with the original TI-Nspire software release. Being a big fan of sliders, I had to construct one each time I wanted to use this feature. By updating my device, I was able to take advantage of this and many other features.

You have two options when it comes to updating your handheld:

✔ Update from the Web.

✔ Update from a file.

To update from the Web, follow these steps:

1. **Establish a connection between your handheld device and TI-Computer Link software.**

2. **Choose Tools⇨Check for Web Updates.**

3. **The software checks the Web for a newer version of the OS currently installed on your device.**

   If one is found, you are prompted to update your device or cancel the operation. You also have the option to save a copy of the OS to your computer to a default location or the location of your choice.

4. **Click Update to update the device or Cancel to cancel the operation.**

5. **Accept the terms of the license agreement and initiate the update.**

6. **Click Yes at the warning prompt or No to cancel the operation.**

   The update may take several minutes.

7. **After the update finishes, a message appears telling you that the OS has been successfully transferred to the handheld. Click OK to complete the process.**

   The first time you use your TI-Nspire handheld device after an update, you are taken through a setup process, much like the one when you turned on your device for the first time.

To install a new operating system from a file, follow these steps:

1. **Establish a connection between your handheld device and TI-Computer Link software.**

2. **Choose Tools⇨Install OS.**

3. **Browse your computer to locate the OS file and double-click the file.**

4. **Follow Steps 4 through 7 from the previous list.**

When you update your TI-Nspire numeric device, all apps (except for those that came pre-loaded on the TI-84 keypad), data, and settings associated with the TI-84 keypad are erased. To avoid losing this data, use TI-Connect to back up your TI-84 keypad. You can use TI-Connect again to restore the TI-84 after upgrading the TI-Nspire software.

Chapter 25

TI-Nspire Computer Software

. . . .

In This Chapter

▶ Understanding the benefits of using TI-Nspire Computer Software

▶ Discovering the basics: Launching the software, creating and editing documents, managing files

▶ Deciding which view best suits your needs

▶ Adapting what you know about TI-Nspire handhelds to TI-Nspire Computer Software

. . . .

*T*I-Nspire Computer Software (and TI-Nspire CAS Computer Software) is a computer application that enables you to experience the same functionality contained on your TI-Nspire device in a computer environment.

When you purchase a TI-Nspire handheld device, you have the option of purchasing a single TI-Nspire device or the TI-Nspire device bundled with the companion TI-Nspire Computer Software. You can also purchase TI-Nspire Computer Software as a separate product.

Unlike the TI-Nspire Computer Link software, this software is not free. However, as you see in this chapter, you have several reasons to consider purchasing TI-Nspire Computer Software.

Do not confuse TI-Nspire Computer Software with TI-Nspire Computer Link software. TI-Nspire Computer Link is a free download from TI's Web site and allows you to perform file management, take screen captures, back up your device, and upgrade the operating system. See Chapter 24 for more information about TI-Nspire Computer Link software.

For the remainder of this chapter, I refer to the numeric TI-Nspire Computer Software, not TI-Nspire CAS Computer Software. Keep in mind, however, virtually no difference exists between these applications when you are trying to master them.

Three Great Reasons for Using TI-Nspire Computer Software

Whether you are a student using TI-Nspire or an educator, you have several reasons to opt for acquiring TI-Nspire Computer Software. Here are my top three reasons:

✔ **Time savings:** With TI-Nspire Computer Software, you can create a document on your computer and transfer it to your handheld device using TI-Nspire Computer Link software. Working on your computer gives you the advantage of using a full QWERTY keyboard. Additionally, your computer mouse replaces the NavPad on the handheld device. As much as I like the NavPad, it simply does not compare with the mouse from a speed standpoint. And speed is very desirable when working with documents that contain complex constructions and lots of text. As you see later in this chapter, files created on your computer have exact compatibility with those created on your handheld.

Here are two more reasons for considering using TI-Nspire Computer Software, both of which apply more to educators rather than to individual users.

✔ **Classroom demonstration:** More and more classrooms are being equipped with computers and projection systems. If you have this technology available to you, then TI-Nspire computer software can be projected to the entire class. This is a good option if you want to demonstrate a concept to your students. Or, perhaps your students may have the same document on their handheld devices. You can project the document to the class from your computer for the purpose of summarizing the activity or to provide students with some instruction as they work through the activity.

✔ **Computer lab:** If you are lucky enough to have a computer lab available in your school, you may want to consider purchasing several copies of TI-Nspire Computer Software. Students can use TI-Nspire Computer Software to create their own documents or to work with a document created by the teacher. At the conclusion of the period, these documents can be e-mailed to the teacher or student or saved to a storage device. Or, students can transfer their work to their handheld device (via TI-Nspire Computer Link software) and finish their work at home.

Connect-to-Class and TI-Navigator

TI has two other products that allow for the quick transfer of `.tns` files to your students.

Using Connect-to-Class software, files can be transferred to up to 14 students at a time. This software also enables teachers to delete student files and to upgrade their devices. A USB hub with multiple ports is used to create the handheld-to-computer connection.

TI-Navigator for TI-Nspire is a souped-up version of Connect-to-Class. This software uses a wireless system to communicate with all students in a classroom. TI-Navigator can perform the same tasks as Connect-to-Class and contains several other features that allow teachers to engage students in a variety of interactive activities.

Both of these products work very well with TI-Nspire Computer Software.

Installing TI-Nspire Computer Software

Before purchasing TI-Nspire Computer software, I recommend you download a free 30-day trial from TI's Web site. Just go to www.ti-nspire.com and click the Downloads and New OS Upgrades link.

TI-Nspire

To install a purchased version of TI-Nspire Computer Software from a CD, insert the CD and follow the prompts. I recommend that you select the default options that pop up during the installation process. A shortcut is automatically placed on your computer desktop, unless you deselect the check box during the installation process.

Launching TI-Nspire Computer Software

In this section, I show you two ways to launch TI-Nspire Computer Software:

✔ **Creating a new document:** Double-click the TI-Nspire Computer Software icon to launch TI-Nspire Computer software. An untitled document opens, with a prompt to select an application, as shown in Figure 25-1. To select an application, click the words Click Here to Add an Application and select one of the five TI-Nspire applications from the list.

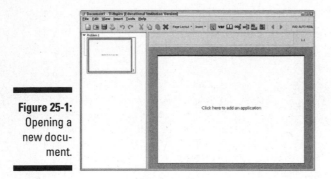

Figure 25-1:
Opening a new document.

In Figure 25-2, I show you a typical TI-Nspire Computer application screen with annotations describing its various components.

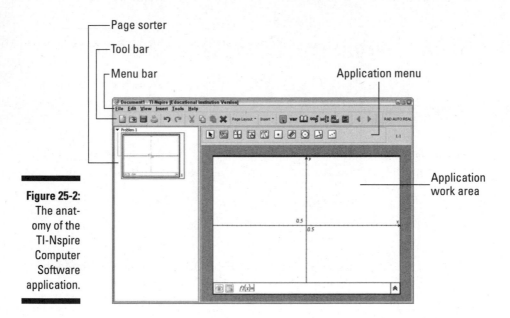

Page sorter

Tool bar

Menu bar

Application menu

Application work area

Figure 25-2:
The anatomy of the TI-Nspire Computer Software application.

✔ **Opening an existing document:** To open an existing TI-Nspire document, locate the file on your computer and double-click it.

The .tns extension convention

Sample.tns

All TI-Nspire files are identified by a `.tns` file extension. This extension is only viewable if the file resides on your computer and cannot be seen in the My Documents view on your handheld device.

While browsing for files on your computer, consider using the Detail view. By clicking the Type heading, all files are sorted by type, allowing you to quickly spot those that have a .tns extension.

Where to get your .tns files

Here are four ways a .tns file may end up on your computer:

- ✔ **You transfer a file from a handheld device to your computer using TI-Nspire Computer Link software.**

- ✔ **You create a file using TI-Nspire Computer Link software and save it to your computer.**

- ✔ **You mine the Internet (especially education.ti.com) for .tns files created by someone else and download them to your computer.** Why do the work if someone else has already done it?

- ✔ **A friend or colleague e-mails a .tns file to you as an attachment.**

Managing Files

TI-Nspire Computer Software manages files in a way that is virtually identical to any computer-based application. If you have some experience working on a computer, then by all means, skip this section.

Saving a document

To save a document that has not been previously saved, choose File⇨Save or click the save icon located on the toolbar. Type a filename and determine the location to which you want to save the document. See Figure 25-3.

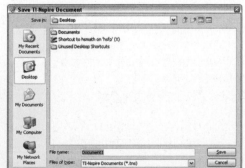

Figure 25-3:
The Save
Document
dialog box.

After saving a document, periodically press Ctrl+S to save your work to the same filename and location. Keep in mind that this process overwrites the last saved version of the current document.

To save your document to a new location or with a different name, choose File⇨Save As and follow the same steps I just described.

The Windows file management system

You can manage files located on your computer using the Windows file management system. That is, you can rename, copy, paste, delete, and so on, just as you do with other files that reside on your computer. Most of these options are available using the *right-click* feature. Move your cursor over a .tns file, click the right button on your mouse, and select an option.

Are you noticing the similarities between your computer and your TI-Nspire handheld? Not only are there similarities in terms of how you manage files, as you see later in this chapter, but much of what you have learned about your TI-Nspire handheld applies to TI-Nspire Computer Software as well. This is no coincidence, considering both environments produce compatible files.

TI-Computer Software Views

In this section, I talk about the three ways to view files in the TI-Nspire Computer Software application. I also make sure to let you know the advantages that each of these views has to offer.

The Normal (default) view

TI-Nspire Computer Software opens new or existing TI-Nspire documents in the Normal (or default) view. If you are not planning to send your file to a handheld, this is a very good choice of views. I like to use this view to project files using the computer projector when doing classroom demonstrations.

As can be seen in Figure 25-4, the Normal view offers quite a bit of space with which to work. In fact, this view is the likely choice if you want to include four applications on a single page.

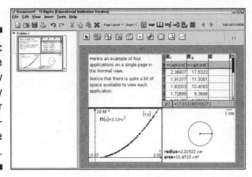

Figure 25-4:
Using the
Normal view
to display
up to four
applica-
tions on one
page.

TI-Nspire Handheld view

Choose View⇨Handheld Screen to view an image of a document exactly as it looks when viewed on the handheld device. As you can see from Figure 25-5, this view offers much less room to work. In fact, if I create a document in the Normal view and then switch to the Handheld view, I usually need to spend quite a bit of time resizing objects to fit the screen.

However, this is by far the best choice of views to work with if you plan on eventually transferring your file to a TI-Nspire handheld device. You can expect that what you see on your computer screen in this view is exactly how it looks on a handheld device.

If I am creating an activity for my students to use on their handhelds, this is the view I must use. Additionally, I often use this view when projecting to the whole class if my students are simultaneously working on the same document on their handhelds. I want them to see the same thing at the front of the classroom that they see on their handhelds.

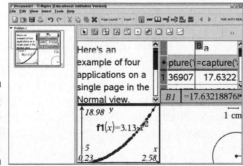

Figure 25-5:
The
Handheld
view.

Presentation view

Referring to Figures 25-4 and 25-5, notice the Page Sorter located on the left side of the screen. Choose View⇨Presentation to hide the Page Sorter. Choose View⇨Presentation again to turn off the Presentation view and reveal the Page Sorter.

The Presentation view always displays in handheld screen mode.

Transitioning to the Computer

The transition from working on your handheld to working on your computer is quite seamless. In this section, I point out some of the key differences. However, I also encourage you to open a new document and start playing around with it. You'll likely find these key differences for yourself in short order. And you'll see that these differences allow you to complete tasks with the computer software even more efficiently than on a handheld device.

Using your mouse

I mention earlier in this chapter that your computer mouse replaces the NavPad on your handheld. Here are some key tasks that you can perform with a mouse and a brief description as to how these tasks differ when performed on the handheld.

- ✔ **Click and drag.** This is probably the most obvious difference. On the computer, move your mouse to an object, press and hold the left button on your mouse to select the object, and move the mouse to manipulate it. On your handheld, you must use the NavPad to move the cursor to an object, press ⒸⓉⓇⓁⒼⓇⒶⒷ to grab it, and use the NavPad again to manipulate the object.

  To release an object on the computer, just release the left button on the mouse. To release an object on your handheld, press the ⒺⓈⒸ key.

- ✔ **Right-click.** As you know, I'm a big fan of the right-click context menu. To access the context menu on the computer, move to an object or area and click the right button on your mouse. On your handheld device, use the NavPad to move to an object or area and press ⒸⓉⓇⓁⓂⒺⓃⓊ.

- ✔ **Accessing menu items.** Whether you are accessing Page Tools or Application menu items, just move your mouse to the menu item and click to activate it or to view drop-down menu items. On the handheld device, you must press ⓂⒺⓃⓊ, ⓗⓞⓜⒺ, or ⒸⓉⓇⓁⓂⒺⓃⓊ to access menu items. Then use the NavPad and the ⓖ or ⓔⓝⓣⒺⓡ keys to activate the command.

Other items (such as the catalog) can be accessed quickly by clicking buttons located on the toolbar.

✔ **Performing a Custom Split.** If you have two or more applications on a screen, move the cursor to the border of an application until the ✛ or ✚ symbol appears. Then click and drag to change the split. On your hand-held device, choose ⌨(ctrl)⌨(⌂)⇨Page Layout⇨Custom Split to activate this tool. Then use the NavPad to adjust the layout.

Managing problems and pages

Part I of this book covers everything you need to know about how to manage problems and pages on your TI-Nspire handheld. Rather than repeat this information, in this section I highlight some of the key differences that you find when performing similar tasks using the TI-Nspire Computer Software.

On your handheld device, press ⌨(ctrl)▲ for a Page Sorter view of a problem. With TI-Nspire Computer Software, the Page Sorter is located on the left side of the screen. Referring to Figure 25-6, the Page Sorter reveals thumbnail pictures of the four pages that comprise Problem 1. Notice that this document contains two problems. To reveal the contents of Problem 2 in the Page Sorter, just double-click Problem 2. Double-click a second time on a problem number to hide its contents.

You may also notice that Page 2 of Problem 1 is displayed in full view on the right side of the screen. Click any page in the slider sorter to bring the page into full view. To perform work in the full page area, you must move the mouse to the full page view and click once.

To change the page order, click and drag a page in the Page Sorter and drop it to a new location.

Here is a brief description of a variety of additional tasks related to the management of problems and pages.

✔ **Insert Page:** Choose Insert⇨Page (or use the shortcut key sequence Ctrl + I) to insert a new page after the current active page. Then, select the application for the page you insert.

If you know the type of application you want to add to your new page, click Insert and select the desired application for the page.

✔ **Insert Problem:** Choose Insert⇨Problem to insert a new problem after the current active problem. You are prompted to select an application for the first page of the new problem.

✔ **Delete a Page or Problem:** Select a page or problem in the Page Sorter view and choose Edit⇨Delete.

✔ **Cut, Copy, or Paste a page:** Select a page from the Slider Sorter view and choose Edit⇨Cut or Edit⇨Copy. A copy of the page is stored to the clipboard. Choose Edit⇨Paste to paste the page elsewhere. Pasted pages are always inserted after the current selected page.

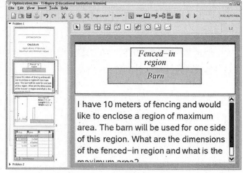

Figure 25-6: Using the Page Sorter to manage pages and problems.

Using the Virtual Keypad

Choose View⇨Keypad to open the Virtual Keypad shown in Figure 25-7. As the name suggests, the keys on the Virtual Keypad are active, and you can use them to create or edit a document. It's also a good visual aid if you want to point out the physical location of certain keys to your students.

Figure 25-7: The Virtual Keypad.

As you can see in Figure 25-7, the top four buttons (ⓔˢᶜ, Ⓣⁱᵃᵇ, ⌂, ᵐᵉⁿᵘ) are missing as is the NavPad. Your mouse certainly takes the place of the NavPad. The ⓔˢᶜ and Ⓣⁱᵃᵇ keys are replaced by the equivalent keys on your computer keypad. The ⌂ and ᵐᵉⁿᵘ keys are missing because the menus associated with these keys are located on the menu bar and toolbar of the TI-Nspire Computer Software window. I talk more about accessing these menus in the next section.

Here's another thing to keep in mind about the Virtual Keypad. Because I know it so well, I often choose to use it to access items that are a bit tricky to find (or I don't have the patience to try to find them). Consider, for example, the Store Variable operator (⊠). To access this symbol on the Virtual Keypad, just click ⓒᵗʳˡ sᵗᵒʳᵉ. To find this symbol without using the Virtual Keypad, choose Tools⇨Symbols (or click the Symbols icon on the toolbar) to open the Symbol Palette as shown in Figure 25-8. Scroll down to find the Store Variable operator and press Enter to paste it to your application.

Figure 25-8:
Accessing
symbols
without
the Virtual
Keypad.

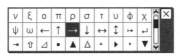

Accessing menus, catalog items, templates, and symbols

In this section, I talk about how to find any menu item, catalog item, template, or symbol.

The application menus for all five TI-Nspire applications are shown in Figure 25-9. Depending on the current active application, you see one of these five application menus. Hover the cursor over any application menu icon to reveal the name of the item. For each application menu shown in Figure 25-9, I've expanded a menu item to reveal its contents. Take, for example, the Calculator application menu in the first image in Figure 25-9. I've clicked the Probability menu icon to reveal its contents.

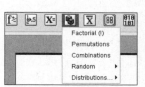

The Calculator application
with the Probability menu
expanded

The Graph & Geometry application
with the Measurement menu
expanded

The Lists &
Spreadsheet
application
with the
Actions menu
expanded

Figure 25-9:
The Five
TI-Nspire
Computer
Software
application
menus.

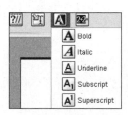

The Notes application
with the Format menu
expanded

The Data & Statistics
application with the
Actions menu expanded

The Catalog menu is accessed by choosing Tools⇨Catalog (or by pressing the Catalog icon located on the toolbar). Everything about the Catalog is identical to what you see on the handheld device. You can move through different fields using the mouse rather than pressing the ⓣᵃᵇ key.

From within the Catalog you can access the Math Templates and the Symbol Palette. Alternatively, you can access the Math Template by choosing Tools⇨Math Template (or press the Math Template icon on the toolbar) and the Symbol Palette by choosing Tools⇨Symbols (or press the Symbols icon on the toolbar).

Part VIII
The Part of Tens

The 5th Wave   By Rich Tennant

"Of course your current graphing calculator plots graphs, solves equations, and is programmable. But does it shoot silly string?"

In this part . . .

This part is one of my favorite sections of the book. Here I get to pull together a bunch of great ideas (in packages of ten) as well as some warnings about what to watch out for. These great ideas come in the form of ten activities and ten shortcuts that are sure to get you thinking about taking your TI-Nspire experience to the next level.

I also share ten mistakes and issues that I stumbled upon as I acclimated myself to TI-Nspire. It is my hope that you will avoid these same issues by reading this chapter.

Chapter 26

Ten Great Activities That Realize the Power of TI-Nspire

In This Chapter

▶ A preview of ten Action Consequence documents

▶ Searching TI's Web site for more great activities

*A*t the time of this writing, TI-Nspire has just hit the stores. Already, TI's Activity Exchange is full of pre-made activities. Many of these activities contain .PDF and Word files, in addition to the `.tns` device files that end up on your handheld device. These additional files provide suggestions and instructions for using the activities in the classroom. I talk about how to download these activities toward the end of this chapter.

I spend most of this chapter giving you a preview of ten great Action Consequence documents. These documents represent a special resource provided by TI and written by a team of talented educators.

An *Action/Consequence document* is a TI-Nspire file that is dynamically linked and connects two or more objects (perhaps across representations) so that changes in one are immediately reflected in the others. These dynamic links provide:

✔ Settings for mathematical exploration

✔ Immediate visual consequences

✔ Opportunities for prediction

Of course, TI-Nspire provides an authoring platform for you to create your own documents that embrace the action-consequence principle.

Ten Great Action Consequence Documents

Here they are — ten truly powerful Action Consequence documents that are sure to inspire you to use TI-Nspire with your students. As you read this section, you see that these documents really tap into TI-Nspire's strengths using very creative and complex constructions. Don't think for a minute that you can replicate these constructions. Just go ahead and steal them for your own personal use!

Algebraic Number Line

The Algebraic Number Line Action Consequence document is intended to assist students in distinguishing between the input value and the corresponding value of a linear expression. It also helps to distinguish between the acts of evaluating an expression and solving an equation. This activity investigates linear expressions in one and two variables. It involves substituting values for variables, evaluating expressions, and finding solutions to a linear equation. Students select points on a number line via a slider and observe changes in the value of an expression.

Figure 26-1 contains some screen images from the .tns file that accompanies this activity. The following list contains a brief description of each image as well as some intriguing questions.

- ✔ **Figure 26-1a:** Drag the slider to change the input value, x. As you do so, observe that, as x increases by 1, the value of the expression increases by 4. Try to find a value of x that produces a result of 12. Is there another value of x that also produces a result of 12?

- ✔ **Figure 26-1b:** Drag the slider and observe the corresponding results from the two expressions. How do the values of each expression change as x is incremented by 1? Find a value of x that makes both expressions equal.

- ✔ **Figure 26-1c:** Drag the sliders for both x and y and observe the values of the two-variable expressions. Can you find a pair of x-y values for which the two expressions are equal? Can you find a different x-y pair that makes both expressions equal?

Figure 26-1:
The
Algebraic
Number
Line activity.

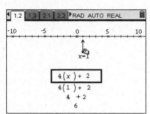 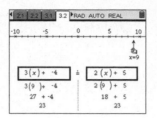 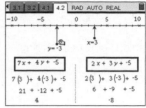

Figure 26-1:
The
Algebraic
Number
Line activity.

The Derivative Explorer

The Derivative Explorer Action Consequence document is intended to help students understand the relationship between a function and its derivative. Students drag a slider in each example and observe and reflect upon the changes to the function and its derivative which results from changes in the focus variable.

Figure 26-2 contains some screen images from the .tns file that accompanies this activity. The following list contains a brief description of each screen image.

- **Figures 26-2a and 26-2b:** The thick graph is the graph of the function $f1(x) = base x$. The thin graph is the graph of the derivative of $f1(x)$. Drag the slider to change the value of the base. What value of the base causes the function and the base to coincide? For what values of the base is $f1(x)$ increasing? Concave up? For what values of the base is the derivative increasing? Concave up?

- **Figure 26-3c:** The thick graph is the graph of the original function and the thin graph is the graph of the derivative. Drag the slider to change the value of a. How is the value of a related to the period of the original graph and the graph of the derivative? How is the value of a related to the amplitude of the original graph and the graph of the derivative?

Figure 26-2:
The
Derivative
Explorer
activity.

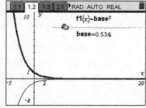 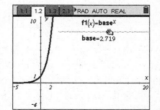 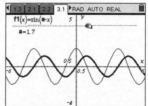

This activity also explores the relationship between $\mathbf{f1}(x) = \mathbf{a} \bullet \sin(x)$ and its derivative where **a** is a slider value.

The Equation Builder

The Equation Builder Action Consequence document is intended to deepen student understanding of the process of solving a linear equation. This activity involves the concept of equation as a balance of two equal quantities. Students drag algebra tiles onto the two sides of a virtual balance in order to build a linear equation. They establish the equality of the two sides by dragging a point (representing the value of x) along the base line until the two sides of the scale are equal. They may then solve the equation by doing the same thing to both sides until they have a simplified form.

Figure 26-3 contains some screen images from the .tns file that accompanies this activity. The following list contains a brief description of each screen image.

- **Figure 26-3a:** Build the equation $5x - 2 = 3x + 4$ by dragging five x-tiles and two −1 tiles to the left side of the scale and three x-tiles and four 1 tiles to the right side of the scale.

- **Figure 26-3b:** Drag the Control Point until the two horizontal lines coincide. This action is the equivalent of balancing the scale.

- **Figure 26-3c:** Drag two 1 tiles to the left and right sides of the scale. Balance is maintained because the same action was taken on both sides. Drag the two −1 tiles and two 1 tiles from the left off the scale. Because the net result of these four tiles is zero, balance is still maintained. Drag three x-tiles from the left and right side of the scale off the scale. Again, balance is maintained. Finally, drag three 1 tiles from the right and one x-tile from the left, the equivalent of dividing both sides by two. The resulting equation, $x = 3$, is balanced and represents to the solution to the original equation.

Figure 26-3:
The
Equation
Builder
activity.

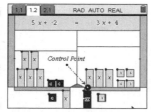 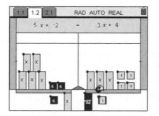 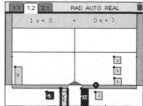

Exploring Box Plots

The Exploring Box Plots Action Consequence document is intended to deepen students' ability to interpret box plots. This activity involves the concept of distributions of data. Students drag a data point and observe the corresponding changes in the box plot and the mean and median.

Figure 26-4 contains some screen images from the .tns file that accompanies this activity. The following list contains a brief description of each screen image.

- ✓ **Figure 26-4a:** A box plot and corresponding dot plot are revealed on the right side of the page. Clicking any part of the box plot reveals the points contained within that part and highlights the same points on the dot plot.

- ✓ **Figure 26-4b:** Click the vertical line on the dot plot to reveal the mean of the data set. Is it possible to grab and move one point on the dot plot to make the mean less than the median?

- ✓ **Figure 26-3c:** Drag points so that there are more points in the upper segment of the box plot than in the lower segment of the box plot. Describe what happens to the box plot when you do this.

Figure 26-4:
The
Exploring
Box Plots
activity.

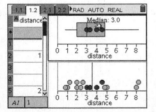 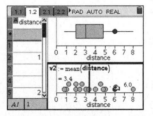 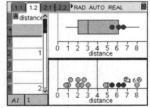

Algebra Expression Builder

The Algebra Expression Builder Action Consequence document is intended to develop student understanding of algebraic expressions. This activity involves the concepts of variable and constant terms, combining like terms, and evaluating algebraic expressions. Students drag algebra tiles onto the *Stage* in order to generate and evaluate algebraic expressions. They first investigate expressions using only positive terms (Problem 1). In Problem 2 the expressions extend to include negative terms, and in Problem 3 the expressions extend to include quadratic terms.

Figure 26-5 contains some screen images from the .tns file that accompanies this activity. The following list contains a brief description of each screen image.

✔ **Figure 26-5a:** Drag tiles onto the stage to create the expression $2x + 3$. What is the value of this expression when $x = 3$? Edit the text and determine the value of the expression when $x = 5$. Add the expression $x + 3$ to the existing expression. What is the resulting expression? How might you represent $2 \cdot (2x + 3)$?

✔ **Figures 26-5b and 26-5c:** Build $2x - 1$ and add $x + 3$. How could you write $2x - 1 + x + 3$ more simply? Drag tiles off the stage to see if you are correct. What does this expression equal when $x = 4$?

Figure 26-5:
The Algebra
Expression
Builder
activity.

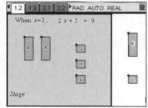
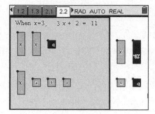
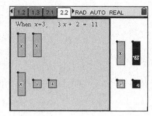

Locus Builder

The Locus Builder Action Consequence document is intended to assist students in understanding that the solution set to an equation of the form $ax + by = c$ can be represented as a set of collinear ordered pairs in the plane. Students drag a point P in the plane searching for solutions to a target linear equation. For each solution found, students press CTRL-dot (.) to drop that point on the plane. They continue to do so until a pattern emerges.

Figure 26-6 contains some screen images from the .tns file that accompanies this activity. The following list contains a brief description of each screen image.

✔ **Figures 26-6a and 26-6b:** This sequence of screens shows the appearance of a set of points that satisfy the equation $2x + 3y = 5$. Make a conjecture about the geometric nature of the solution set. Can you find a solution with abscissa 9? Can you find a solution with ordinate 4?

✔ **Figure 26-6c:** This page allows you to configure your own equation of the form $ax + by = c$ by inputting the values of a, b, and c in the Lists & Spreadsheet cells A1, A2, and A3, respectively. A set of points representing a partial solution set to $-2x + y = 6$ is displayed on the screen.

Figure 26-6:
The Locus
Builder
activity.

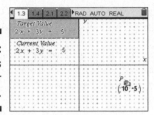
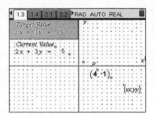
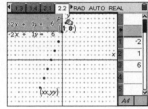

Percentage Builder

The Percentage Builder Action Consequence document is intended to deepen student understanding of percentages and percentage calculations. This activity involves the concept of percentage as a proportional part of a whole. Students drag a point to vary the amount of the smaller part and observe corresponding changes in the percentage part.

Figure 26-7 contains some screen images from the `.tns` file that accompanies this activity. The following list contains brief description of each screen image.

- ✔ **Figure 26-7a:** Drag the point to find 40% of 50 dollars. Write an equation that represents this situation.
- ✔ **Figure 26-7b:** Edit the text box to change *50 dollars* to *60 dollars*. Find 30% of 60 dollars. Which is larger, 40% of 50 dollars or 30% of 60 dollars?
- ✔ **Figure 26-7c:** Drag the point to create a percentage greater than 100%. Describe what happens to the percent model.

Figure 26-7:
The
Percentage
Builder
activity.

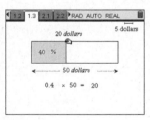
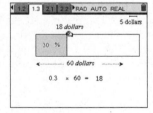
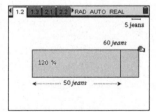

Takeoff of an Airplane

The Takeoff of an Airplane activity allows students to investigate the relationships between acceleration, velocity, and displacement. Acceleration data for a Boeing 737 is used to calculate the plane's velocity as it taxies down the runway. The calculated velocities are then used to determine the plane's displacement during taxiing.

Figure 26-8 contains some screen images from the `.tns` file that accompanies this activity. The following list contains a brief description of each image.

- ✔ **Figure 26-8a:** Time versus acceleration data contained in a Lists & Spreadsheet page is graphed as a scatter plot in a Graphs & Geometry page. The time interval between data points is a constant 0.5 seconds.

- ✔ **Figure 26-8b:** Use the formula $a = \Delta v/\Delta t$ (rewritten as $\Delta v = a \cdot \Delta t$ with $\Delta t = 0.5$) to construct a list with the change in velocity for each time point. The cumSum command is used to add each successive Δv value and store the data in another list which yields total velocity for each corresponding time value. A scatter plot of this data reveals a linear graph.

- ✔ **Figure 26-8c:** Use the formula $v = \Delta s/\Delta t$ (rewritten as $\Delta s = v \cdot \Delta t$ with $\Delta t = 0.5$) to construct a list with the change in displacement for each time point. The cumSum command is used to add each successive Δs value and store the data in another list which yields total displacement for each corresponding time value. A scatter plot of this data reveals a graph that is nonlinear.

Figure 26-8:
The Takeoff
of an
Airplane
activity.

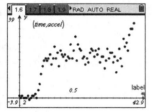 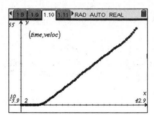 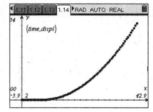

Temperature and Trigonometric Functions

The Temperature and Trigonometric Functions Action Consequence document is intended to deepen student understanding of trigonometric functions. This activity involves the concept of cyclic change as described by a sinusoidal function. Students drag a point to vary the time over a 24-hour period and observe corresponding changes in temperature.

Figure 26-9 contains some screen images from the `.tns` file that accompanies this activity. The following list contains a brief description of each screen image.

- ✔ **Figures 26-9a and 26-9b:** As the point on the *x*-axis is dragged, the time and temperature are displayed as well as the corresponding point on the *x-y* graph. Describe what is happening to the temperature during the day. When is the temperature the warmest? The coolest? How are these temperatures represented on the graph? Find two times during the day when the temperature is the same. How can you tell this from the graph?

> ✔ **Figure 26-9c:** The equation that models the time versus temperature (in degrees Celsius) scenario is displayed.

Figure 26-9:
The Temperature and Trigonometric Functions activity.

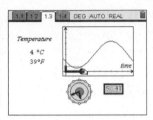 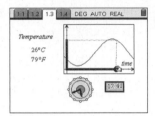 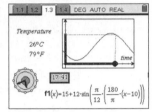

"Proof" without Words

The "Proof without Words" Action Consequence document is intended to deepen student understanding of three important geometric facts. This activity involves the concepts of interior angles of a quadrilateral, the Pythagorean Theorem, and triangles inscribed in a semicircle. Students drag a point on a geometric figure or a slider bar and observe a transformation that represents a geometric property of plane figures.

Figure 26-10 contains some screen images from the `.tns` file that accompanies this activity. The following list contains a brief description of each screen image.

> ✔ **Figure 26-10a:** Each slider in this sketch is dragged to the right. The first slider (Step 1) rotates the top-left and bottom-right triangles to the top-right corner. The second slider translates the triangle located in the bottom left to the top right. The third slider translates the resulting quadrilateral down to the right. As a result of moving the sliders, you see that the sum of the interior angles of a quadrilateral is 360°.

> ✔ **Figure 26-10b:** The darkest regions are originally located in the squares whose sides form the legs of the right triangle. As the indicated point is dragged down, this region morphs into the region shown in Figure 26-10b. Eventually, this region moves to the bottom square and takes the shape of the large square whose side is equal to the hypotenuse of the right triangle. The result of this activity provides visual proof of the Pythagorean Theorem.

> ✔ **Figure 26-10c:** Drag the slider to the top of the segment to rotate the dark-shaded triangle. What inscribed figure is created by the original triangle and its image? What does this say about the original triangle? What important geometric fact does this illustrate?

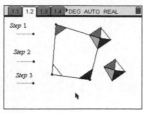  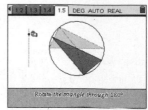

Figure 26-10:
The "Proof"
without
Words
activity.

How to Find and Download More Great Activities

If you are motivated to find more Action Consequence documents or activities like those featured in the previous section, I encourage you to visit TI's Activities Exchange. Here are the steps to follow to find and download an activity:

1. **Go to TI's Web site at** `education.ti.com`.

2. **In the Classroom Activities drop-down list, click Activities Exchange.**

3. **Search for an activity using one of these options:**

   • *Browse by Subject:* Click a broad topic area (such as Algebra II) and select a subtopic (such as Exponential Functions). All the activities associated with this subject area are displayed.

   • *Click the link called TI-Nspire Search:* Activities that specifically use TI-Nspire technology are displayed, although you may have to click through several pages to see them all.

   • *Quick Search:* Type some keys words in the Quick Search field and press Enter to display the activities.

   • *Advance Search:* Click the link for Advanced Search, fill in the information, and click Search to display the activities.

4. **Click the desired activity from the list of displayed activities.**

   You are directed to a page that gives an Activity Overview and a list of downloadable files as well as some other useful information.

5. **If you are searching for a TI-Nspire activity, download the associated .tns file. Also download any additional files, including .pdf and .doc files.**

6. **Transfer the .tns file to your handheld device using TI-Nspire Computer Link software or open the .tns file using TI-Nspire Computer software.**

   Don't forget to read the documentation that accompanies the .tns file.

Chapter 27

Ten Great Tips and Shortcuts

• •

In This Chapter

▶ Using your computer to save time

▶ Other shortcuts that get you where you want to go — faster

• •

No doubt, TI-Nspire is a powerful machine. Fortunately, Texas Instruments has put a lot of effort into developing a keypad, navigational tools, and menu structure that allow you to harness this power and create documents quickly and efficiently.

In this chapter, I talk about some of the additional shortcuts and time-savers that may not be apparent to a new TI-Nspire user. Most of these shortcuts are consolidated from other areas of this book.

One Great Timesaver

There's no substitute for working with a computer. Consider purchasing the TI-Nspire Computer software (or at least download a 30-day free trial of the software). Create your documents using this computer software and transfer them to your handheld device using TI-Computer Link software. Make sure you work in the Handheld Screen view on your computer to ensure consistency when you transfer documents to your handheld. You will save an incredible amount of time, especially if you are just learning TI-Nspire or working with complex constructions.

Seven Sets of Wonderful Shortcuts

In this section, I feature seven sets of additional shortcuts that are sure to improve your efficiency. The first shortcuts are grouped by task and are taken from the resources provided by TI when you purchase your TI-Nspire device. Within each task are several shortcuts associated with that particular task. The last two shortcuts are my own.

Shortcuts for editing text

Here are several editing shortcuts, the same ones that used with most computer applications:

- **Cut:** (ctrl)(X)
- **Copy:** (ctrl)(C)
- **Paste:** (ctrl)(V)
- **Undo:** (ctrl)(Z) (or (ctrl)(esc))
- **Redo:** (ctrl)(Y)

Shortcuts for inserting characters and symbols

These shortcuts help you access some common characters and symbols that are not found on the primary and secondary keys:

- **Display the Symbol Palette:** (ctrl)(⬚)
- **Not equal to (≠):** (ctrl)(=)
- **Underscore:** (ctrl)(◡)
- **Greater than or equal to (≥):** (ctrl)(>)
- **Less than or equal to (≤):** (ctrl)(<)
- **Semicolon (;):** (ctrl)(:)
- **Display the Math Template:** (ctrl)(⬚)
- **Infinity symbol (μ):** (ctrl)(*i*)
- **Dollar sign ($):** (ctrl)(″)
- **Degree symbol (°):** (ctrl)(/)

Shortcuts for managing documents

Here are shortcuts to access the Tools and Context menus as well four shortcuts to help you manage documents:

- **Access the Tools menu:** (ctrl)(⌂)
- **Access the Context menu:** (ctrl)(menu)
- **Create New Document:** (ctrl)(N)

- Insert New Page: (ctrl)(I)
- Select Application: (ctrl)(K)
- Save Current Document: (ctrl)(S)

Shortcuts for navigation

These shortcuts help you move around within pages, problems, and documents quickly and efficiently:

- Move through fields in reverse order: (caps shift)(tab)
- Home: (ctrl)(7)
- End: (ctrl)(1)
- Page Up: (ctrl)(9)
- Page Down: (ctrl)(3)
- Up a level in the hierarchy (such as from Full Page view to Page Sorter view): (ctrl)▲
- Down a level in the hierarchy: (ctrl)▼

Shortcuts for navigating in documents

Use these shortcuts to move from application to application (on the same page), from page to page, and from problem to problem:

- Switch between applications on a split page: (ctrl)(tab)
- Display previous page: (ctrl)◀
- Display next page: (ctrl)▶
- Display page sorter: (ctrl)▲

Shortcuts for wizards and templates

Use these shortcuts when working with matrices, the integral template, and the derivative template:

- Add a column to a matrix: (caps shift)(↵)
- Add a row to a matrix: (↵)
- Definite integral template: (caps shift)(⎙)
- Derivative template: (caps shift)(⎙)

Shortcuts to modify the display

These secondary key shortcuts help you adjust contrast and turn off the device:

- ✔ **Increase contrast:** (ctrl)(+)
- ✔ **Decrease contrast:** (ctrl)(−)
- ✔ **Power off:** (ctrl)(off/on)

And Two Helpful Hints

Here's my two cents' worth . . . no pun intended.

- ✔ **Use the Save As feature:** If you are working on a document, and you want to add something that you are not sure will work out, choose (ctrl)(⌂)⇨File⇨Save As to invoke the Save As command. Choose a different filename, and then try out your idea. If it doesn't work out, choose (⌂)⇨My Documents and open the original file. This brings you back to where you were before you tried out this new idea. The Undo feature is another similar option, but it may take longer to restore your position than the Save As feature.

- ✔ **Search for your idea in TI's Activities Exchange:** In Chapter 28, I showcase 10 great activities. I also tell you how to use the search feature in TI's Activities Exchange to find these and other existing activities. There's a good chance that a downloadable .tns file already exists that performs the task you hope to accomplish. Or, with a little editing on your part, you can configure an existing .tns file to suit your exact needs.

Chapter 28

Ten Common Problems Resolved

1 f you are like me, mistakes are part of the learning process when it comes to getting to know a new tool such as TI-Nspire. Some of the mistakes that you make with TI-Nspire result in an error message. Others mistakes are a bit more insidious — it's not necessarily that you've done something wrong; it's just that the device isn't doing quite what you want it to do. I talk about both types of issues in this chapter. You can also be assured that the material presented in this chapter comes strictly from personal experience. It is my hope that by sharing the issues I dealt with during the learning process, you may be spared some aggravation.

Think Like a Computer, Act Like a Computer

TI-Nspire is so similar to a computer that many of the methods and procedures you have acquired while working on a computer can be applied to TI-Nspire. You can access a variety of shortcuts to work efficiently, navigate documents using a variety of computer-like actions (such as Page Down), and save documents using methods that are virtually identical to those found on a computer.

My favorite computer-like feature happens to be my number-one remedy when it comes to dealing with mistakes: the Undo feature. Just as with a computer, you can press the shortcut key sequence (ctrl)(esc) or (ctrl)(Z) repeatedly to back out through a series of steps. This fixes the majority of problems. At least, it gets you back to a point where you can try a different tactic. If you back out through a series of steps only to realize you were correct, you can use the Redo feature (press (ctrl)(Y)) to move forward through the steps that you've just undone.

Ten Common Problems and Their Remedies

The following subsections contain a list of ten specific errors or problems and their accompanying solutions.

Conflicts between the independent variable *x* and variables containing *x*

Consider that you have just created a slider for the purpose of investigating the effect that *b* has on the graph of $y = x^2 + bx + 1$. You configure the slider and type $x^2 + bx + 1$ next to the first available function line. To your dismay, your graph does not appear. This is because TI-Nspire does not assume the implied multiplication of two letters as it does with a number and a letter (such as 2*x*). Rather, TI-Nspire treats *bx* as a single variable. You must press ⬚ between *b* and *x* to force TI-Nspire to multiply these two quantities. When you do so, you see the letter **b** turn bold (as in $x^2 + \mathbf{b}{\cdot}x + 1$). Bold font is a sure sign that TI-Nspire recognizes **b** as the variable defined by your slider.

You see a similar effect when working with TI-Nspire CAS. For example, the command expand(($a + bc)^2$) returns $a^2 + 2{\cdot}a{\cdot}bc + bc^2$ whereas the command expand(($a + b{\cdot}c)^2$) returns $a^2 + 2{\cdot}a{\cdot}b{\cdot}c + b^2{\cdot}c^2$. In the first case, TI-Nspire CAS treats *bc* as a single variable. In the second case, TI-Nspire CAS treats *b* and *c* as two different variables.

Removing a function table

When working in the Graphs & Geometry application, I often choose (menu)⇨View⇨Add Function Table (or press (ctrl)(T)) to add a Function Table. This action adds a Lists & Spreadsheet application containing a Function Table to the current page. After using the Function Table, I typically wish to remove it and restore the screen to its original layout, but it's not always obvious how to accomplish this task. Here are the steps:

1. **Press (ctrl)(tab) to activate the Lists & Spreadsheet application.**
2. **Press (ctrl)(K) to select the Lists & Spreadsheet application.**
3. **Press (clear) to delete the Lists & Spreadsheet application.**

   You see the words *Press Menu* in the vacated spot.
4. **Choose (ctrl)(⌂)⇨Page Layout⇨Select Layout and select a layout with one less application on the page.**

Use these steps any time you want to reconfigure a page to show one less application.

Crowding multiple applications on one page

Consider you have three applications on one screen, and it's simply too crowded. To move one application to a separate page and reconfigure the existing page with one less application, follow these steps:

1. **Press** (ctrl)(tab) **until the application you want to move is active.**

   Active applications are surrounded by a dark border.

2. **Press** (ctrl)(K) **to select the application.**

   The selected application flashes.

3. **Press** (ctrl)(X) **to cut the application.**

   The cut application is stored to the clipboard. The words *Press Menu* take the place of the cut application.

4. **Choose** (ctrl)(⌂)⇨**Page Layout**⇨**Select Layout and choose a layout with one less application on the page.**

5. **Press** (ctrl)(I) **to insert a new page. and press** (esc) **to remove the chosen application menu displayed in the top-left corner of the screen.**

6. **Press** (ctrl)(V) **to paste the copied application to this new page.**

The pasted application appears as a full page.

Making right angles in the Plane Geometry view of the Graphs & Geometry application look like right angles

If your right angles don't appear so, you probably haven't actually made a mistake. Rather, TI-Nspire is in radian mode. Press (⌂)⇨System Info and change your Document Settings or System Settings from radians to degrees.

You may experience a similar problem when working in the Analytic Window. By default, TI-Nspire uses a square window. At some point, you probably changed the scale on one axis only, resulting in a non-square window. Choose (menu)⇨Window⇨Zoom – Square to restore a square window.

Storing a variable to the wrong name

Consider that you named a column in the Lists & Spreadsheet application only to realize that you want to use this name as a variable elsewhere in the same problem. You try moving to the column heading and deleting the name, but the name is still a defined variable (you press ⬡ and see it still sitting there in the list of defined variables). The Undo feature doesn't work either.

To permanently delete a variable from a problem, open a Calculator page and execute the command delvar (*variable name*). Choose ⬡⇨Actions⇨Delete Variable to access the delvar command.

Viewing objects created with TI-Nspire Computer Software on the handheld

If you are planning on shipping TI-Nspire Computer Software documents to your handheld, make sure that you work in the Handheld Screen view (press View⇨Handheld Screen). This ensures an exact correspondence between the two environments. The default Normal view on the Computer allows for significantly more space than the Handheld Screen view does.

Manipulating objects in the Graphs & Geometry application

If you can't manipulate an object in the Graphs & Geometry application, check out the top-left corner of the screen. In all likelihood, you see an icon indicating that a tool is currently open. Press ⬡ to close the current tool and restore the Pointer. Alternatively, choose ⬡⇨Actions⇨Pointer to close an open tool and access the Pointer.

Properly entering the arguments for a function

If the argument of function is not properly entered, you get an error message. For example, nderiv(x^2, x, 2) returns the error message "Error: Variable is not defined." Press ⬡⬡ to access the alphabetical listing of functions in the Catalog. Highlight the function to reveal the syntax associated with it.

Graphing a scatter plot of lists contained in Lists & Spreadsheet application

You must name your lists in the Column/list name area of the Lists & Spreadsheet application to access them in the Graphs & Geometry or Data & Statistics applications.

Giving results in fractional form (or simplified radical form) rather than as decimals

It's great to have the option to see the exact form of a rational and irrational number. However, sometimes you prefer to view results as decimal approximations. In the Calculator application, press (ctrl)(enter) to force approximate results. Alternatively, include a decimal point somewhere in your expression to trick TI-Nspire into displaying a decimal approximation.

Appendix A

Working with Libraries

. . . .

In This Appendix

▶ Understanding what libraries are and why they are helpful

▶ Creating a library document with a private and public library object

▶ Using your library objects from within any document

. . . .

*I*n this appendix, I talk about how libraries provide global access to a function, variable(s), or program. I also talk about the difference between public and private libraries and how a library is created. Finally, I show you the steps used to call a library into play from any open document.

How Libraries Improve Efficiency

Libraries are TI-Nspire documents that reside in the MyLib folder of the My Documents view. Libraries contain variables, functions, or programs available from within any open document. These are different from ordinary variables, functions, and programs, which are available only from within a single problem within a single document.

If you find yourself defining the same function, storing the same variables, or performing a series of steps repeatedly, you may want to consider defining a library object. For example, you can create a program defined as a library object that takes the inputs a, b, and c and uses the discriminant to give information about the number and nature of the solutions to an equation of the form $0 = ax^2 + bx + c$. By defining this program as a library object, it is available in any document, not just the document in which is was created. Using the discriminant is a fairly common task and one that warrants defining the program as a library object.

Here's an overview of the process used to create private and public library objects.

1. **Open a new document and define one or more private or public library objects.**

   Select a name for each library object that helps describe its purpose.

2. **Save the document to the MyLib folder.**

   Use a name that describes the library objects contained within the document. This document is referred to as a *library document*.

3. **Open a new or existing document.**

4. **From the Calculator application, choose (menu)⇨Actions⇨Library⇨Refresh Libraries to refresh the library list.**

5. **Type the long name of the private library object or use the Catalog to quickly access a public library object.**

   Only the Calculator can run library objects that are programs. You can access variables or functions defined as library objects from any application.

Creating Public and Private Libraries

A *public library object* is a variable, function, or program that appears in the Catalog. A *private library object* is one that does not appear in the Catalog and is typically used to perform basic, low-level tasks.

Consider you want to define a public library object that enables you to find the area of any triangle using Heron's formula. Heron's formula states that the area of a triangle, *A*, with sides *a*, *b*, and *c,* is given by the formula

$$A = \sqrt{s(s-a)(s-b)(s-c)}$$

where *s* is the semi-perimeter defined as

$$A = \frac{a+b+c}{2}$$

In this section, I create a public library program called `heron` that calculates the area of a triangle. Within this program, I define a private library function `sp` that calculates the semi-perimeter, *s*.

Here are the steps used to create the private library function `sp`:

1. **Open a new document with a Calculator page.**

2. **Choose (menu)⇨Actions⇨Library⇨Define LibPriv.**

3. **Type the command shown in the first screen in Figure A-1.**

    This creates a function that takes the lengths of the sides of a triangle, *a*, *b*, and *c*, and determines the semi-perimeter.

At this point, I have the option of saving the current document to the MyLib folder, the location to which all library objects must be saved. However, I have chosen to first define the public library program heron and then save the document.

When defining a public library object that is a variable or a function, choose (menu)⇨Actions⇨Library⇨Define LibPub (Show in Catalog) from within the Calculator application and then define the variable or function. To create a public library object that is a program (which is true in this situation), follow these steps:

1. **Choose (ctrl)(⌂)⇨Insert⇨Program Editor⇨New to open the Program Editor dialog box.**

    You can also choose (menu)⇨Functions & Programs⇨Program Editor⇨New

2. **Type the name of the program.**

    I use heron for the name of the program.

3. **Configure the Library Access field for LibPub (Show in Catalog).**

    I also have the option to save my program as a private library object.

4. **Click (enter) to close the dialog box and open the Program Editor in a new Calculator page.**

    If you choose (menu)⇨Functions & Programs⇨Program Editor⇨New to access the Program Editor, the Program Editor opens in a split page. I prefer to work with the Program Editor on a separate page.

5. **Type the program as shown in the second screen in Figure A-1.**

    The third line from the bottom of the heron program, in its entirety, is

$$A = \sqrt{sp\left(a,b,c\right)\left(sp\left(a,b,c\right)-a\right)\left(sp\left(a,b,c\right)-b\right)\left(sp\left(a,b,c\right)-c\right)}$$

Notice the private library function $sp\left(a,b,c\right)$ is called into play for the purpose of calculating the semi-perimeter. I certainly could have calculated the semi-perimeter within this program but wanted to show you how a library object can be accessed from within another library object.

See Appendix B for more information about programming.

6. **Choose (menu)⇨Check Syntax & Store⇨ Check Syntax & Store (or use the shortcut key sequence (ctrl)(B)).**

This step is important. Saving the document does not automatically store the program.

7. **Save the document to the MyLib folder.**

As you can see in the third screen in Figure A-1, I have named my document `geo_formula`. This document contains both library objects. I have chosen to define these library objects in the same library document because they are related to one another.

Figure A-1: Creating private and public library objects.

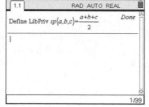 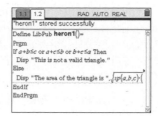 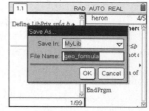

Library objects must be defined in the first problem of a library document.

Use the GetVarInfo command from within the Calculator application of a library document to view a list of all stored variables, including those that have been defined as library objects. This is particularly helpful if you did not create the library document and wish to view the library objects contained within it.

Library documents can also be created using TI-Nspire Computer software. The default save location for computer-based library documents is `My Documents\TI-Nspire\MyLib` (**Windows**) and `Documents\TI-Nspire\ MyLib` (**Macintosh**).

Using Library Objects

In this section I show you how to access privately and publicly defined library objects from any open document.

Private libraries

To access the private library object sp(a, b, c) follow these steps.

1. **Open a new or existing document.**

2. **Choose ⓒtrl⌂⇨Refresh Libraries.**

   This refreshes the libraries and provides access to those libraries that have been previously defined.

3. **Type the name of the document that contains the private library object, the backslash symbol (\), the name of the private library object, and the argument(s) for the private library object, if necessary.**

   Referring to the first screen in Figure A-2, geo_formula is the name of the document that was used to create the private library object sp(a, b, c). Recall that this library object requires three inputs that are the sides of the triangle.

   Choose ⓜenu⇨Actions⇨Library⇨Insert "\" character to insert the backslash symbol.

4. **Press ⏎ to execute the command.**

The first screen in Figure A-2 shows that the semi-perimeter of a triangle with sides 5, 6, and 7 is 9.

Public libraries

You can access the public library object heron(a, b, c) from any open document. First, if you haven't already done so, choose ⓒtrl⌂⇨Refresh Libraries to refresh the libraries. You then have two options:

- ✔ Use the long name. You can do this as follows:

  1. **Open a Calculator page and type** geo_formula\heron(a,b,c) **where** a, b, **and** c **are the sides of the triangle.**

  2. **Press ⏎ to execute the command.**

- ✔ Use the Catalog. You can do this as follows:

  1. **Open a Calculator page and choose ⓐ⑤ to access the public libraries (press ⓐ⑥ if you are using TI-Nspire CAS).**

  2. **Highlight** geo_formula **and press ⓡ to reveal its contents.**

All public libraries defined in the document `geo_formula` are listed here.

3. **Highlight** `heron` **and press** ⏎ **to paste it to the Calculator application.**

See the second and third screens in Figure A-2.

4. **Type the argument(s) for the program, if necessary, and press** ⏎ **to execute the command.**

The third screen in Figure A-2 shows that a triangle with sides 5, 6, and 7 has area of approximately 14.6969.

Figure A-2: Using private and public library objects.

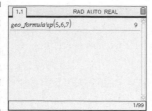 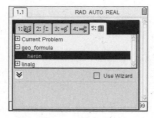 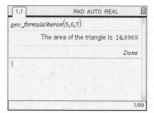

 If the current open document is the same document that was used to create a library object, then you can access this library object via its short name. For the example used in this chapter, the short name for the private library object is $sp(a,b,c)$ and the short name for the public library object is $heron(a,b,c)$. The long names for these library objects are `geo_formula\`$sp(a,b,c)$ and `geo_formula\`$heron(a,b,c)$, respectively.

 The program $heron(a,b,c)$ is written to check if the inputted sides form a valid triangle. Recall that the sum of any two sides of a triangle must exceed the length of the remaining side. If the triangle is not valid, the message "This is not a valid triangle" appears.

 Library objects that are programs can only be used with the Calculator application. Library objects that are variables or functions can be accessed from any TI-Nspire application.

Appendix B

Basic Programming

*T*here are two ways to write functions and programs using TI-Nspire: by typing statements directly on the Calculator Entry line or by using the built-in Program Editor. The Program Editor has several advantages, including having its own application menu, which allows for quick access to a variety of programming tools. Consequently, I focus strictly on using the Program Editor to write functions and programs.

In this chapter, I cover all the programming basics, including what you need to know to work with existing programs and functions as well as how to write your own programs and functions.

The Difference between Programs and Functions

Functions and programs have many similarities. However, there are a few notable differences. Here's how you differentiate between a function and a program:

✓ **Functions must return a result, whereas programs cannot.**

✓ **Functions can be used within mathematical expressions.** For example, consider a function called func( ) and a program called pgrm( ). The expression 4func(5) is valid whereas 4pgrm(5) is not.

✓ **Programs can be run only from the Calculator application. Functions can be used with any application.**

> ✔ **A function can use another function as part of its definition or as part of its argument.** However, a function cannot refer to another program or use a program as part of its definition. Looking at the previous example, `func(func(5))` is valid whereas `func(pgrm(5))` is not.
>
> ✔ **Programs can store local or global variables. Functions can store only local variables.**
>
> ✔ **A function can define a local function. A function cannot define a global function.**

If the information contained above leaves you a bit confused, then here's another way to think about a function. A function basically takes an input(s), does some work to it, and spits out an output — which sounds a lot like the mathematical definition of function.

Working with the Program Editor Menu

The Program Editor is where you work with new or existing functions and programs. Additionally, the Program Editor has its own application menu associated with it, just like the five core TI-Nspire applications.

Here are two ways to invoke the Program Editor:

✔ **Use the Tools menu:** From any page, choose ⓒⓣⓡⓛ)(ⓐ)⇨Insert⇨Program Editor and select one of the first three options: New, Open, or Import

   When this method is used, the Program Editor opens in a separate page.

✔ **Use the Functions & Programs menu from within the Calculator application:** Choose ⓜⓔⓝⓤ)⇨Functions & Programs⇨Program Editor from within the Calculator application and select one of the first three options: New, Open, or Import.

   When this method is used, the current page is reconfigured for one more applications, and the Program Editor application is added to the current page. If four applications are already on the page, the Program Editor opens in a separate page.

If prefer to work with the Program Editor on a separate page. Therefore, I almost always choose the first option.

The first screen in Figure B-1 shows the result of choosing ⓒⓣⓡⓛ) (ⓐ)⇨Insert⇨Program Editor⇨Import and selecting the public library program `heron` from the document `geo_formula`. (See Appendix A for more about this and other library objects.)

The second screen in Figure B-1 shows the application menu (press ⓜⓔⓝⓤ)) associated with the Program Editor.

Status line

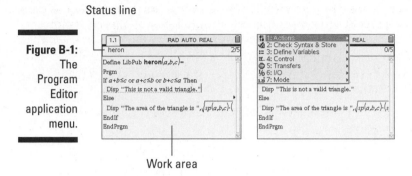

Figure B-1:
The
Program
Editor
application
menu.

Work area

The first screen shows the two main areas of the Program Editor view:

- ✔ **Status line:** This area shows the name of the current program or function and the line number corresponding to the current cursor location. An asterisk (*) indicates that something has changed since the last time the syntax has been checked and the function or program has been stored.

- ✔ **Work area:** The location of the function definition or program.

Here's a brief description of the contents associated with each top-level item contained in the Program Editor application menu:

- ✔ **Actions:** This submenu allows you to create new functions or programs. It's also where you open, import, and view existing functions and programs as well as create copies, rename, and change the library access of existing functions and programs. Editing tools in this submenu enable you to insert comments, find/replace text, and go to a specific line.

- ✔ **Check Syntax & Store:** Here you check the syntax for errors and store the program or function. TI-Nspire tries to put the cursor near the first error it finds.

- ✔ **Define Variables:** This submenu is where you define local variables. It's also where you can insert the `Func...EndFunc` and `Prgm...EndPgrm` templates. Keep in mind that these templates are automatically inserted if you choose (ctrl)(⌂)⇨Insert⇨Program Editor⇨New.

- ✔ **Control:** This submenu contains several functions that allow you to control the flow of a function and program. It includes conditional statement templates and looping commands.

- ✔ **Transfers:** Here are commands that allow you to terminate a function or program, jump to a different location, or alter the flow of a loop.

- ✔ **I/O:** This submenu contains the Disp (display) command.

✔ **Mode:** This submenu allows you to temporarily change the mode settings associated with a function or program. For example, you can configure a function or program to display numerical results in binary form.

In this appendix, I give specific examples of how to use most of the various Program Editor application menu items.

Working with Existing Programs or Functions

You can access a public or private library function or program from any document. Any function or program that is not defined as a library object can only be accessed from within the same problem that it was created.

Contained within this section are all the options available with existing programs and functions.

✔ **Opening an existing program or function:** To open a program or function that has previously been defined in the current problem, choose (ctrl)(⌂)⇨Insert⇨Program Editor⇨Open. Or, from the Calculator application menu choose (menu)⇨Functions & Programs⇨Program Editor⇨Open.

Select a function or program from the list of available items. Use this option if you want to edit a program or function that resides in the current problem.

✔ **Importing an existing program or function:** To import a program or function that is defined as a library object, choose (ctrl)(⌂)⇨Insert⇨Program Editor⇨Import. Or, from the Calculator application menu choose (menu)⇨Functions & Programs⇨Program Editor⇨Import.

A dialog box opens. Select the name of the library document that was used to define the library object (see first screen in Figure B-2). Then select the library object name as shown in the second screen in Figure B-2. The third screen shows that I am importing the library object heron from the library document geo_formula. After pressing (enter), I get the image shown in the first screen in Figure B-1.

Figure B-2: Importing an existing library object.

 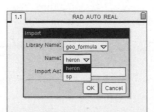 

See Appendix A for more information about library objects.

↳ **Viewing an existing program or function:** To view a program or function that has been previously defined in the current problem or as a library object, choose (ctrl)(⌂)⇨Insert⇨Program Editor⇨View. Or, from the Calculator application menu choose (menu)⇨Functions & Programs⇨Program Editor⇨View.

This option does not allow for editing of a program or function. Rather, the program or function opens in a separate dialog box for viewing only.

↳ **Making a copy of an existing program or function:** Sometimes, it's easier to modify an existing program or function rather than create one from scratch. Follow these steps to perform this task:

1. **Open or import an existing program or function in the Program Editor.**

2. **Choose (menu)⇨Actions⇨Create Copy.**

3. **Type a new name in the Save As field and press (enter) to create the copy.**

4. **Edit the program or function as needed.**

The new copy is saved to the current document. If the copy came from a library object and you want the edited copy to remain a library object, you must save the current document to the MyLib folder.

↳ **Renaming an existing program or function:** To rename an existing program or function, follow these steps:

1. **Open or Import an existing program or function in the Program Editor.**

2. **Choose (menu)⇨Actions⇨Rename.**

3. **Type a new name in the Rename As field.**

4. **If desired, change the access level by selecting the appropriate setting from the Library Access drop-down menu.**

5. **Press (enter) to close the dialog box and put the changes into effect.**

↳ **Changing the library access settings of an existing program or function:** To change the library access settings of an existing program or function, follow these steps:

1. **Open or import an existing program or function.**

2. **Choose (menu)⇨Actions⇨Change Library Access.**

3. **Select the appropriate setting from the Library Access drop-down menu.**

4. **Press (enter) to close the dialog box and put the changes into effect.**

If you change the library access settings to LibPriv or LibPub (Show in Catalog), you must save the current document to the MyLib folder for your function or program to be available as a library object.

✔ **Closing an existing program or function:** To close an open program or function, follow these steps:

1. **Choose ⒨⇨Actions⇨Close.**

2. **If you have not already done so, you are greeted by the prompt: "Do you wish to check the syntax and store?"** Press ⒠ to check the syntax and store or ⒯⒠ to close the program or function without checking the syntax and storing.

If you close a function or program without storing, all your work is lost.

✔ **Running an existing program or function:** You can run a function from any application. You can only run a program from the Calculator application.

To run a program or function defined within the current problem, follow these steps:

1. **Press ⒱ to access a list of current problem functions and programs.**

2. **Select a program or function and press ⒠ to paste it to the current application.**

   You can also type the program or function name using the keypad.

3. **Include parenthesis after the name and include one or more arguments, if needed, within the parentheses.**

   You must include parenthesis after the function or program name, even if it does not require an argument.

4. **Press ⒠ to run the program or function.**

See Appendix A for information on how to run a function or program defined as a library object.

Writing Programs

Now that you know how to manage existing programs and functions, it's time to look at the tools and techniques available when writing programs.

Getting values into a program

Most programs look for some input when performing a task. For example, consider that you want to write a program that calculates the volume of a cylinder for the inputs *radius* and *height*.

Figure B-3 shows three different configurations of this program. Here's a brief description of how these configurations differ:

- **First screen:** When the program volume( ) is run, the variables *radius* and *height* are stored to the values 3 and 4, respectively, directly in the program. Likewise, the variable *vol_cyl* is stored with a value of 113.097.

- **Second screen:** Here, the user must store the values of the variables *radius* and *height* before the program volume( ) is run. The program stores a value to the variable *vol_cyl* based on the values of *radius* and *height* supplied by the user.

- **Third screen:** When the program volume(*radius,height*) is run, the user must *pass the variables* to the program by entering the values if the variables *radius* and *height* in the argument. For example, the command volume(3,4) calculates the volume of a cylinder with radius 3 and height 4. Notice that the order of the values in the argument is important. I like this option best.

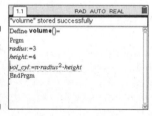 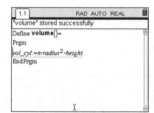 

Figure B-3: Using values with a program.

Displaying information

In the previous example, the volume of the cylinder, represented by the variable *vol_cyl*, is not displayed when the program is run. To display a value from a program, use the Disp command.

The first screen in Figure B-4 shows how the Disp command is used with the Volume program. Enclose text in quotation marks and make sure that calculations or numerical values variables are not included in quotation marks. Notice that I've mixed text with the variable *vol_cyl* by separating the two components with a comma.

The second screen in Figure B-5 shows the result of using the Disp command with this program.

Figure B-4:
Using the
Disp com-
mand to
display text
and numeri-
cal values.

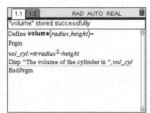
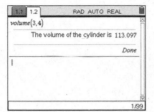

Using local variables

The variable *vol_cyl* can be accessed from within any application within the same problem, and its current value is determined by the value assigned to it the last time the program volume was run. To see the value of *vol_cyl* in the Calculator application, press (var), select *vol_cyl*, and press (enter).

Sometimes, it's advantageous to define a *local variable* within a program. Local variables are variables that cannot be accessed from outside a program. It's a good idea to use local variables when they are used as counters in a program. In such cases, there's no reason to make this variable accessible outside a program — its only purpose resides within the program.

To specify a local variable, choose (menu)⇨Define Variables⇨Local from within the Program Editor. Next, type the name of the variable. For example, Local *x* defines *x* as a local variable.

Calling one program from within another

You can call out a separate program from within a program or embed a program within another program to define an internal subroutine.

Here's an overly simple example of how to call out an existing program from within another program. In the first screen in Figure B-5, I've created a program called test1( ) that calls into play a second program test2(*x,y*) (shown in the second screen in Figure B-5) that generates a list of numbers and their squares.

The third screen in Figure B-5 shows the result of running the program test1( ).

Figure B-5:
Calling a
program
from within
another
program.

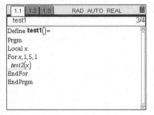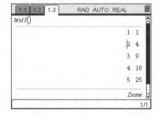

To define a program or subroutine within the body of another program, choose (menu)⇨Define Variables⇨Define to access the Define command and choose (menu)⇨Define Variables⇨Prgm...EndPrgm to insert the Prgm...EndPrgm structure. It's a good idea to define a subroutine toward the beginning of a program and call it into play later.

Controlling the flow of a program

Typically, programs or functions execute commands in sequential order. However, sometimes you want to redirect the flow of the program. In this section, I talk about how conditional statements, the Label and Goto commands, and loops can alter the flow of a program and enhance the efficiency and functionality of a program or function.

Using conditional statements

The Control submenu of the Program Editor application menu includes four conditional commands. These commands test a condition and, based on the result, decide which part of a program to execute.

If you only want to execute a single command based on a true condition, choose (menu)⇨Control⇨If to access the If command. The following is a simple example that uses the If command:

```
If x > 10
Disp "x is greater than 10"
x:=x+1
```

In this example, the program displays x is greater than 10 if the current value of x is greater than 10. If not, Line 2 is skipped and the program moves on and executes the command in Line 3.

Keep in mind that you must store a value to *x* before executing the If command.

If you only want to execute multiple commands based on a true condition, choose (menu)➪Control➪If..Then...EndIf to insert an `If...Then...EndIf` structure. The following is a simple example that uses this command:

```
If remain(x,10)=0
  Disp "x is divisible by 10"
  Disp "x is also divisible by 5"
EndIf
Disp "x is not divisible by 5 or 10"
```

In this example, the program tests to see if *x* divided by 10 has a remainder of 0. If this condition is met, the block of commands that precede EndIf are executed. Otherwise, the program skips to the line immediately after EndIf.

Sometimes, you want to execute one command for a true result and a different command for a false result. In such cases, choose (menu)➪Control➪If.. Then...Else...EndIf to insert an `If...Then...Else...EndIf` structure. Take a look at the example that follows:

```
If x>10 Then
  Disp "x is greater than 10"
  x:=x+15
Else
  Disp "x is less than or equal to 10"
  x:=x+5
EndIf
Disp x
```

Consider that *x* initially has a value greater than 10. The program executes Lines 2 and 3, skips Lines 4 through 6, and executes Line 8. If *x* initially has a value less than or equal to 10, the program skips Lines 2 and 3, executes Lines 5 and 6, and executes Line 8.

To perform multiple tests, consider using an `If...Then...ElseIf...EndIf` structure. Here's an example in which I test for divisibility by three different numbers:

```
If remain(x,2)=0 Then
  Disp "x is divisible by two"
ElseIf remain(x,5)=0 Then
  Disp "x is divisible by five"
ElseIf remain(x,7)=0 Then
  Disp "x is divisible by seven"
EndIf
```

Choose (menu)➪Control➪ElseIf...Then to insert an `ElseIf...Then` structure.

Using the lbl to Goto commands to jump to different locations in a program

The lbl and Goto commands work in conjunction to direct the program to jump from one section to another. You can type these commands using the keypad or access them from the Transfers submenu (choose (menu)⇨Transfers⇨Lbl and (menu)⇨Transfers⇨Go To Lbl).

Because the Goto command is not conditional, it is often used in conjunction with an If command. This way, the Goto command is only executed if a certain condition is met. Check out the simple example that follows:

```
If x < 10 Then
Goto line5
Disp "The number is less than or equal to 10."
Stop
Lbl line5
Disp "The number is greater than 10"
```

In this example, if $x < 10$, the program executes Line 2, jumps to Line 5, and continues on from there. If $x \geq 10$, the program skips Line 2 and executes Lines 3 and 4 (Line 4 stops the program).

You can use multiple lbl and Goto commands within the same program. Just make sure pairs of lbl and Goto commands have the same label. Follow standard variable-naming conventions with the lbl and Goto commands.

Using loops

To repeat a set of commands in succession, use one of the loop commands found in the Control submenu (choose (menu)⇨Control). Each of the available loop commands uses a conditional test (often with a counter) to determine when to exit a loop.

The For...EndFor loop uses a counter to control the number of times the loop is repeated. Choose (menu)⇨Control⇨For...EndFor to paste the For... EndFor structure to the cursor location. Here's an example of how this loop is used:

```
For x,0,10,2
   Disp 3·x+1
EndFor
Disp x
```

The syntax associated with the first line is For *variable, begin, end [, increment]*. I set up this loop to start at $x = 0$, increment by two, and exit the loop when x exceeds 10. If I omit the increment value, the increment is assumed to be 1. This loop displays the values 1, 7, 13, 19, 25, and 31, followed by 12 — the value of x that finally breaks the loop.

The `While…EndWhile` loop repeats a block of commands as long as a condition remains true. Choose (menu)⇨Control⇨While…EndWhile to paste the `While…EndWhile` structure to the cursor location. Here's an example of how this loop is used:

```
x:=1
While x<5
   Disp x+3
   x:=x+1
EndWhile
Disp x
```

Because *x* is initially 1, the two commands that precede `EndWhile` are executed. The second command increases *x* by 1. When *x* reaches a value of 5, the loop breaks and the program executes Line 6. The program displays 4, 5, 6, 7, 5. The first four values come from the Display command contained in the loop. The last value comes from the Display command located in Line 6.

The `Loop…EndLoop` command sets up an infinite loop. The only way to break this type of loop is to include a command such as If, Exit, Stop, or Goto. Choose (menu)⇨Control⇨Loop…EndLoop to paste the `Loop…EndLoop` structure to the cursor location. Here's an example of how this loop is used:

```
x:=1
Loop
   If x<5 Then
      Disp 2·x
      x:=x+1
   Else
      Exit
   EndIf
EndLoop
Disp x
```

Here, I initially store 1 to the variable *x*. After I enter the loop, the program checks to see if *x* is less than 5. If so, it displays the value of 2*x,* and increments *x* by 1. This continues until *x* = 5, at which point the program executes the Exit command and breaks the loop. The Exit command takes the program to the line immediately following EndLoop. The program displays 2, 4, 6, 8, 5. The first four values come from the Display command contained in the loop. The last value comes from the Display command located after EndLoop.

The Exit command can be used to break any loop that uses a `For…EndFor`, `While…EndWhile`, or `Loop…EndLoop` structure.

Changing the mode settings from within a program

The setMode( ) function uses two numerical inputs to temporarily set specific mode functions. Here's how to use this function:

1. **Position the cursor at a point where you want to insert the setMode ( ) command.**

2. **Choose (menu)⇨Mode to view a list of mode settings.**

   This list includes Display Digits, Angle, Exponential Format, Real or Complex, and so on.

3. **Highlight a mode setting and press (enter) to view the specific settings.**

4. **Select a setting and press (enter) to paste the command to the cursor location.**

   For example, choose (menu)⇨Mode⇨Auto or Approximate⇨Approximate to set the program or function to display results in decimal form. The syntax associated with this action is setMode(5,2).

Keep in mind that mode changes made within a program or function do not affect the document or system settings.

Putting It All Together: A Sample Program

In the previous sections of this chapter, I give you little snippets of code for the purpose of illustrating how to use a particular command or sequence of commands when writing programs. The real trick when writing programs is to combine a series of commands in a logical format for the purpose of performing more complex and sophisticated tasks. The example given in this section certainly is not the end-all. Rather, it is intended to show how some of the commands covered in this chapter can be used to perform a task that may be of interest to you.

Listing B-1 shows the code for a program called simulation. This program performs x simulations of rolling two dice 50 times and displays the number of times a sum of y occurs for each simulation.

Listing B-1: The simulation program

```
 1. Define simulation(x,y)=
 2. Prgm
 3. If y≠iPart(y) or y<2 or y>12 Then
 4. Disp "Please enter an integer between 2 and 12
         inclusive for the sum."
 5. Stop
 6. EndIf
 7. If x≠iPart(x) or x<1 Then
 8. Disp "Please enter an integer greater than or equal to
         1 for the number of simulations."
 9. Stop
10. EndIf
11. Local i
12. Local n
13. Local m
14. For i,1,x,1
15. m:=0
16. n:=1
17. While n≤50
18.    If randInt(1,6)+randInt(1,6)=y
19.    m:=m+1
20.    n:=n+1
21. EndWhile
22.    Disp "A sum of ",y," occurred ",m," times."
23. EndFor
24. EndPrgm
```

Here's a description of each of the numbered regions of the program:

1. This If...Then statement checks to make sure that the value of y is an integer between 2 and 12, inclusive. This represents the possible outcomes when rolling two dice and recording the sum. If the condition is true, the user inputted an incorrect y-value, and the program displays the error message and stops.

2. This If...Then statement checks to make sure that the value of x is an integer greater than zero. This represents the possible number of simulations that can be run. If the condition is true, the user inputted an incorrect x-value, and the program displays the error message and stops.

3. Here, I define variables used in the program as local variables. These variables are basically used as counters and are not needed outside the program.

4. This outer loop statement repeats a number of times equal to the user input x. Recall that x represents the number of simulations to be performed.

5. The variable m is used to count the number of times a sum of y occurs. It is initially stored to zero.

6. This loop runs 50 times, which is the number of trials for each simulation. I could have also made the number of simulations a user-defined input. The conditional statement in this loop checks to see if each trial has a two-dice sum equal to y, the value specified by the user. If this condition is true, the value of m is incremented by one. After the 50th loop cycle, the program displays the number of times y occurred in the simulation. The program then goes back to the For...EndFor loop until i exceeds x at which point the program ends.

The first screen in Figure B-6 shows a result when simulation(6,3) is executed. The scenario performs six simulations of rolling two dice 50 times and records the number of times a sum of 3 occurs with each simulation. The second screen shows the error message that is displayed if the number of simulations is inputted incorrectly. The third screen shows the error message that is displayed if the sum is inputted incorrectly.

Figure B-6: Two-dice sum simulation program results.

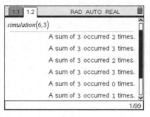
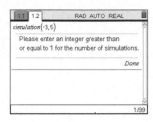
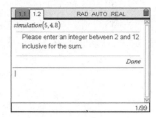

Index